Brand Journalism

Responding to the newly emerging trend of organizations hiring journalists to create content on their behalf, *Brand Journalism* is the first comprehensive, practical guide to this hybrid form of traditional journalism, marketing and public relations.

This textbook takes a direct and practical approach to the subject, showing journalists and journalism students how they can apply their skills to working for a brand, and showing those who work for non-media organizations how their organization can acquire the skills necessary to become a multimedia publisher.

Areas covered include:

- establishing the audience your brand wants to engage with
- identifying your organization's business goals
- developing a brand journalism strategy to help deliver those business goals
- measuring the results of your brand journalism strategy.

The book also features a wealth of case studies on the subject and offers an invaluable companion website – www.brand-journalism.co.uk.

Andy Bull has held senior positions at *The Times*, AOL, *The Independent*, the *Mail on Sunday* and the *Sunday Express*. He has produced brand journalism on behalf of organizations including Amnesty International, HSBC, Harrods, 20th Century Fox and Parlophone. He currently teaches at the London School of Journalism and is author of *Multimedia Journalism: A Practical Guide* (2010).

Brand Journalism

Andy Bull

Routledge
Taylor & Francis Group

LONDON AND NEW YORK

First published 2013
by Routledge
2 Park Square, Milton Park, Abingdon, Oxon OX14 4RN

Simultaneously published in the USA and Canada
by Routledge
711 Third Avenue, New York, NY 10017

Routledge is an imprint of the Taylor & Francis Group, an informa business

British Library Cataloguing in Publication Data
A catalogue record for this book is available from the British Library

Library of Congress Cataloging in Publication Data
Bull, Andy, 1956–
Brand journalism / Andy Bull.
pages cm
Includes bibliographical references.
1. Branding (Marketing) 2. Advertising. I. Title.
HF5415.1255.B85 2013
658.8'27–dc23
2013000999

ISBN: 978-0-415-63809-8 (hbk)
ISBN: 978-0-415-63810-4 (pbk)
ISBN: 978-0-203-08357-4 (ebk)

Typeset in Goudy
by Taylor & Francis Books

Printed and bound by CPI Group (UK) Ltd, Croydon, CR0 4YY

This book is dedicated to Lisa Clark.

Contents

Introduction

What the *Brand Journalism* project is about

This book is about how to do journalism for a brand. And by brand, I mean any organization: any corporation, B2B (business-to-business) or B2C (business-to-customer) company, any government department or quango, any third-sector body, any charity, cause or campaign. The book demonstrates how any organization can use brand journalism to help it attain its business and marketing goals, and shows how it can function effectively as a publisher.

What brand journalism is

Brand journalism is a hybrid form of traditional journalism, marketing and public relations. It has emerged as a reaction to what Tom Foremski, a former *Financial Times* journalist now reporting on Silicon Valley, has dubbed EC = MC: every company is a media company.[1] Brand journalism is a response to the fact that any organization can now use journalistic techniques to tell its story direct to the public.

But while it is rooted in some of the main principles of traditional journalism and good storytelling, creating stories that are timely and compelling, it also differs from traditional journalism. There are serious issues over balance, independence and fairness that must be addressed, and we shall.

Brand journalism's hybrid nature also sees it incorporate core elements from strategic public relations (PR) and marketing communications: visionary planning, research, incisive messages, a defined purpose, and a requirement to quantify what has been achieved through it. The result is an integrated brand journalism-driven communications strategy.

Because brand journalism is a new and still-evolving discipline, there is much disagreement about its validity, the form it should take, the value it represents and the threats it may pose to traditional journalism. This book takes a direct and practical approach to its subject. By bringing together 97 case studies of how a wide range of small and large commercial organizations, charities, campaigns, government departments, public bodies and others are actually using it, this book aims to be the first comprehensive, practical guide to how to do brand journalism.

Who this book is for

This book, and its companion website, are designed for journalists, for brands, and for those working for brands: in brand management, marketing, public relations, communications and customer service.

For journalists, it's about how to bring the skills you learned, or are learning, on your undergraduate or postgraduate journalism course into the alien environment of an organization that is not principally a media company. It also provides an essential guide for any working journalist who is switching from employment by a media organization to working for a brand.

For brands and their non-journalist employees, it shows, now that every company is (or could be) a media company, how brand journalism can be made to work for you.

What we cover is also known variously as content marketing, inbound marketing, brand storytelling or – most colloquially – how to sell without selling. Whatever you call it, our focus is on how journalistic techniques can be used to transform the quality of the material brands employ to communicate with their communities of customers, clients, supporters, whatever.

We focus on those areas of content where journalism can do most to help; where journalists' skills and creativity can have the most impact. We don't deal directly with the wider context of content strategy – for example, the processes surrounding the creation and maintenance of the many hundreds of pages of basic service or product-focused information that many brand websites have to carry. That's not to say good journalistic writing can't help in any context. It can, and what we cover here can be applied across the content-creation board.

What the book will teach

To exploit the enormous potential of brand journalism as a business tool, a brand will need to introduce a new skill set within the organization. It will need an editor-in-chief and a team of brand journalists, either in-house or run externally by a third party. It will need to give brand journalism training to those within marketing, public relations, communications and customer service who will be creating content and engaging with customers or clients via social media and other platforms.

The book puts creating journalism for a brand in the context of the organization's business or marketing goals. It covers establishing brand journalism strategies to help deliver those goals; monitoring the performance of that journalism; and using monitoring and analytics to demonstrate the return on investment that the brand journalism strategy has delivered.

How and why this book is different

As far as I am aware, there are no other books on brand journalism. There are a number on content marketing, but they tend to be heavy on process and light on how to create the right content. This book aims for a better balance. While we cover the processes involved in creating, implementing and managing a brand journalism strategy, we put greater emphasis on analysing how particular brands are writing on their websites and blogs, developing customer magazines, engaging on Twitter, Facebook and other social media, creating video, apps and games.

Most journalism textbooks are written from the perspective of students getting a job with a publisher or broadcaster. That made sense when most journalism jobs were offered by media companies. It makes a lot less sense now that jobs in traditional journalism are nose-diving, while this large new market in brand journalism is developing. The *Brand Journalism* project is designed to address and correct that mismatch.

What this book won't do is teach the basics of doing modern social, mobile and multimedia journalism. I covered all that in *Multimedia Journalism: A Practical Guide*, (www.multimedia-journalism.co.uk, Routledge, 2012), which is a comprehensive programme that takes journalism students through from day one to graduation, covering every practical journalistic aspect of a journalism course.

This book, *Brand Journalism*, is about applying those broad journalistic skills to working for a non-media organization. But its companion website, www.brand-journalism.co.uk, will offer a full range of support for any reader who has gaps in their training, or whose skills need updating.

The website will feature guidance in the use of the platforms we cover here, plus many links to sources of further teaching and information, including to *Multimedia Journalism* itself. There will also be essential updates to keep everything entirely current as brand journalism develops as a discipline.

You'll find this learning programme most valuable if you are able to apply what we cover to a real-life brand journalism operation or to a brand-specific project you are working on.

Web links

All web links included here were active at time of writing. Where links have subsequently become broken, we will, wherever possible, update with alternative, active links on the *Brand Journalism* website: www.brand-journalism.co.uk

Note

1 Tom Foremski, Silicon Valley Watcher: www.siliconvalleywatcher.com/.

Part I

How to Develop a Brand Journalism Strategy

In Part I we begin by demonstrating the development of brand journalism as a discipline before covering the key stages in the development and implementation of a brand journalism strategy. We don't look in any detail at content creation – that comes later. First we need to analyse the elements that make up a strategy. In Parts II and III we will look at many examples of the kind of brand journalism that is created in support of that strategy.

Chapters in Part I will cover:

- how brand journalism was invented and has developed
- researching audiences – deciding whom you want to talk to and how to reach them
- assessing your business and marketing goals
- developing a brand journalism strategy to support those business goals
- creating the infrastructure and skill set you need to achieve your brand journalism strategy
- learning the storytelling skills that will enable you or your brand journalism team to implement the strategy; and
- the ethics of brand journalism.

You'll find this learning most valuable if you are able to apply what we cover to a real-life brand journalism operation or to a brand-specific project you are working on.

1 How McDonald's Invented Brand Journalism, and How Brand Journalism Saved McDonald's

Goals of this module

- Examine the coining of the phrase "brand journalism" and the development of the concept.
- Map the development of the brand journalism strategy at McDonald's.
- Show that brand journalism was a key part of an almost total reinvention of McDonald's as a company.
- Outline how adopting a brand journalism strategy brought the end of brand positioning for McDonald's and a move to market segmentation.
- Demonstrate how the brand journalism approach transforms marketing and makes a marketer akin to the editor-in-chief of a magazine.
- Provide a detailed demonstration of what brand journalism means in practice for the marketing of McDonald's, with key case studies.

On the website

Find further resources, updates and links to all the sources quoted here.

In 2003, McDonald's was a global corporation in decline. A brand that had built its reputation on the simple slogan that it was a happy place to be, and which had democratized eating out, had forgotten what it was about.

Its restaurants were scruffy and tired, its staff poorly trained and demoralized, its food produced with an eye to economy, not quality. That food had become anachronistic at a time when consciousness about good diet and health were growing rapidly. What was worse, its senior management didn't see a problem. In a *BusinessWeek* article, Michael Quinlan, then chairman and CEO, said: "Do we have to change? No, we don't have to change. We have the most successful brand in the world."[1]

As sales in each restaurant fell, McDonald's responded not by improving those restaurants, and what it sold in them, but by opening more and more new ones. When regular evaluations showed that the brand experience was declining, McDonald's dropped the evaluations. Instead of making the brand better, it just made it bigger.

In March 2003, *BusinessWeek* wrote about these problems under the headline "Hamburger Hell". There were plenty more reports like it. As Larry Light, then McDonald's chief marketing officer, recalls in his book *Six Rules for Brand Revitalization*: "Article after article described the unfortunate conditions of McDonald's. Reporters, analysts, observers, activists, franchisees, employees, marketing consultants, everyone had something negative to say: McDonald's was 'out of date'; 'too large to be turned around'; 'its time is passed'."[2]

And yet … a year later everything had changed.

When Larry Light spoke at an *Economist* conference in 2004, he was able to quote headlines such as: "'The Sizzle Is Back'; 'Eye Popping Performance'; and 'McDonald's Leaves Analysts Upbeat on Prospects'. And after another year, McDonald's was being described as an incredible turnaround business case." What had happened in the meantime? Light had initiated a transformation of the company. Just about everything had changed – from staff training to restaurant refurbishment; the food that was sold and the way in which McDonald's was advertised and marketed. That marketing now followed what Light said was something very new: a brand journalism approach.

The McDonald's transformation

Why did everything have to change? Because everything communicates. Light says that all the changes he initiated were in pursuit of one central goal: McDonald's had to be demand rather than supply driven. He says: "The mindset had to change from selling what we want to provide, to providing the brand experience customers want." In taking this approach to restoring the brand, he was rejecting the then current orthodoxy of brand positioning in favour of a multifaceted approach involving market segmentation.

USP

The outmoded brand positioning approach saw a brand as having one USP (unique selling point) that was relevant to everyone who used that brand. For McDonald's, that brand positioning approach would translate to the slogan: "Burgers and fries for everyone." That no longer worked, he said, because brands actually appealed to many different markets in many different ways. So a revolutionary new approach to marketing was needed.

Light said: "We need to reinvent the concept of brand positioning by instituting the new concept of brand journalism. Mega brands are multi-dimensional, multisegment, multifaceted brands. No one communication can tell the whole, multifaceted megabrand story."[3] In essence, he explains: "The process of market segmentation is about dividing people into different markets that share common needs and are differentiated from people in other segments who share different needs."

The end of mass marketing and mass media

Light explained that mass marketing no longer worked: "We no longer live in a world where mass marketing to masses of consumers with a mass message delivered through mass media makes money. In fact, mass marketing as we know it is dead."

That's just as true for mass journalism. Journalism has always been seen as serving a mass audience. Newspapers, magazines, television and radio – they are all mass media. Or they were. Now journalists are facing just the challenge that Light defined for marketers.

How Larry Light used the language and concepts of journalism to shape his concept of brand marketing

One of the first things journalists learn as they begin to write news is to apply what Kipling, its originator, called his "six little friends", or six questions. Six questions that everyone wants answered when they read a news story are: who, what, when, where, why and how. Answering those questions is essential if a news story is to deliver the essential information the reader wants. They provide the framework for writing that story.

Light took the language of journalism, and core concepts about structuring a story, identifying and serving a particular audience's interest in a given subject, and editing a journalistic product, and applied these concepts to marketing, making what he did immediately recognizable and comprehensible to journalists. While Light's brand journalism is actually about a new way to market a brand, and was addressed to marketers rather than journalists, it very neatly fits journalists' way of working. This is why journalists are just as good at creating content for brands as they are doing it for publishing and media companies.

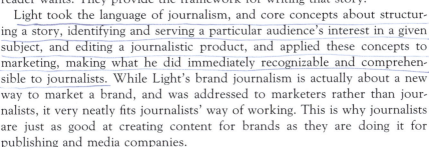

How Larry Light adapted the who, what, when, where, why and how from journalism to marketing

Whereas journalists use the formula to shape a story, Light uses it to shape a marketing strategy – to help marketers identify market segments in order to determine their needs and serve them. In traditional journalism, the elements are these:

- What: is happening (or has happened or will happen)?
- Who: is it happening to?
- Why: has it happened?
- How: will it happen?
- When: will it happen?
- Where: will it happen?

Light adapts this approach to give what he calls the brand segmentation, brand marketing or brand journalism approach. First, you must understand a customer's needs by asking:

- Why: does the customer use this product or service?
- What: are the wants that using the product or service satisfy?

And:

- What: are the problems with what the customer currently uses?
- Who: are the people with these needs?

How Larry Light's brand journalism approach to serving an audience draws from journalistic concepts of adapting information to fit any given audience

So far Light has adapted the five whys and how (5Ws and H) to look at needs and who has them. Next he defines the context of those needs. According to him, marketers must ask:

- How
- When
- Where

do these different needs exist?

Light's brand journalism approach to serving an audience draws from journalistic concepts of adapting information to fit any given audience. It uses journalists' understanding of writing for niche audiences, and for adapting information to not just the people consuming it, but to how, when and where they are consuming it.

It's like a multimedia journalist deciding what content should go in a print product, what is relevant to Twitter or Facebook, where video will be useful, how content can be served by location, via a smartphone app and so on. This, in Light's terms, is "needs-based segmentation".

Here's how Light explains the change. As we mentioned, before it took this new approach, McDonald's was a "Burgers and fries for everyone" brand. Light says: "This [description] is wrong. It is product categorization, not needs-based segmentation. And brands cannot appeal to every person for every occasion. By trying to appeal to an undefined mass market, the result is inevitably a mass message of mediocrity." With segmentation you get to identify key audiences, with clearly defined needs. Light says: "We [created] a multidimensional view of the market: what people buy and use is a function of why they need it, who they are, context of use (how, when and where)."

Here is how McDonald's identified some consumer segments, the needs it could fulfil, and when and where it could fulfil them. It decided to focus on three key segments with different needs:

- "Great tasting food and fun for kids."
- "Healthful eating for young adult moms."
- "Satisfying food for young adult males."

And it decided on four key contexts in which it could satisfy those needs:

- lunch
- breakfast
- late hours; and
- snacking.

Let's bring this back to journalism – specifically, brand journalism – for a moment. This process gives the person who is creating content for a brand a clear idea of who the audience is, and what they are interested in, in a range of contexts and situations. Every journalist needs to know this context in order to do their job as well as possible. In media companies, such research is rarely available to content creators. With brands, it can be.

How McDonald's got a new tag line

The tag line usually appears beneath the title of a magazine or website, and it acts to explain exactly what the title is about. For example, the magazine *Country Living* has the tag "For when your heart's in the country". That suggests to me an audience which may actually live in town, but which love the idea of country life and aspire to share in it. So if you are creating content for this audience, items about achieving the switch to country living – achieving the dream they've bought into by purchasing the magazine – are highly relevant.

At McDonald's, Light didn't talk about a tag line, he talked about brand essence, but it amounts to the same thing. McDonald's developed, as a key part of its rejuvenation, a brand essence which was "to appeal to the child in our hearts". We can think of it like a tag line – the line under the title, or brand logo – that says what the brand is about. That was a crucial step in starting to address the key markets they had identified: kids, adult mums and young adult males.

From the brand essence came the slogan "i'm lovin' it", which turns the "child in our hearts" brand essence into something that can generate content: content for advertising, marketing and brand journalism. Give any content creator the starting point of "i'm lovin' it" and they can begin to create content that fits the image and personality the brand wishes to project.

How Larry Light's concept of marketing a brand is modelled on how an editor edits a magazine

When Light talks about rejecting the concept of brand positioning in favour of brand journalism, a process we discussed above, he draws examples from traditional journalism and journalism products. He says:

> For mega-brands like McDonald's, Coca-Cola, Kellogg's, GE, Samsung, Sony, HP, and Visa, we need to reinvent the concept of brand positioning by instituting the new concept of brand journalism. Mega brands are multi-dimensional, multisegment, multifaceted brands, No one communication can tell the whole, multifaceted megabrand story.

Talk of unique selling propositions was old fashioned, he said. Journalism can show us why that is so: "Think about journalism for a moment. Journalism is the collection and communication of news, events, and happenings. Journalism provides order to otherwise disparate or unconnected events. Journalism informs, entertains, and persuades."

Light says we should think of a brand as we think of a magazine. You could also think of one of those fat multi-section Sunday newspapers. Each magazine or multi-section newspaper has its own brand character and direction – broad parameters on what content is and is not right for that title. But within this, a wide range of topics is covered, which chime with the interests of a wide range of readers.

Not every reader looks at every article in the magazine or every section in the newspaper. And as those readers move through life, and their interests and concerns change, they are interested in different aspects of a magazine's content. Ask a dozen people why they read a magazine/newspaper and you are likely to get 12 different answers. Ask those same 12 people at different points in their lives – when they are looking for their first home; when they are starting a family; when they are looking for good schools for their children; when those children go to university; when they themselves are about to retire – and you'll get different answers again.

It's the same, says Light, with brand journalism: "Brand journalism is a chronicle of the varied things that happen in a brand's world, throughout the day, throughout the years. This is how we create real customer-perceived lifetime value for a brand." Different people want different things from a brand (or a magazine) at different times in their day, their week, their lives.

Light says that the motivation to go to McDonald's varies for each customer segment: kids, teens, young adults, parents and seniors. McDonald's also appeals for different reasons at breakfast, lunch, dinner, snack time, on a weekday and at the weekend. The appeal is different when you are with children, without them, or on a business trip. And the question of who rivals McDonald's for a person's custom also differs, depending on their given need and situation at any one time. The brand journalism approach to marketing involves appealing to "different people with different desires in different contexts". The communications plan – the content element of the brand journalism approach – "consists of a compilation of varied messages, different subjects, and different topics, that all come together in a dynamic, ever-evolving, overall relevant brand story".

"Brand journalism allows us to express the multidimensional essence of a brand in a way that is appealing and compelling to specific audiences with their specific needs." And those brand journalism communications need to use the full range of media, including the traditional mass media outlets of TV, radio, the press, advertising in all its forms, online and social media, events, educational situations and more – and all of those in an international, national and local context.

All those messages, delivered on all those platforms, need to be integrated within a coherent brand story, which is quite a challenge.

How news drives brand journalism and brand revitalization

Clearly, McDonald's wanted people to gain a fresh impression of the brand – to discover that it had something to offer that was new and better – and better suited to them, particularly if they fell into one of the segments we've been talking about. To tell people McDonald's had changed, and to give them a chance to revise their opinion of the brand, the corporation used news. Light says: "New food news provides this tangible opportunity for people to change their minds."

What McDonald's came up with were things such as salads with Paul Newman's dressing, apple slices, yoghurt, better coffee and bottled water. The needs-based market segmentation gave McDonald's segments and occasions at which to aim new products.

McDonald's brand journalism in action

So how does the brand journalism approach filter down into what McDonald's does in the media? How does it conduct itself online and on social platforms? What content does it come up with? And, most importantly, how successful is it at the thing Larry Light invented and which so many brands have now adopted?

We won't look here at the mechanics of its brand journalism – who does what; we'll cover that in Chapter 4. For now, let's look at a number of brand journalism strategies and how they have worked out for McDonald's.

First, let's discuss an initiative that is clearly designed to work towards reaching two of the three key customer segments that McDonald's decided it needed to appeal to via the provision of "Great tasting food and fun for kids" and "Healthful eating for young adult moms".

McDonald's Mom Quality Correspondents[4]

McDonald's knew its food had to be healthier, and perceived to be so. One way it achieved this was to appoint a group of ordinary mothers who were given full access to McDonald's. They would go behind the scenes of the company's operations, meet senior executives and then communicate what they saw. They would be like independent reporters whose unedited journals, stories and comments would be published on McDonald's branded websites, in YouTube videos and discussed across social platforms.

Here's how McDonald's described the initiative:

> With unprecedented access to our food supply system, the Moms' Quality Correspondents saw first-hand how McDonald's successfully serves quality food to millions of customers every day … Like you, moms everywhere want to know that they're providing quality, nutritious food to their families. A few years ago, we launched Moms' Quality Correspondents, an exciting project to address questions that moms – and dads – have been asking about what their kids are eating. Representing real families from across the country, a group of moms came with different backgrounds but a common concern: they care about what their kids eat.

Here's how the *Washington Post* covered the story:

> So here is Debra DeMuth, McDonald's global nutrition director, mounting a spirited defense of fries to five mothers of young children at a McDonald's in Baltimore.
>
> "They are probably one of the most victimized foods", DeMuth says.
>
> Plausible reason: A medium order at McDonald's, besides the delectable taste, includes 380 calories, 270 milligrams of sodium and a color preservative called sodium acid pyrophosphate. But DeMuth presses her case, pointing out that fries are rich in potassium, adding, "They are also a really good source of fiber."
>
> One mom replies, "Once you throw them in grease, you kind of ruin it."
>
> Another says, "Potassium is good in bananas."
>
> This is the tricky dialogue that results when the world's largest fast-food chain extols the quality of its food to a group of people – busy moms – who often need food fast but don't necessarily trust fast food, especially with worries over obesity sweeping the nation. But McDonald's thinks it has a positive case to make.[5]

The online comments that the initiative drew were not always positive, but they were published on McDonald's sites. Here's one on a video in which the mothers look at the McDonald's production process: "It's a shame that your tour of McDonald's didn't include a visit to the abattoir to see animals being slaughtered that go into the burgers or to the rainforests in South

America that are destroyed to make way for cattle ranches. But hey, that would have been a reality."[6]

The *Washington Post* article quoted above had this from New York University nutritionist Marion Nestle, author of *What to Eat*:

> McDonald's has a problem ... They're big, so they are an easy target. They sell junk food, and they market it to kids at a time when public obesity is a major public concern. So what are they going to do? Turn into a health-food company? I don't think they can do that. Somebody must have figured out that what they need is good PR on transparency. Those mothers are willing to be used for that purpose.

Here's what one of those mothers thought of the process she took part in, published on McDonald's website:

> My impressions of McDonald's have changed since the beginning of my Moms' Quality Correspondents experience. Before our trips, I didn't think I would learn anything, really, that would change my perception that McDonald's was anything but junk food. Going into McDonald's to grab a meal doesn't leave me feeling completely guilty any more. I know I have options to feed my family a nutritious meal out, just as I am able to feed them a nutritious meal at home. It's all about my choices.
>
> Moms should know that they can choose, and help their children choose, healthier options at any restaurant. I love the Big Mac sandwich just the same as everyone else, but I know, and now my children know, you can't eat it every day. Balance is the key to any eating regimen.[7]

What did McDonald's achieve with this brand journalism initiative?

Food Bubbles, a blog about food politics, reports on what McDonald's goals were:

> McDonald's says the program is not a response to the negative portrayal of its restaurants in [the Morgan Spurlock documentary] *Super Size Me*, nor is it in response to New York's new menu laws where its 380 calorie medium fry bares its shame to the world. "This program wasn't in response to anything", said Tara Hayes, manager of US communications at McDonald's. "We saw this as a great opportunity to give the facts and let people make up their minds for themselves. You can take it or leave it."[8]

We'll look in detail in Chapter 6 at the ethics of brand journalism. One of the tests of whether the journalism element in brand journalism can be described as ethical is transparency. We'll discuss that and other issues there.

My impression is that the mom correspondents initiative has brought increased transparency and an increase in trust in line with that enhanced transparency. But while transparency can help to remove misconceptions about a brand, it can also highlight truths. Food Bubbles says: "the campaign seems to be making some inroads into reassuring parents that McDonald's food is not as bad as they think. With absurdly low expectations, though, McDonald's doesn't have to try very hard to impress."[9]

Transparency won't change the fact that McDonald's produces highly processed foods on an industrial scale. There will always be those who refuse to accept McDonald's because of that fundamental fact, and those people can be vociferous. McDonald's presence on Twitter and other social platforms often seems like a fire fight, as they seek to correct misconceptions, to counter negative views and to quash false rumours. So there are limits on what such brand journalism can achieve. The reality is that brand journalism – indeed, all journalism in the modern world – is conducted in an open arena in which anyone can challenge what is said.

Did it succeed? This comment from the Marketing Profs blog is pertinent to that question:

> Whether this effort "succeeds" or not (and how will they measure that?), McDonald's will definitely end up with a much better understanding of how the minds of their mom-customers work, what language they use when they are talking about providing meals for their families, and how they can work to be more relevant in the daily, more health-aware lives of today's women, in general.[10]

That strikes me as a fair example of success in the real world of brand journalism. Let's look at another initiative.

Our Food, Your Questions

McDonald's Canada set up a forum called Our Food, Your Questions where customers could ask about their products. They say: "We'll answer any questions about our food – even the tough ones – then post a personal reply from McDonald's Canada."[11] Often the questions are challenging and concern factory farming of animals and fish, and about the calorie content of meals. So, ask them how many calories there are in a large strawberry milkshake and they'll tell you: 1110. And add: "truly ... indulgent".

One question that attracted a lot of interest on social media, and coverage in press and broadcasting, was: "Why does your food look different in the advertising than what's in the store?" McDonald's Canada got Hope Bagozzi, its director of marketing, to address the question in a YouTube video.[12] In it she is filmed buying a quarter pounder with cheese in a store, then taking it over to the studio of the food stylist used by McDonald's. The bought burger is photographed; a second one is then prepared under the perfect conditions required for a shoot. The first was made in a matter of minutes, the second takes hours. And then they are compared. The stylist explains why they have to move the elements which aren't visible in the bought burger – pickles, ketchup and so on – to make them visible in the photograph. They reveal the artistry, and also demonstrate why the product you get won't look as great as the one in the picture.

What's the result of this exercise in brand journalism? McDonald's achieves transparency. It's honest. Does it damage its brand? No. McDonald's could have chosen to keep quiet on this subject; but if it did so, it would have no chance of influencing public opinion. As with much brand journalism, the goal is to make your voice heard.

But it's a battle. The (London) *Daily Mail* headlined its report: "One McBurger with lies, please". Yet within the story it gave McDonald's credit for what it was doing, saying "the fast-food giant has taken a candid approach by revealing the secrets of how it makes its burgers look so much juicier, bigger and tastier in its adverts".

Finally, let's look at a McDonald's Twitter campaign that went wrong. We do so partly as an example of the dangers of doing brand journalism on social media.

"Meet the Farmers": When a McDonald's Twitter campaign goes wrong ...

A brand can't control a Twitter campaign, or one on any other social platform, once it has gone live. With "Meet the Farmers", McDonald's used the strategy of placing promoted tweets into the streams of Twitter users during a 24-hour campaign that linked to video on its branded websites and on YouTube featuring farmers who supply the brand.[13] Essentially, they were advertising their brand journalism. It all went horribly wrong.

PaidContent reported:

> The campaign was intended to share happy farmer stories and featured two keyword hashtags. The company used these hashtags in its tweets and also paid for them to appear at the top of the results when a user searched for those terms. The campaign proceeded uneventfully until ... McDonald's switched from its first hashtag #MeetTheFarmers to its second one #McDStories.
>
> "Within an hour, we saw that it wasn't going as planned," said [Rick] Wion [McDonald's social media director]. "It was negative enough that we set about a change of course."
>
> Even though the company used the hashtag only twice, a legion of critics pounced on #McDStories to tell their own tales of weed or animal cruelty. Some offered crass personal accounts like that of

@MuzzaFuzza who wrote "I haven't been to McDonalds in years, because I'd rather eat my own diarrhea."

The hashtag continues to take on a Twitter life of its own – most recently as a social media parable for marketers.[14]

But it's not all negative:

> If there's any consolation for McDonald's, it's that the company's original positive message ("When u make something w/pride, people can taste it") continues to appear at the top of the search results. This is happening not because the company is paying for it to stay there ... but because of the tweet's popularity.

Twitter's Matt Graves told PaidContent: "It's what we call a Top Tweet – a tweet that is getting extremely high engagement when people do a search for a term. These are chosen algorithmically." Promoted tweets are clearly marked in yellow, to differentiate them.

But could McDonald's have done anything to avoid this embarrassment? The Complete Pulse blog saw the campaign as misconceived: "How on earth could McDonald's think that a campaign like this would go well? While there are plenty of people who enjoy McDonald's food, I sincerely doubt that the majority of them feel proud enough to publicly declare it."[15]

McDonald's spokesman told PaidContent the brand took care with Twitter campaigns:

> According to Wion, McDonald's carefully selects the words or phrases used to describe its promoted tweets but that it's inevitable both "fans and detractors will chime in" (although the latter appear to have a clear majority in this case). His point appears to be that a certain amount of social media blowback is unavoidable if a company is a lightning rod in the first place.

The Complete Pulse post goes on: Twitter has proven time and again that once you release a social media campaign into the wild, you no longer control the message. In a way, that's the entire point of a social media campaign: social proof. In a store, when you see someone else admiring a piece of clothing, you're much more inclined to be interested in it as well. Social media marketing works the same way. A successful social media campaign is one that gets people to publicly display their genuine enthusiasm for a brand, which in turn makes their friends curious to find out more about this apparently awesome product:

> The pendulum swings both ways, however, as McDonald's (and many others before them) found out ... The point is, if you're thinking about trying a Twitter campaign that encourages people to tweet warm-fuzzies

about your brand, you'd better be darn sure that most of your followers, and your followers' followers etc., actually *have* warm-fuzzies
about your brand, or are at least neutral on it.

So that's a selective demonstration of how McDonald's – whose Larry Light,
former chief marketing officer, invented this new term for content marketing – does brand journalism. In Chapters 2 and 4 we'll look at the mechanics
of McDonald's content creation efforts, and how it runs its brand journalism
operation.

We'll see many further examples of brand journalism in the rest of this
book. Bear McDonald's in mind as you look at them.

Assignments

These suggested assignments (like others that appear at the end of each
chapter) are designed as potential ways in which the chapter can be used as
the basis for group discussion, university assignments, or as projects within
a training environment.

1 Give your assessment of the potential gains, and attendant risks, in a
   brand adopting a brand journalism strategy.
2 Take as comprehensive a look as you can at McDonald's brand journalism as practised on social media, via websites and elsewhere. Consider
   the quality of the content produced and the topics covered. What is your
   assessment of how well McDonald's does brand journalism?
3 Analyse the brand journalism created by a particular brand, or seek out
   two brands in the same market sector, and compare how successful their
   brand journalism is.
4 Find two brands within a market sector, one which uses brand journalism and one that does not. Develop a brand journalism strategy for the
   latter.

Notes

1 *BusinessWeek* article, 9 March 1998.
2 Larry Light and Joan Kiddon (2009) *Six Rules for Brand Revitalization: Learn How
   Companies Like McDonald's Can Re-Energize Their Brands* (Upper Saddle River, NJ:
   Prentice Hall).
3 Ibid.
4 McDonald's Mom Quality Correspondents: www.mcdonalds.com/us/en/food/
   food_quality/see_what_we_are_made_of/moms_quality_correspondents.html. You
   can read about the programme here: www.mcdonaldscorrespondents.com/, and
   see some of their reports here: www.youtube.com/user/McDMoms?feature=watch.
5 How the *Washington Post* covered the Mom Quality Correspondents story: www.
   washingtonpost.com/wp-dyn/content/article/2008/11/19/AR20081119036 18.html.
6 A video in which the Mom Quality Correspondents look at the McDonald's
   production process: www.youtube.com/watch?v=qIyR6bJ2DDk&feature=plcp.

7 What one of those mothers thought of the process in which she took part, published on McDonald's website: www.mcdonalds.com/us/en/food/food_quality/ see_what_we_are_made_of/moms_quality_correspondents/what_it_means.html.
8 Food Bubbles blog on the Moms initiative: www.foodbubbles.com/blog/2008/11/ 22/moms-blog-for-mcdonalds/.
9 Ibid.
10 Marketing Profs blog: www.mpdailyfix.com/mcmoms-can-mcdonalds-really-handle-the-truth/.
11 McDonald's Canada's "Our Food, Your Questions" forum: yourquestions. mcdonalds.ca/questions/4280.
12 McDonald's video on the subject "Why does your food look different in the advertising than what's in the store?": youtu.be/oSd0keSj2W8.
13 McDonald's Meet the Farmers video: www.youtube.com/watch?v=3xxl EkstcwM.
14 PaidContent on the Meet the Farmers fiasco: m.paidcontent.org/article/419-mcdonalds-social-media-director-explains-twitter-fiasco/.
15 The Complete Pulse blog on the Meet the Farmers fiasco: blog.compete.com/ 2012/02/03/twitter-campaign-amounts-to-mcdefeat/.

2 Who Do You Want to Talk to?

Identifying the Community You Wish to Serve

Goals of this module

- Examine the art and science of defining the audiences with whom you want to communicate.
- Explain the role of analytics, research, surveys, focus groups and interviews in identifying the key groups you need to engage with.
- Explore the vital importance of listening to your community, and demonstrate through case studies how a range of brands have done that.
- Analyse the process through which customer personas are created for each audience segment.
- Demonstrate the importance of learning to speak one to one.

On the website

Find further resources, essential updates and links to all the sources referenced here.

Defining your audience or audiences

Before building your brand journalism strategy you need to know who you are talking to or want to talk to. That's an essential first step if your brand journalism strategy is to succeed. You need to have accurately identified a target audience (or range of audiences) with a specific interest in your goods, services, cause or other offering before you can proceed.

Before selecting the channels to use for your brand journalism, you need to understand the community you are seeking to engage with, how they use media and what they use it for. Identify that community – and how it uses social media, websites, blogs, and traditional media, including TV, radio and print – and you can begin to build a brand journalism strategy that matches their interests and their pattern of media usage. Then you know you'll be fishing where the fish are.

To help you do that you can build what are known variously as customer, marketing or buyer personas. These are representative archetypes of particular sections of your community that help you to focus on particular key audiences with definable needs and interests in relation to your products or services. So, who do you want to talk to? What do you know about the community your brand journalism is designed to serve? How can you learn more about it?

The art and science of defining your audience

It's rare for journalists working for a traditional publisher to be given much information about the audience for their work. It's often said that really good journalists instinctively know the audience, who they are, and what their interests and concerns are. That instinct is just as useful in brand journalism, but it is not enough on its own. And as we have access to so much data that can confirm or correct our instincts, it would be mad not to use it.

Social media helps us enormously in building our understanding of our audience. Because we have so many multiple engagements on so many platforms, it has never been easier to speak to our community, ask them questions, get their responses, and understand their interests and concerns from the things they tell us, the things they respond positively or negatively to.

The scientific approach involves qualitative and quantitative research into your audience (we'll look in detail at how analytics can help us in Part IV). We need to build up profiles of each clear category of user within our overall community. And to get meaningful profiles, we need to gather both quantitative and qualitative data.

Quantitative data includes such things as the information we can gather online: the visitor demographics to our websites and blogs. We can learn how people found us: whether by search, via our presence on a social platform, from a link on another site, as a result of our advertising, or directly by typing in our URL. We can see where visitors go on our websites and how long they stay. We can also analyse the stats from social media sites on follows, re-tweets, likes, talking about and so on. This is bare bones information, but it can tell you a lot.

Demographic information – the age range, gender split, geographic location, education, work and salary profile of your community – can help you to visualize them. It may alert you to the fact that your community is actually different than you had thought – younger, maybe, or in another country than you had anticipated. You can get some demographic information from analytics some of the time – social platforms such as Facebook and YouTube, where subscribers have given them a good deal of information about themselves, will feed that knowledge into the analytics they give you. But to get a full picture and create customer profiles you need to do more – as we'll discuss in a moment.

Data can also show us who our most active community members are. It will reveal who comments on our content and shares it the most; who has the most social connections within the community we seek to serve. That makes these individuals key influencers. We need to know about them and their interests. We should cultivate them because they are demonstrating a strong connection with us and can help us to build relations with the rest of our community. We should connect with them wherever appropriate – if they blog, we should read and comment on their posts; if they run Google+ hangouts, we should join them.

But data alone is never enough. We need to understand the interests and desires of our community members. In an article on the Wall Blog, Albert Pusch wrote:

> Marketers must learn more about their target audiences than just basic demographic data. Over the course of time, brand managers must be able to develop a comprehensive picture of the interests and desires of their consumers. Howard Schultz, chief executive of Starbucks, which has been extremely successful in social media, describes this as breaking a code, in order to give people opportunities to feel good about themselves.[1]

That concept of allowing people to feel good about themselves is not one that works for all brands, but it does play a key part in the brand journalism strategies of youth-orientated brands such as Red Bull and Coke Zero, as we shall see later.

The desires of users of other brands will differ widely, depending on the nature of the brand and what need it satisfies. But Schultz's concept of breaking a code is one that is relevant to any brand. All brand journalists need to break the code and fully understand the interests, desires and aspirations of the community we seek to serve. This is where qualitative data comes in. Qualitative data puts flesh on the bare bones of quantitative data. It is gathered, in part, from the comments readers leave on our blogs, the content of their interactions with us on Twitter and other social platforms, plus material we may gather from interviews, focus groups and surveys. Qualitative data can help us to understand why people visit us, what they need or want from us, and what they expect from us.

Do they come to research a subject, to learn, to look for a job, to buy something, to express support for a cause? Qualitative data can tell us how happy they are with the service we provide. If the quantitative data showed us that content on a particular topic gets a lot of traffic, qualitative data can tell us why those who consume it like that content. It can also tell us why visitors come to our website, read our customer magazine, consume our product, support our cause, prefer us to a rival or a rival to us.

Qualitative data is very useful if we have yet to build a presence on a particular social platform or are considering building a website for a particular sector of the community we want to serve.

The importance of listening to your community

One way of getting to know your audience is to listen to them. McDonald's did just that before it launched into social media. Rick Wion, director of social media at McDonald's USA, told Mark Schaefer at the Social CMO blog:

> We actually worked tracking conversations [through social media monitoring, which we'll cover in Part IV] for more than a year before we ever actually reached out and started reacting to people ... What we found is that people talk about McDonald's a lot, obviously. We also were trying to find out what topics do they talk about the most. Was it things around the experience in the restaurants? Was it things around the products? We even found out that specific products get more conversation than others. People talk about fries more than salad. What was really important is the style of conversation. So we wanted to make sure that we really understood the vernacular, and how people were engaging with each other, before we stepped into it because we didn't want to step in awkwardly.[2]

What he's talking about when he mentions the vernacular could also be described as the tone of voice of the community that engages with McDonald's in social media. Why is that important? If we can hear how our community talks, as well as what they talk about, we can get our own voice right. Adopting the correct tone of voice when we create content is another of the key things we learn in traditional journalism. We'll have more to say on this point in a moment, when we look at creating customer personas.

TES Connect, the web and social version of the *Times Educational Supplement*, a teachers' newspaper, found what its community wanted from it online by reading the site's forums and running focus groups. The TES's Edward Griffith explained in an interview with the Online Journalism Blog how the site came to be as it is:

> Someone noticed in the forums there were two big conversations going on. People were seeking support and ideas from each other. Second was sharing teaching tools and resources. So we thought, hang on, there are over half-a-million teachers, and there aren't that many classes, so we thought: what can we do? We had a resources section, but it was a bit of a dog. So we developed a prototype resources sharing tool, and it went through the roof. It's grown 200 per cent year on year ever since. The really weird thing was that, in some focus groups we ran, teachers were telling us how isolated they were. They were spending a huge amount of time planning their lessons in the evenings and at weekends, and doing it all alone. Link that with what the teachers are looking for in the forums, and we've got the premise for the biggest single professional social network in the UK.[3]

A combination of listening and monitoring can show you why one particular platform might work for one segment of your community. The 14- to 24-year-olds who drive decorative tape manufacturer Duck Tape's growth love to connect with the brand on Facebook. Success.com used Duck Tape as a case study for building your brand on Facebook. David Rodgers, Duck Tape's digital marketing manager, told Success.com:

> We honed our message by culling Google Reader alerts to see what bloggers and other media were already saying about our product. Today I read through each and every post, checking the site at least three times a day. It gives me a real sense of who our customer is and who we should be focusing on.[4]

Brands know that they need more than the raw qualitative and quantitative data they gather to understand their community members and to communicate with them effectively. The soft-drink manufacturer Red Bull defines its primary audience as males aged 12 to 34. That's OK as a starting point; but how does a Red Bull brand journalist know how to talk to that community, and what content will work well?

A lot comes from what is called the "Me Statement". Red Bull's Me Statement is: "I'm cool under pressure and can conquer any challenge." As Karlene Lukovitz wrote on Mediapost, Red Bull engages so successfully with its audience because "their messaging across all contact points consistently reflects and conveys an 'idealized self' or 'Me Statement' embodied by the brand – the reason that users want to be associated with it."[5] We'll look in detail at Red Bull's brand journalism strategy in Chapter 7.

The Coca-Cola Company has what it calls a "brand vision and architecture" which forms a blueprint for brands such as Coke Zero. Jonathan Mildenhall, Coke's vice-president for global advertising strategy and creative excellence, explained how the vision shapes its brand journalism (actually, Coke uses the term liquid content, but it amounts to the same thing) in a YouTube video:

> The Coca-Cola Zero brand is positioned to target 18–24 year old males who are fuelled by an unprecedented belief in what they can achieve, and driven by an impatience with the status quo. Coca-Cola Zero speaks to individuals who are in their formative years of change and discovery, and who are actively taking the lead in determining who they can be.[6]

Like the Red Bull "Me Statement", that gives a pretty good starting point for creating effectively targeted content.

The easily defined audience

Let's take as a first example something a world away from the mega-brands we have been talking about up to now. Mark Taylor had this advice for a small business – actually a wedding photographer – in a post on Hub Pages:

> Similar to knowing who your target audience is, you also need to uncover the specific attributes of that audience. If you are a wedding photographer who specializes in small-budget weddings, consider who those specific brides are as individuals and hone in on that. It might be: between 18 and 22 years old; freshly out of college; small families; new in their career; etc. Creating this kind of a profile will help you fine-tune, not only who your customers are, but what they need.[7]

You might also consider other key types of customer, such as older brides, those embarking on a second marriage or same-sex couples entering civil partnerships, and gather data about them as well. There could also be other people, apart from bride and groom, involved in the decision-making process about using a wedding photographer. Maybe the bride's mother or father are paying for the wedding and want to make sure the occasion is photographed in a particular way.

Gathering information on each of those core customer categories enables you to create an archetype – a typical customer – with particular needs, concerns and requirements. As you create brand journalism in support of such a business, you can focus on these distinct customer sectors and their particular requirements. Doing so will help you to communicate as if in a one-to-one conversation.

The multifaceted audience

If you do brand journalism for a big corporation, you'll probably find that you have many different audiences, and that they have different needs at different times, so the brand journalism you produce for them must be carefully targeted and developed from an understanding of not just who they are, but what they are interested in at a given time.

In Chapter 1 we looked at how McDonald's identified some consumer segments, the needs it could fulfil, and when and where it could fulfil them. It decided, if you remember, to focus on three key segments with different needs:

- "Great tasting food and fun for kids."
- "Healthful eating for young adult moms."
- "Satisfying food for young adult males."

And it decided on four key contexts in which it could satisfy those needs:

- lunch
- breakfast

- late hours; and
- snacking.

So a McDonald's brand journalist needs to know which of these community segments he or she is creating content for, and to which of the key contexts their content should relate. Are you creating content addressing mums who might get together at a McDonald's for coffee after doing the morning school run, for example, or football fans looking for a burger on the way home from a match?

To create effective content, and to really engage with a particular audience with a particular need at a particular time, we need to be able to picture them, really understand them and what they want, and talk to them not as some anonymous mass, but as if we were chatting one to one. In order to do that, we need to create what are known as customer, marketing or buyer personas for each audience segment.

Creating customer personas for each audience segment

We get back to the art of targeted brand journalism here, or, rather, art with a solid scientific base. All the quantitative and qualitative data is great, but it doesn't put a face on the person whom you are trying to talk to; it doesn't give them a name. And if we want to create brand journalism that works on a one-to-one basis, we really need a very clear idea of to whom we are talking.

Many brands, having divided audiences into categories, create customer personas for each category: profiles that give a typical customer within a segment a name, a face and a three-dimensional existence – someone the brand journalist can have in mind as they create content. The emphasis on customer personas represents a key shift in marketing, away from products and services and towards an understanding of our customers: what they need or want from us and how, by listening to them carefully, we can create brand journalism that fulfils the needs they have expressed.

We need a lot of information to create a meaningful customer profile. Heidi Cohen, a digital and direct marketer, gives a full list of information requirements for creating marketing personas in a blog post.[8] I am summarizing her key points here:

- *Demographics:* where they live, their sex, level of education, income, family situation.
- *Lifestyle:* how they spend their money – are they into conspicuous consumption or thrift?
- *Interests:* what do they do in their free time? What religious and/or political affiliations do they have? What hobbies or pastimes? For instance, if they travel, where to, how often, and how much do they spend?

- *Who influences their product choices*: are they the primary purchaser for the household? Whom do they consult about purchases? Influencers can include close family members, friends, those they trust and respect on social media, groups they belong to, professionals they consult.
- *What are their personal goals*: as defined in Maslow's five-tier hierarchy of needs, and where does the use of your product fit into that hierarchy?

Maslow, briefly, divided needs into five categories, ranging from the most basic survival needs up to what he called self-actualization, or self-development and realization. He argued that it was only when a lesser need had been fulfilled that a person could think about fulfilling a higher need. So the basic physiological needs of gaining shelter, finding water and curbing hunger must be satisfied before a person can think about the next level, the safety needs of security and protection. Above this come the social needs of love and family, followed by esteem needs – self-esteem, recognition, status and the respect of others. Finally, there is the self-actualization need we've mentioned.

So, regarding your product or service, does it help to fulfil an individual's self-actualization, esteem, social, safety or physiological needs?

- *What are they like from an emotional perspective*: how do they respond emotionally to positive or negative events?
- *Past behaviours*: how do they spend money and how does that relate to your brand? What have they bought from you, and did they buy at full price or in a sale or via some other discounted offer?
- *Why they interact with you and your competitors*: do they like or dislike your products? What do they feel about your competitors' products? Are there barriers to their buying your products that can be removed?
- *What they want from your brand*: it could be low-cost, basic products or more exclusive or specialist items. Do they want help from you in using your products? Do they want to be actively involved with your brand – as fans or followers, perhaps?
- *Where do they look for information about your product category*: do they research online, use search engines? If so, what search terms do they use? Do they participate in social media as part of their shopping process?
- *The information they want*: it could be product details, customer reviews, product support.
- *Where they are when they look for information*: do they research on the fly with mobile devices or at leisure on a home computer? How much time do they have for research?

These are general areas that will apply to most brands, but it is also possible to be more specific, depending on the nature of your brand.

Every brand needs to identify the distinct groups it has within its overall customer base and to create personas for each of them. Take an institution such as a university. It has customers, or potential customers, in each of these categories: potential students, the parents of potential students, current students, academic staff, alumni and (in the increasingly commercial world of higher education) potential commercial partners such as funders of research and subscribers to appeals for funds.

We could subdivide these categories further – such as dividing potential students into undergraduate, MA and PhD categories – and for particular business goals that might be necessary. But if we take the list above as our starting point, a business goal can be set for some of them – such as the overall number of undergraduates being recruited at the start of the next academic year. A buyer persona could be drawn up, a business goal set for the number of undergraduates recruited, and a brand journalism strategy developed which was designed to help deliver that business goal.

Whatever the business you work in, one key element of creating effective customer personas is to listen to the way in which those customers talk – the language and tone they use. As BuzzedUp says:

> Crucially, buyer personas consider and describe the type of language and phrases such prospect groups use. By seeing the world through the eyes of buyers, and not via the lens of product features and marketing jargon, a more human and realistic visualisation of the people that form customer segments is revealed.[9]

How do we get all this information?

We can gather some of this information from the observable online habits of those who come to our sites. We can also observe their interaction with us on social media. And there will be much we can gather from those within our organization who interact with the community we serve: those involved in customer service, sales and other departments. But none of that will tell us enough.

To gather so much information about individuals, a brand will need to conduct professionally led surveys, focus groups and interviews. It is really only through such in-depth contact with people – particularly through open-ended interviews – that we can build up a full picture of our community.

Your brand will need to use a market research organization or in-house expertise to identify and interview a representative range of people in order to produce reliable information on your customers. Relevant interview questions can be drafted for each customer sector that is identified. So, to take the university example, interviews could be conducted with new students during fresher's week which asked them in detail how they had decided to attend this university. It could ask about the process they went through in deciding upon this institution – when they started researching universities and which resources they used, who or what influenced them, by which means they connected with this university (social media, printed material, website), what convinced them that this university was right for them. It would also be enormously valuable to know why those prospective students who decided not to enrol came to that decision.

In small organizations where there isn't the budget for such research, you may have to just do what you can, gathering information from those who deal with customers, trawling through analytics and inviting users to complete online or in-magazine questionnaires, perhaps with the chance of winning a prize.

Examples of customer personas

Once we have all that data, how do we use it? We use it to build up a short but detailed biography of a typical customer – or a customer who is typical of one group among your overall customer base.

Often these archetypes are given a label – in politics we have seen, in the US, hockey moms; and in the UK, Mondeo man; among many others. Parties and candidates use these personas to identify key groups among the many millions of voters and then build communications campaigns designed to appeal to each.

I prefer to give personas a name. As the Content Marketing Institute says: "To help people relate to your personas, add images and give names to your buyer profiles. Assigning a name to the persona helps everyone on the team think of this buyer as a real person, not just a piece of business."[10]

In order to build an accurate customer profile, we must work within the information that we have discovered. So, for example, if the target audience segment you have identified is young couples aged in their 20s, who live in a rented apartment in an inner-city area, you can give them names, ages and pick an appropriate area of a particular city for them to live in. If the data reveals that they are educated to undergraduate level at a university, you can name that university. From the range of subjects they read, pick one that a good proportion of your survey group studied, and so on.

If we take the list of required information we identified in "Creating customer personas for each audience segment", we can demonstrate how a persona can be created. Let's say your brand is the upmarket British supermarket chain Waitrose, which is seeking to persuade shoppers who mainly use mid-market rival Sainsbury's and brand leader Tesco that, because of a new keen pricing policy, plus a mix of quality, high ethical standards and support for British farmers, they should shop with Waitrose. Your target audience are shoppers who might be persuaded to shop regularly with you if they could see that the barriers to their doing so had been removed or substantially reduced. You are introducing a new range of grocery products so that a careful shopper will spend no more with you, on many items, than they would with your mid-market rivals.

The persona is designed to help staff across the brand, including marketers and those working as brand journalists on the customer magazine, newspaper, website and app, to understand the customer whom this business strategy is directed at, and to create content that will chime with that person's information needs, interests and concerns.

Demographics

Nancy McDouglas is 41, lives in Beckenham, Kent, with her husband James. They have two children, Harry, aged 14, and Lucy, aged 9. Nancy graduated with a degree in history from the University of Birmingham and a postgraduate certificate in education from the University of Southampton. She teaches at Tindale Primary School in Beckenham and earns £33,000. James is an administrator at the local National Health Service (NHS) Trust and earns £38,000.

Lifestyle

Nancy and James McDouglas have a disposable income after tax of £51,000. Their main outgoing is the mortgage on their four bedroom semi-detached Victorian house. Payments are £1300 per month. Their remaining disposable income is £2000 per month, after all household and other bills, plus provision for holidays, is taken into account. Their budget for groceries is £150 per week.

Interests

Nancy and James are politically in the centre. They have voted for both major parties and are influenced by the social programme of the parties, their perceived grasp of economic matters, and crucially by their treatment of teachers and the NHS.

They are keen on keeping fit, and exercise two to three times a week. They take part in fun runs and events associated with their children's schools. They holiday in France, either at campsites or by hiring *gites*, sometimes with friends. They enjoy French and Italian food, and both old and new world wines.

Who influences their product choices?

Nancy and James do a big supermarket shop every Sunday morning. Nancy is keen to buy organic wherever possible, but finds it too expensive to do so all the time. She would also like to buy products that are sustainably sourced and is against factory farming. She looks for fair-trade wherever possible, and on meat for labels that reassure her that the animal has been humanely treated. She sees the Red Tractor logo and other animal welfare categorizations on products but is not sure what standards of welfare they represent. The couple's buying habits have been affected by campaigns against, for example, battery hens.

What are their personal goals?

Nancy's food shopping habits are a mix of physiological needs: providing for her family; social needs: the importance of sustaining a happy, healthy family around her; but, more importantly, the higher needs of esteem and self-actualization. Nancy would like to see herself as someone who shops responsibly, and to be seen by others as fitting that category. There is also an element of self-actualization – she feels good about herself when she does all she can to shop responsibly, and would feel even better about herself if she could afford to buy entirely in line with her high ethical standards.

What are they like from an emotional perspective?

Nancy and James are practical people, and when presented with an issue that is of concern, they seek to act to resolve the problem. In relation to foods, they worry in general about issues such as obesity. Nancy sees the impact upon children, and James is aware of the costs to the NHS of treating those whose illnesses are, in part, due to poor diet. They worry, in particular, about the impact of poor diet upon their children, and strive to ensure the family diet is good.

Past behaviours

They have bought from your brand, but not consistently. They have taken up discount vouchers printed in newspapers for shopping over a certain value.

Why do they interact with you and your competitors?

They respect your brand and like your products. They dislike shopping with the brand leader, Tesco, whose quality they suspect and who they consider to have low ethical standards and to behave aggressively towards farmers and other suppliers. They shop at Sainsbury's because it gives them the optimum combination of affordability, quality and ethical standards. When Tesco offers them discounts on their weekly shop, they take them up, on one occasion using offers over six consecutive weeks before returning to shop at Sainsbury's once the offers ran out.

What do they want from your brand?

They would like to be able to afford your brand. Nancy has a friend who has Waitrose credit and loyalty cards. She enjoys the free magazine and has shown Nancy the website, which has many recipes that Nancy likes the look of, and the smartphone app, which Nancy believes could help her with her food and recipe research, and compiling shopping lists.

Where do they look for information about your product category?

Nancy does not research food purchases, but she does use the Mumsnet website regularly and follows discussions about food matters. She is also on Facebook, but mainly to keep in touch with family members. She has noticed some of her Facebook friends liking brands, but can't imagine doing so herself. She watches TV chefs and has been influenced by the campaigns some of them have got involved in, particularly against battery hens and unsustainable fishing. Nancy likes the cook Delia Smith, who used to be the face of Sainsbury's but is now associated with Waitrose. James uses Twitter and Facebook, mainly in relation to work issues and keeping in touch with colleagues. They usually pick up a national newspaper on a Sunday, alternating between the *Observer*, *Sunday Times* and *Sunday Telegraph*. Nancy reads *The Guardian* on a Wednesday, when it has an education section. They also read a number of relevant trade magazines that they see at work. Nancy subscribes to the weekly *MoneySavingExpert* e-bulletin.

The information they want

Nancy would be persuaded to use Waitrose more if she felt it was price competitive. If she were presented with this information from Waitrose, she would experiment with doing her main shop at the brand to see if the price claims were true.

Where they are when they look for information

Nancy picks up food information from TV news, cookery programmes, TV advertisements from supermarkets and discount offers. She always checks the *MoneySavingExpert* bulletin and has followed tips she found there for getting discount vouchers for Waitrose and other supermarkets. Discounts of 10 per cent or more on her weekly shop will persuade her to switch to the brand making the offer.

Where do we go from here?

Once you have established customer personas, you can create business or marketing goals related to them. We'll look at business goals in detail in the next chapter. You can then build brand journalism strategies designed to help deliver on these goals, and we'll discuss that in Chapter 4.

Assignments

1 Take a brand – ideally one you work with, that you know a lot about, or which will give you access to data – and build up as complete a picture as you can of the audience for its products or services, and hence for its brand journalism.

2 Create an archetype for the McDonald's mum who is into healthy eating. Find out all you can about young mothers and their concerns about healthy eating through researching qualitative and quantitative data. Perhaps an appropriate forum such as Mumsnet – which we feature in detail in Chapter 11 – will let you post a link to a survey? From that information, create a customer persona by giving that young mother a name, age, location, family situation, educational and career background, and fill in as much other information as you can about her. Then develop a brand journalism strategy to engage with her on the subject of healthy eating for busy mums.

Notes

1 Wall Blog: wallblog.co.uk/2011/05/17/brand-journalism-how-the-marketing-department-of-today-is-tomorrows-social-media-newsroom/.

2 Social CMO blog: www.thesocialcmo.com/blog/2011/03/mcdonald%E2%80%99s-scales-t.

3 TES's Edward Griffith in an interview with the Online Journalism Blog: online-journalismblog.com/2008/08/22/the-teachers-are-online-interview-with-edward-griffith-of-tesconnect/.

4 Success.com on Duck Tape's Facebook performance: www.success.com/articles/1425-how-to-build-your-brand-with-facebook.

5 Karlene Lukovitz of Mediapost on Red Bull's "Me Statement": www.mediapost.com/publications/article/171130/top-social-engagement-brands-make-me-statements.html.

6 Jonathan Mildenhall, Coke's vice-president for global advertising strategy and creative excellence, on Coke's liquid content strategy: www.youtube.com/watch?v=LerdMmWjU_E.

7 Mark Taylor's advice for a small business: markwtaylor.hubpages.com/hub/Developing-a-Social-Media-Content-Strategy.

8 Heidi Cohen on creating marketing personas: heidicohen.com/marketing-persona/.

9 BuzzedUp: www.buzzedup.co.uk/index.php/what-are-buyer-personas/.

10 Content Marketing Institute guide to building buying personas for B2B organizations: www.contentmarketinginstitute.com/2011/04/4-questions-answered-about-buyer-personas/.

3 Establishing Business Goals and Developing Brand Journalism Strategies to Support Those Goals

Goals of this module

- Demonstrate that brand journalism goals must emanate from business goals.
- Outline six common business goals.
- Present detailed case studies of brand journalism strategies that have been designed to help achieve those common business goals.

On the website

Find further resources, essential updates and links to all the sources referenced here.

This chapter is about determining what you want to achieve with your brand journalism, how you plan to get there and how you judge your success. Brand journalism goals start with the big picture of a brand's business goals. As a brand journalist, you may not be party to the creation of that big picture, but to do your job well you need to know what the business goals are so that you can work effectively towards them.

If you are in a commercial business, those underlying goals are likely to do with the bottom line. A target will be set for increased revenue. That target may be quantified in terms of increased prospects, leads and customers (we'll define these terms in a moment). If you work for a charity, cause or campaign, those goals could be rooted in raising donations, but they might also be about increasing awareness of your message, gathering support for your cause, or building momentum for your campaign. Again, targets need to be set so that you can measure your success. There are many other goals, and we'll look at a range of them in a moment.

There may also be different goals emanating from different departments within an organization. There may be conflicts between what marketing, advertising and other departments want to achieve with brand journalism. And if there is no one who has ownership over the content that is created – no content director or chief content officer – it may be that those who don't understand brand journalism have control over it. As a consequence, content may fail to meet your community's needs; it may be promotional in tone rather than informative, educational or simply entertaining. We'll look at these issues further in the next chapter.

Once the business goals are clear, you can form a brand journalism strategy to achieve them. That strategy will use an appropriate combination of the platforms, both online and offline, and techniques in using them that we will cover in detail in Part II.

With most of the case studies that follow, the journalistic element is apparent and central. With one or two, it is less so. But as brand journalism is a hybrid medium, incorporating elements of marketing, public relations and customer service among other disciplines, that is inevitable. If you find yourself thinking, at some points, "but that's not journalism", you may be right – but it is brand journalism. It will not always be conducted by a brand journalist, but it will involve whoever is creating the content using brand journalism skills. With a brand that has an ongoing brand journalism strategy, realistic goals can be set with reference to what has been achieved in the past. If your organization is new to brand journalism, if it hasn't used the techniques you have chosen before, then it is harder to quantify what positive outcomes can be expected. There is often an element of experimentation with brand journalism.

Exploring examples of business goals and the brand journalism strategies used to achieve them

Let's take a look at six widely set business goals and case studies of the brand journalism strategies used to reach them.

1 Launching or reintroducing a brand, and building brand awareness

This goal is about building visibility and awareness or changing perception.

2 Becoming a trusted news source

Establishing yourself as the place people come to for reliable information is a key goal for many business-to-customer (B2C) and business-to-business (B2B) organizations. Spreading news about you is a part of that, but it's mainly about becoming a trusted information hub where the community you seek to serve can get all the information it needs.

3 Improving customer service and engagement with your community

This goal is not just about responding swiftly to customer complaints – something that can be done very effectively on social media – but also about protecting and managing your reputation, forging meaningful relationships with members of your community, attaining a particular level of engagement on each of a range of social media platforms, and possibly building a community of advocates.

4 Becoming a thought leader within an industry

Key individuals can be established as thought leaders – as authoritative and influential sources of information, knowledge and wisdom. So can brands. This goal is about leveraging the expertise within your organization and making it available to your community.

5 Driving sales and leads

This goal is about identifying prospects and leads, and achieving a certain level of conversions to paying customer status, membership, charitable contributions or other measures of success appropriate to your organization:

- Prospects are people who have shown an interest in your products or services. They may have become a Facebook fan or followed you on Twitter.
- Leads have completed a task, such as downloading a White Paper or subscribing to an email bulletin, which you have specified in your conversion funnel (the process designed to turn prospects and leads into customers).
- Customers are people who have completed a purchase, made a donation or performed some other activity that you have defined as the ultimate goal of your engagement with them. Such people have completed their journey through your sales or marketing funnel.

6 Building customer loyalty

Success with any of the goals above is likely to build customer loyalty; but another focused strategy involves making a community feel valued by offering promotions, coupons or other rewards. The belief is: make your network feel valued and they will value you.

A combination of goals

Those are big picture or headline goals. Brands often want to achieve several of them, and there is often a great deal of overlap between them. Move towards realizing one goal and you'll begin to achieve others as a by-product of that – as we shall see in the examples below.

There are plenty of other smaller or less focused goals. And in a major brand journalism strategy, there will be many intricate elements, all designed to work towards the goals set: the number of follows on Twitter, say, of likes on Facebook, comments on a blog, shares of video and other content, subscriptions to a customer magazine, products sold, amongst others. All can be measured, so you can quantify what you have achieved.

Let's look in more detail at the six key goals listed above, with examples of how particular brands have developed and implemented their brand journalism strategy in order to achieve them.

Launching or reintroducing a brand, and building brand awareness

Brighton and Hove council had a big problem with its brand. John Shewell, head of communications at the council, told *The Guardian*:

> We went out and asked focus groups what they thought of the city and what they thought of the council. They absolutely loved Brighton and said it was creative, vibrant, youthful, exciting. What about the council? They had this image of the faceless bureaucrat, it was just the stereotype view of public services.[1]

The council decided it needed a new, effective brand identity: it needed a human face. Its strategy to get that human face involved social media – particularly Twitter and YouTube. The council worked with a social business consultancy to map the conversations that people were having about it, and to identify social media influencers among local citizens. John Shewell said: "We wanted to get a better understanding of where the conversations were and who were influencing those conversations. We didn't want to get into a place where we were broadcasting stuff – you know, the spray and pray method, just pitch it out there – we wanted to understand who was having the conversation, with whom, what were they sharing and how influential were they."

Shewell has an interesting point to make about the quantitative and qualitative research it did before launching its new brand identity. He decided that collecting statistical, evidence-based information to support the new direction the council was to take was not only very difficult on social media, but unhelpful and outdated. He told *The Guardian*: "I've got this real issue about organisations truly believing in the metric-based approach, because sometimes the conversations can give you a much more powerful insight into how people actually feel about something. Numbers won't tell you that."

Much of Brighton's strategy did not require actual brand journalists to implement it, but it did use brand journalism communication skills. Once the council had an idea of the issues and concerns being expressed, it was able to train staff to use social media to respond to issues raised.

Shewell says the turning point for its strategy came when a citizen tweeted a problem with traffic lights. The council replied on Twitter, asked for a picture and fixed the problem within hours. That citizen tweeted: "Completely shocked, I'm amazed, thank you so much."[2] The post went viral and was hailed as a landmark, not just in Brighton's rejuvenation of its brand image, but for local government in general.

The council also created a YouTube channel which helps to overcome the "faceless bureaucrat" image by putting individual faces to roles and services.[3] Officers explain how to recycle and use other council services. Key communities are identified and served. There is Wastebuster, an animated character who explains issues such as food composting to school children, and information for potential investors in the city. The council uses YouTube to communicate with its citizens over important local concerns. It initiated a Big Alcohol Debate – about antisocial drinking in public areas – by setting up video pods where anyone could go and be interviewed on camera about their views. Those videos are on the council's YouTube channel.

Concrete results from successful interaction on social media include a fall in calls to call centres. Waste-related calls fell by 30 per cent. John Shewell says that by devolving communications to the front line, the council could potentially do away with call centres and bespoke communication departments. Implementing the strategy meant trusting many staff members who had not previously been in a communications role to handle the concerns of residents effectively; in doing so, they became ambassadors for the organization.

Becoming a trusted news source

One major objection to putting the words "brand" and "journalism" together stems from the question of impartiality. We'll look in detail at this and other important questions in Chapter 6, when we consider ethics in relation to brand journalism. For now, I'd like to take a practical look at how a brand might be considered a trusted – if not an entirely independent – news source.

Trust is important to all effective engagement, but it is essential if your brand goal is to become a respected information source. Trust has to be earned. The news you produce must be as reliable as that from an independent news source.

Gatwick Airport wanted to become a trusted news source. To do so it used a combination of social media and branded websites to offer all the information a user of the airport, and visitors to the region it serves, might need. One key element in that strategy was breaking news and travel updates on Twitter.[4] It succeeded to the extent that, as *The Drum* reported, it became the first UK airport to be recognized by Twitter as a trusted news source.[5] Twitter awarded Gatwick a blue tick logo for its efforts to communicate flight details, weather warnings and terminal information to passengers.

Lindsay Baldwin, head of airport communications, told *The Drum*: "We recognise the importance of providing accurate and timely communication – not only during times of disruption but also in responding to broader enquiries or passenger feedback. Twitter provides us with an immediate and effective communications platform to do just this."

On Twitter, Gatwick treats the platform as the breaking news service it is at heart, but communication is two way. On its profile, Gatwick says: "We love to hear your views, so please ask us a question".[6] It also uses Twitter for customer service. As Wall Blog reported: "The airport runs its Twitter customer service support 24-hours a day, which includes the #askgatwick campaign. It says that no matter what time of the day or night, if a passenger requires help then Gatwick can respond. And that's better than most."[7]

While the news Gatwick posts on Twitter is highly targeted towards breaking news, on its own branded site it concentrates on a wider range of information that any passenger might need at any time.[8] There is live flight information, access to arranging airport services such as parking, the situation on the roads around the airport, and so on. It has also widened its chosen role as a deliverer of trusted information through a partnership with local tourism organizations to create a site with a much wider brief.[9] The site, which is presented as a subsidiary to the Visit South East England site, is called Around Gatwick, and has the tag: "Gateway to the beautiful south". It's a rich resource for visitors to the area: a one-stop travel shop not just for users of the airport, but for anyone interested in a wide range of tourist and traveller attractions and facilities.

Contrast these channels with how Gatwick uses its Facebook page and you see a clear distinction.[10] On Facebook, Gatwick is more social, the status updates are more about competitions, things you might enjoy doing at the airport, links to less newsy content on the branded sites such as shopping reviews, and engagement with key community sectors such as business travellers and local residents. On Instagram, which is linked to from the Facebook site, they take fun pictures of stylish travellers, among other things.

Improving customer service and engagement with your community

Both Brighton and Hove council and Gatwick Airport achieved this alongside other goals, but let's focus now on this as a primary goal.

Key to achieving improved customer service and engagement is knowing what people are saying about you and responding to it appropriately. Dell, the computer company, was shown to be poor at both when the blogger and Columbia University New York (CUNY) journalism professor Jeff Jarvis had problems with a new computer from them. As Community Toolbar reported, when Jeff couldn't get Dell to address his problems through their own company channels, he blogged about his experience.[11] Unfortunately for Dell (or, actually, fortunately in the long run), Jeff was a key influencer, widely followed in media circles and a trusted source for information. He called his post "Dell Is Hell" and it was quickly picked up by the *New York Times* and *Business Day*.[12]

What Jeff did – this was back in 2005 – was highly influential for Dell on customer service levels, and the extent to which they engaged with their community. Here's Jeff's account of what happened following his blog post:

> I chose to see whether Dell is listening.
> They are not.
> Their media people were not reading the media that matters – media written by their very own customers. This page is already No. 5 in Google under Dell sucks. I gave them time. They failed.
> So then I emailed their media department and told them to read this blog. I gave them a cheat sheet. They didn't. They failed …
> You know what: If Dell were really smart, they'd hire me (yes, me) to come to them and teach them about blogs, about how their customers now have a voice; about how their customers are a community – a community often in revolt; about how they could find out what their customers really think; about how they could fix their customers' problems before they become revolts; about how they could become a better company with the help of their customers.
> If they'd only listen.

His conclusion was prescient: "Public relations has to take on a new meaning. It can no longer be about the press and publicity, which just separate companies from the public they are supposed to serve. Public relations must be about a new relationship with the public, with the public in charge."

How Dell then responded is a model for any company whose business goal is to improve customer service and engagement with their community. The company created a Dell Community website where customers could post problems and browse blogs, forums and groups to find solutions and advice.[13] That meant unhappy customers could bring their problems straight to Dell, making them easy to identify and facilitating quick resolution. Dell also created the position of corporate blogger, who talked to Jeff and worked to resolve his problem. As Community Toolbar reported:

> In the end, Jarvis felt he was listened to and respected, and praised Dell's response on his blog. Not every company can afford a corporate blogger, but every company, no matter how big or small, can respond quickly to customers and provide a satisfactory resolution.[14]

According to Payal Chanania:

> The latest news is that Dell has launched a "Social Media Listening Command Centre", to leverage the power of social networking in

customer service! As Laura Thomas, marketing communications senior consultant at Dell propounds, "Thanks to social media, customers have a voice like never before. When customers wanted to discuss a product or service in the past, they'd dial a call centre and their problem would be addressed behind closed doors. Only the customer and the company would hear the complaint or praise. Now, these issues are aired publicly to potentially huge audiences of potential buyers. At Dell, we still rely on a number of traditional channels for help desk services, but are increasingly looking to social networking to actively engage with our customers and ensure they have a good experience with us!"[15]

Dell uses forums, blogs and Twitter, with the community website as the hub that links them all.[16] There are also groups and wikis and an Idea Storm area where customers can help the company to innovate. They explain Idea Storm sessions like this: "Storm sessions are hyper focused idea generating sessions centered on a specific topic or theme and open for a limited time. You can also submit ideas for future sessions to the 'Storm Sessions Topics' category." When I looked there were around 17,500 ideas submitted and over 500 implemented. So Dell's effort with customer service and engagement is also fulfilling another goal – facilitating research and development.

Payal Chanania has further advice for any brand seeking to improve customer service. Listening is vital:

> If the management were to tap into these valuable public mentions by monitoring where their company name pops up (Facebook posts, Twitter feeds, etc.), not only can it directly address the issues or concerns but also spot crucial opportunities for product improvement. A definite win–win for the organisation. This can go a step further when customers can directly post comments on the product/service's Facebook page to voice their queries, complaints, demands or suggestions. The organisation can capitalise on the ideas, expectations of change or even bad experiences and criticisms by regarding them as valuable insight and dealing with them accordingly.[17]

Such an approach embodies one of the core requirements for successful brand journalism: transparency. If anyone can see how problems are dealt with, they can draw their own conclusions about the brand.

Becoming a thought leader within an industry

This is where your in-house expertise comes into play. Individuals can become thought leaders; so can brands if they achieve leadership on an organization-wide basis.

Ben Boyd of the Edelman PR firm gave four tips for achieving thought leadership status in a *Forbes* post.[18] First, you need the right team –

employees and advisers who question assumptions and ask why you do things a certain way. Second, make sure your company's behaviour meets its aspirations. You can't be a thought leader if your words don't fit your actions. Third, "if you're going to spend the time to build expertise and recognition, it ought to connect to your actual business". Boyd cites the example of Coca-Cola, which has become a thought leader regarding clean water, which is both a worthy cause and key to Coke's supply chain. We'll look in detail at Coke in a moment. Fourth, thought leadership requires long-term commitment.

The platforms for thought leadership are your branded websites and blogs, plus forums – places where expertise is sought and advice can be offered in depth. White Papers and e-books can also be useful. We'll look at these and other platforms in Part II.

So, on to Coke. Coca-Cola was under fire for the high demand it had for water in areas where there was a shortage, often in developing countries. There was a growing environmental movement committed to protecting water supplies. Coke had a business interest in the issue because it needed fresh water for its bottling plants around the world and didn't want to see those supplies denied. There was a public relations interest because if Coke was seen to be depleting these reserves, or failing to act to protect them, that could damage its brand reputation. So, water depletion was an area in which it needed to act. Coke possessed the knowledge and expertise required to tackle the issue.

As Reuters reported, Coke had the data and maps needed to identify threatened watersheds: "The maps, which are powered by previously pro-prietary Coca-Cola data collected over years of research in locations wher-ever the world's biggest soft drinks firm had manufacturing sites, are now publicly available for free on the Internet."[19]

As well as releasing the data needed for action to be taken on this issue, Coca-Cola forged partnerships with governments and non-governmental organizations (NGOs), and took part in initiatives. It used brand journalism on its corporate websites, plus reports and White Papers, to communicate what it was doing.[20] It wrote about its collaboration with charities and aid agencies, in 320 projects in 86 countries, on protecting watersheds and providing clean water.

Such initiatives, and the way in which Coke's brand journalism spread the word about them, helped to establish Coca-Cola as a thought leader in the subject of water use by industry and in action to protect watersheds. The benefits to Coke's business goals are clear. As Fast Company reported:

> Viewed from a certain perspective, Coke's business is really a water-processing operation. The company needs 333 ounces of water to generate $1 of revenue. Coke says that every litre of beverage it manufactures and sells requires 2.43 litres of water. That represents a 9 per cent improve-ment over 2004, which translates into 8 billion gallons of water saved a

year. That's 8 billion gallons Coke didn't have to buy or pump out of rivers or aquifers, clean to food-manufacturing standards, and then dispose of. Reduce water use 9 per cent, and you reduce a flood of costs.[21]

Driving sales and leads

This can include several measures of success, such as achieving a certain level of conversions to paying customer status, membership or charitable contributions. In a post for Coherent Social Media, Neicole Crepeau gave an example of a business goal for a health club and the brand journalism strategies, or what she called social goals, used to achieve it:

> Business goal: Increase new members by 10 per cent.
>   Social goals:
>
> • Increase guest pass registrations: get club members to invite their friends to the club on a guest pass.
> • Increase awareness: get club members to tell other likely customers in the neighbourhood about the club.
>
> Because you can put a figure on the increased revenue the goal would bring in, you can put success criteria alongside the strategies used.
>   That, in turn, can help you to identify a strategy for conducting your social media efforts. By taking a top-down approach and starting with what you want to achieve as a business, you can build a coherent social media strategy.[22]

You can identify the platforms to use by knowing (through the sort of research we discussed in Chapter 2) who your customers and potential customers are and where they can be found online, then look at how much effort you can afford to put in to achieve the set goals.

The Public Relations Society of America gave this example of a company, Catalytic Products International, a manufacturer of air pollution control equipment, that implemented a brand journalism strategy with the very clear goal of gaining new business.[23] The company used newsletters, copy on its website and White Papers (which are authoritative reports or guides that help readers to understand an issue, solve a problem or make a decision) to address topics of value to potential customers. The content created led to 66 requests for quotes and additional $2.2 million in revenue.

The social marketer Jeff Bullas looked at how a similar strategy can be developed in the case of charities seeking increased donations and subscribers.[24] He was writing specifically about a strategy for the use of Facebook in a social media marketing initiative, but the approach would stand for any of the platforms you choose to use. Once you have defined your target audience (which will tell you whether Facebook is the place to reach them), you need to determine your goals and objectives. Jeff lists these possible goals for a charity:

- Increase traffic to the organization's website and blog.
- Improve the "call to action" conversion rates for the donate button.
- Increase donations.
- Save money on traditional marketing costs.
- Deepen the relationship with possible donors and benefactors.
- Grow the brand's Facebook "likes".
- Increase email subscriptions to the newsletter.
- Run a successful event.

He gave these possible measures of success:

- Increase donations by 20 per cent.
- Reduce marketing costs by 30 per cent.
- Grow Facebook "likes" by 50 per cent per month.
- Increase newsletter subscribers by 40 per cent per annum.

He gives as an example Marie Curie Cancer Care with, at the time of writing, around 4000 likes and 3000 "talking about this". He says:

> Strategy goals translate into tactics with two calls to action that are about achieving two goals on the Facebook landing page:

1 Running a successful event with an invite to "Hold a Blooming Great Tea Party".
2 Acquiring new email subscribers and potential donor information with a subscriber form on the Facebook landing page.[25]

Build customer loyalty – give consumers a reason to interact with you by offering promotions, coupons or information

The EIC agency blogged these suggestions on how to build customer loyalty through social media:

- Develop rewards programmes: "You can choose from different models, like offering deals and special offers if a customer buys a certain amount of your products in a specific period of time."
- Encourage interaction: "In order for customers to connect with your brand they have to feel that you're accessible to them ... [interact] with them on your brand's social networks."
- Show appreciation: Offer thank yous and, where appropriate, gifts.[26]

Incentive Mag featured a case study of Dairy Queen, the US quick-service restaurant chain, and how it used social incentives to boost its fan base: "Using targeted consumer incentives, [it] ... was able to massively grow its customer fan club and encourage customer loyalty over the long term."[27] The company had a long-established Blizzard Fan Club, whose 2.8 million members receive emailed special offers, discounts and news.

But the company wanted to increase that membership and engage more closely with existing members. It set itself the goals of increasing the number of coupons printed via email by fan club members by 300,000 and to grow the number of fans by 300,000 overall. Emails were sent out offering existing fan club members the option to post a buy-one-get-one-free coupon on their Facebook pages. They went out in July, a busy month when Dairy Queen didn't normally issue offers.

Incentive Mag reported: "To ensure the coupons went viral, [Dairy Queen] offered free ice cream for a year to the individual who got the most friends to sign up and made a promotion for five other participants chosen at random." Kristin Olson, a media planner who worked on the strategy, told *Incentive Mag*: "We wanted our current customers to share the good news about the coupons. Our consumers are really passionate about the product and were really instrumental in achieving our aggressive goals."

The campaign was more successful than expected, beating the 300,000 goals for both new members and printing of coupons by 22 per cent and 37 per cent, respectively.

Assignment

Create a brand journalism strategy for a brand you know. Begin with a business goal and then fit a detailed brand journalism strategy to it. Set goals and determine how you will measure success.

Notes

1 *The Guardian* on Brighton's initiative: www.guardian.co.uk/government-computing-network/2012/feb/27/social-media-brighton-hove-council?newsfeed=true.
2 See twitter.com/BrightonHoveCC/.
3 See www.youtube.com/user/BrightonandHoveGovUk.
4 See twitter.com/Gatwick_Airport.
5 *The Drum*: www.thedrum.co.uk/news/2012/04/24/gatwick-recognised-twitter-trusted-news-source.
6 Gatwick on Twitter: twitter.com/Gatwick_Airport.
7 Wall Blog: wallblog.co.uk/2012/04/24/gatwick-is-the-first-uk-airport-to-be-recognised-by-twitter-for-excellent-customer-service-support-infographic/.
8 Gatwick's own branded site: www.gatwickairport.com/.
9 Gatwick's partnership with local tourism organizations: www.visitsoutheastengland.com/gatwick/.
10 Gatwick's Facebook page: www.facebook.com/GatwickAirport.
11 Community Toolbar: toolbar.conduit.com/social-media-marketing/customer-service.aspx.

12 "Dell Is Hell" post from Jeff Jarvis: buzzmachine.com/2005/07/01/dell-hell-seller-beware/.

13 Dell community website: en.community.dell.com.

14 Community Toolbar: toolbar.conduit.com/social-media-marketing/customer-service.aspx.

15 Payal Chanania's report: payalbytes.blogspot.co.uk/2012/02/published-on-february-22-2012-social.html.

16 Dell community website: en.community.dell.com/.

17 Payal Chanania has further advice for any brand seeking to improve customer service. Listening is vital: payalbytes.blogspot.co.uk/2012/02/published-on-february-22-2012-social.html.

18 Ben Boyd on thought leadership: www.forbes.com/sites/dorieclark/2012/06/06/four-steps-to-become-a-corporate-thought-leader/.

19 *Scientific American* on Coke and water: www.reuters.com/article/2012/07/24/us-water-maps-idUSBRE86N13C20120724 and maps on the Internet: insights.wri.org/aqueduct/atlas.

20 Coke's community water programmes: www.thecoca-colacompany.com/citizenship/community_initiatives.html.

21 Fast Company on Coke's water initiative: www.fastcompany.com/magazine/154/a-sea-of-dollars.html.

22 Coherent Social Media: blog.coherentia.com/index.php/2011/10/business-goals-should-drive-social-media-goals.

23 Public Relations Society of America: www.prsa.org/Intelligence/Tactics/Articles/view/9647/1045/The_newsroom_approach_Make_customers_care_with_bra.

24 Jeff Bullas: www.jeffbullas.com/2011/08/05/how-to-create-a-facebook-marketing-strategy-for-your-non-profit/.

25 Marie Curie Cancer Care: www.facebook.com/MarieCurieUK.

26 The EIC agency on how to build customer loyalty through social media: www.onlineadvertisingagency.info/2012/05/09/how-to-build-customer-loyalty-through-social-media/.

27 *Incentive Mag* on Dairy Queen: www.incentivemag.com/Incentive-Programs/Consumer/Articles/Case-Study–Dairy-Queen-Uses-Social-Incentives-to-Boost-Fanbase/.

4 Making the Case for Brand Journalism Within an Organization

Putting the Structure in Place to Achieve Your Brand Journalism Goals

Goals of this module

- Establish the place of brand journalism within a brand's overall content strategy.
- Discuss the question of who owns the brand journalism project within an organization.
- Outline the roles of an editor-in-chief and a chief content officer within a brand.
- Guide editors and chief content officers in how to make the case for brand journalism within an organization.
- Lay out the processes in getting your brand journalism/editorial strategy successfully implemented.
- List the skill sets you'll need to be able to draw upon.
- Demonstrate how to obtain buy-in from throughout an organization.
- Itemize the processes involved in planning, implementing and managing a brand journalism operation.
- Show, through case studies, how a number of companies' brand journalism operations are structured and how they operate.
- Provide a model social media engagement policy.
- Outline the training needs of non-journalists now engaging in content creation and social media engagement.

On the website

Find further resources, essential updates and links to all the sources referenced here.

A brand needs to understand what brand journalism is, what it can achieve and how a brand journalism department must be organized and run. One thing you have to be absolutely clear about is that developing and implementing a brand journalism strategy takes time. It takes time to build a community and to gain its trust and respect. Don't let the boss think brand journalism can be a quick fix. And it can't be done without the budget, the time, the staff and the tools.

Your goal in making the business case for a brand journalism strategy is to demonstrate the results you can achieve and, hence, to justify the budget you need. One key question to answer right at the start is who owns the brand journalism project? Is it marketing? What about customer services? Or should there be a new division, headed by a chief content officer or content director, that oversees the work of a brand journalism editor-in-chief? Brand journalism is likely to be one element within a brand's content strategy. The question for any brand is this: how big a part of our content/communications strategy should the brand journalism element be? And, as a supplement to that, how does the brand journalism element fit within that overall content strategy?

While journalists and journalistic techniques can be used to optimize any type of content, for a large amount of very routine material, a journalist's skills would be wasted. So although a journalist could, in theory, polish, say, the many hundreds of pages of basic product information your e-commerce site might contain, you don't want your brand journalism team tied up with that. Instead, a brand can instil an understanding of good communications practice throughout its content-creating and customer-facing teams. That involves training, and it may well be that the brand journalism team can help.

So how does brand journalism fit within a brand's overall content strategy? Let's remember what Larry Light said when he developed the concept of brand journalism. He spoke about a brand as if it were a multi-topic magazine, and of brand journalism as "a chronicle of the varied things that happen in a brand's world, throughout the day, throughout the years."[1]

Like an editor in traditional publishing, the focus of an editor at a brand is on creating great content that the audience will love. Rather than being pulled this way and that by marketing, advertising and other stakeholders in the brand's content strategy, it is best if brand journalism comes under a director of content. While the brand journalism editor must never lose sight of the business goals of the company they work for, they must be given the same freedoms within those business parameters as an editor at a publishing company gets.

Shel Holtz, in a post at *Social Media Today* called "Marketers Keep Your Hands Off Your Company's Brand Journalism" argued the need for independence for the brand journalism project: "Marketing is what companies do to promote and sell products or services. Organisations produce plenty of it. Brand journalism, though, is different." He distinguished brand journalism content from marketing messages, saying: "people will want to link to it, share it, talk about it precisely because it's *not* trying to pitch something. As soon as it begins to smack of The Pitch, it loses its appeal ... The companies that get this – and there is an ever-growing number of them – have taken to hiring content strategists and journalists to execute the strategy." And while he stresses that brand journalism content must support key marketing strategies, "for marketers to insist on control over brand journalism just doesn't make sense. In fact, smart marketers will *want* to keep their fingers out of this content, focusing instead on strategizing the *kind* of visibility brand journalism should attract, then leaving the brand journalists to do their jobs."[2]

Making the case for brand journalism within an organization

If a brand isn't yet doing brand journalism and you are to introduce it, you'll need to make the case for it around the organization. If they are doing it badly, you'll need to show just how it can be done better.

For many brands, the idea that they might become a publisher is a disconcerting one. Publishing is often seen as being way beyond the core competencies of the organization. So you may need to make the case for such innovation. To get support from the CEO and key executives, you need to be able to show them that it works. You need to convince them that they must move beyond conventional selling and into brand storytelling. And to do that you need some solid evidence. There is plenty of that in this book, but what a sceptical CEO will want to know is what it can do for his brand, how, what it'll cost and the ROI (return on investment) he or she will see.

To demonstrate this, you can apply the principles we are covering in *Brand Journalism*: of establishing an audience's needs; identifying business goals; developing brand journalism strategies to support them; and measuring your success. You might need to start small, with a test project focusing on a particular niche audience and a distinct business goal. You may be able to show what a rival is doing successfully with brand journalism.

If you inherit a poorly performing customer magazine, you may be able to dummy up an improved version and get it focus grouped. The same holds if you want to make the case for starting a magazine. You can also use web analytics to show how your community interacts with your online content now, and what may be wrong with that (how often they come, how long they stay, how much content they consume, where the drop-offs in readership come and why, what the barriers are to the achievement of goals): whether it's getting them to a purchase decision, making a donation, sharing your content or whatever.

The processes in getting your brand journalism strategy successfully implemented

Let's stick with the editor function as we outline the processes involved in getting your brand journalism strategy implemented. Editors within traditional publishing companies work with other departments: advertising, marketing, information technology (IT); plus specialists either within or outside their department: website builders, printers, search engine optimization (SEO) specialists and others. Editors within brands have to do the same. The difference is that, while in publishing an editor creates the product, in a brand, the editor creates products that are the means to marketing the brand.

In both environments, those other departments have a stake in the product you create. They'll want influence. In publishing, advertising directors want their ads in prime spots; marketing want their promotions prominently displayed in the newspaper/magazine/on the website. In a brand, departments such as marketing, advertising, customer relations, communications, investor relations, and others are stakeholders. All companies have rivalries between departments. There may be turf wars over content. These departmental stakeholders will want to get their sponsored content onto the platforms that the editor runs. And they may well have staff in their own departments creating and posting content and interacting with customers on social media.

How do you ensure it all works? If you're not careful, you end up with poor quality content that doesn't do its job, swamping and sinking the brand journalism project. That's why you need a director of content who has clear ownership of all content platforms and who ensures that the brand journalism editor-in-chief can get on with his or her job. But the content director and editor need to work with those stakeholders, so that the content you create, and the brand journalism you do, fulfils the goals of the business and each of the stakeholders. Not always easy. For success, content director and editor-in-chief have to hold that ground, and other stakeholders need to believe that the brand journalism strategy can deliver for them.

The first step in developing and implementing a brand journalism strategy is to achieve a broad consensus on what that strategy is to be. This begins with approving the business goals and the brand journalism projects that are to help deliver them. The brand as a whole must decide how you want to appear to your community; how you want that community to perceive you; the relationship you want to have with them. It needs to decide how big the brand journalism project will be, what input there is to be from other departments and, hence, what training is needed in, for example, engaging with customers on social media.

The processes you must put in place

It is essential that you impose editorial standards, structures and processes onto any content that your brand creates as part of a brand journalism strategy. Should you do the same with all content? Arguably, yes, even though that can be a massive task.

First you need to conduct an audit on all the brand journalism you have inherited. An assessment of your owned media, from the way in which the customer magazine looks and feels, to the design and structure of the website, is essential. Any other material you are to be responsible for, from blogs to social media presences, must be assessed. How is it performing? What is below standard; what is missing?

On your branded websites, where there is probably a good deal of standing content – the non-news stuff that is pretty static – a very detailed audit is necessary. You need to analyse the structure and the content on every screen. On structure, you should ensure that the website works, that it presents your brand as you would wish it, and that the needs of visitors are satisfied. On content, decide what needs junking, what needs improving and what is missing. The only way to find out is to have a team, whether from brand journalism or elsewhere, go through and create a full breakdown of the website: every screen, every item of content, grading it for effectiveness.

Where content has been generated by other departments, this can be a challenge. They'll fight their corner for content you know is poorly written or fails for a number of other reasons. You can be objective here – is that content doing its job? Web analytics will show where traffic goes, where it drops off, the pages that are popular and those that are not.

Information architecture experts can demonstrate where navigation is confusing. SEO experts will show whether it is findable. Such an audit can show your brand in relation to rivals in terms of SEO, Google ranking and other measures of effectiveness. Then, from this audit, you can decide what needs to be done to the website and what new static content you need. You can establish those needs from business perspectives, from individual stakeholder requirements and customer needs. And, of course, the brand needs an approval process for all that is done.

Planning the detail of your fluid content creation

We've looked at standing and static content – now for fluid content: the news that you create. You'll need to decide what types of content you create, where and how frequently. You should ask yourself these broad questions:

- Why are you creating this content?
- What business or marketing goals is it designed to deliver on?
- What audience segment or defined information or entertainment need is it designed to satisfy?
- What platforms should you be using to reach that audience?
- How will success be measured?

When it comes to the processes involved in getting and publishing content, there are more detailed questions to consider:

- What content is created – and for which platforms?
- What is the publishing programme?
- What do you do each day, week, month throughout the year? You must plan content that fits your brand's products and services, including launches, promotions and specialist seasonal content as appropriate.
- What platforms do you use?

- How do you coordinate content across printed media, websites, on social media? What storytelling methods do you use: text, stills, infographics, video, audio? What is the process for promoting blog content on social media?
- What is the workflow?
- Who can request content and who approves that request?
- Who commissions the content that is needed?
- Who creates this content?
- How much comes from the brand journalism team and freelancers/ experts hired by them?
- What content is to come from other departments?
- Who are the in-house experts or thought leaders you need material from?
- How do requests for new content come to you from other departments?
- Who edits and sub-edits it?
- What is the approval process before publication?
- Who publishes it?
- What is your content update programme?
- Who is responsible for taking down outdated content?

The skill sets you will need to draw upon

You'll need the same range of skills within your team, or available to that team, as you would as the editor in a publishing house. In terms of content creation and editing skills, that means people who can work in print and online, and use text, still images, infographics and other graphics, video and audio. You'll need web developers, SEO specialists and experts in web analytics. To research your audiences you'll need marketing research, survey, interview and focus group resources.

Getting buy-in from throughout the company

Once you have the senior executives persuaded, you'll need the message to filter down through the organization. For a brand journalism strategy to work, you need buy-in from throughout the company. That's at its most essential where individuals in other departments are to take on roles related to the brand journalism initiative, from content creation to engaging on social media.

Social media involvement is best seen as a part of content creation because it is integral to the successful delivery of content to your audience and to interacting with them about that content. Anyone involved needs to be shown what the brand journalism strategy is and what it is designed to deliver. Their role needs to be explained to them and they should be given all the support and training they need (we'll look at training such people, and establishing a social media policy for them to work to, later in this chapter). The content director and/or editor-in-chief should take the lead in this process.

In a post at *Social Media Examiner* on achieving social media buy-in, Marcus Sheridan recommended that you educate via an event. Sheridan says there is often a lack of understanding of what social media is and what it can do for a brand, and that needs to be addressed if you are to get buy-in. He recommends: "Start a social media campaign and hold a social media summit."[3]

Pull as much of the company together as you can. The first goal is education: "This is where all employees can become familiar with types of social media, the potential power of these platforms, how content marketing works, etc. ... The next step of this summit is to implement an action plan of how each person in the company can make a difference."

Sheridan gives a case study:

> The CMO [chief marketing officer] and I decided content marketing (blogging) would be the main emphasis of their social media marketing efforts. To make this happen, we brainstormed as a group (about 60 people in this case) the common questions received each day from prospects and customers. Within 30 minutes and after much participation and enthusiasm from the entire group, we had well over 100 common questions.
>
> Later on, the CMO turned each one of these questions into the title of a blog post, and assigned each article to different employees, with corresponding due dates for each. Now that everyone in the company understood the power and importance of content marketing, each accepted his or her role in producing the assigned article. And because there were so many employees who were now willing to take part in this activity, it was easy for this company to produce multiple blog articles a week, all without putting too much burden on the shoulders of the CMO/CCO [chief creative officer].

He suggests creating a company social media newsletter: "A big launch is one thing, sustaining interest is another. So send out regular updates about the successes you are achieving." And you should continue training and education. As your brand journalism strategy develops, you need to make sure everyone understands what you are doing and why.

The Content Marketing Institute suggested several ways to get employees involved in content creation.[4] I am summarizing them here:

- Get executives on Facebook answering questions posed by your Facebook fans and supporters [or, indeed, get them to engage with your community on any platform that is important to you]. Repurpose the resulting content as a blog post.

- Poll your staff to see which of them might be willing to write blog posts on a rotating basis.
- Take pictures during your next team lunch and post them on your blog.
- Interview one of your employees every week or every month as a "getting to know us" feature on your blog.
- When anyone on your team attends an industry event, have them write a report on your blog.

You can come up with others that are more appropriate to your brand.

Establishing your brand journalism team

Do you hire experienced journalists, outsource to a third party or enable employees? Outside firms can bring expertise and a clear focus on creating brand content, but they can't know your company as well as you and your team do. Get the right firm, though, and they can train your team in brand journalism.

Hiring experienced journalists who also understand and are in tune with the ethos and goals of brand journalism brings essential skills inside the organization. These hires can also train the rest of your team. Many firms find that employees can become natural brand ambassadors, with the right training. But just as brand journalism won't work unless you are a company that deserves to have a good reputation, you can't make employees into brand ambassadors unless they believe in you.

Your team may include staff from different disciplines – marketing is often the core, plus public relations, customer service, internal communications. We'll look at how to train a disparate team below.

Should you create a brand journalism newsroom?

Should you create a newsroom? That depends, in part, on the size of your organization – whether you are big enough to run one – but more on the type of information world you operate in. Some brands can easily become newsmakers – they have a ready supply of fast-moving information that forms a strong thread linking all other parts of their content creation together. Others find that they move in a much slower information world, where constant updates are not appropriate (we'll look more at this distinction in the next chapter).

If your brand falls into the latter category, a newsroom approach is probably not for you. But if you fall into the former, it could be. There is a growing recognition that in a fast-moving information environment, a brand journalism strategy needs to mirror much of what a traditional journalistic enterprise does. But that takes a big team. Where does it come from? One strategy is to reinvent the marketing department.

In a Wall Blog post headlined "Brand Journalism – How the Marketing Department of Today Is Tomorrow's Social Media Newsroom", Albert Pusch wrote:

> Marketing departments need to operate like newsrooms if they are to reflect the continually changing requirements of today's corporate audience. This means that even established, reputable marketing departments need to accept some things that new start-up companies have already learned, such as working in real time. [A brand newsroom is the obvious answer.] ... The reality is that, if they are to really engage with their customers and drive awareness of their brand, "modern" marketers need to create new content every day that promotes and encourages dialogue with their target audience. They must also monitor new blog entries, videos and other items using, for example, really simple syndication (RSS) feeds or Twitter. Managing this process is only possible when the work is properly organised, much the way that a newsroom is.
>
> What marketers need to realise above anything else is that while many of the tools of the modern two-way conversation may be free to set up, they take time, effort and energy to make work. While every company can now become their own publisher by investing in a Facebook page or a regular e-newsletter, these are only going to be effective if they adhere to the journalistic qualities that magazine editors have been working to for many years. But, if they do this, marketers can create stronger and more meaningful relationships with their clients.[5]

Journalists have the skills you need

Essentially, you need fully trained and qualified journalists to plan and implement your brand journalism strategy. They make the best corporate storytellers. David Meerman Scott, quoted in the *Ryerson Review of Journalism*, said:

> Journalists know how to tell a story, they are very good at taking complex pieces of information and boiling them down so they are easy to understand, and they are efficient at working on multiple stories at one time ... They just make the best corporate storytellers in my opinion.[6]

But how you use those journalists varies. Shel Holtz of the Holtz Blog gives these examples:

> At Intel, three full-time journalists produce the content. At Cisco Systems, the content comes from a host of freelance journalists, coordinating by social media staff, many of whom come from journalism

backgrounds. Dell has brought outside journalists in who are pitched [to] by brand managers, but the journalists make the ultimate decision about the topics they'll address.[7]

Case studies of brand journalism operations

Let's take a look at a couple of brands that have found differing answers to the question of how a brand journalism team is set up and operates, and the other departments it draws expertise and personnel from.

Nissan

First, here's Nissan's take on the brand newsroom approach. Nissan hired television and print journalists from the BBC, CNBC and *Bloomberg Busi-nessWeek*, among others, to set up its in-house newsroom. It is run by Dan Sloan, who spent 17 years at Reuters.

The newsroom sends its crews to cover Nissan stories – for example, Nissan's chief executive Carlos Ghosn touring a car plant damaged by the Japan earthquake of 2011. They live-streamed the visit and Ghosn's announcement that the plant was back to 80 per cent of pre-quake output on YouTube. Two hours later a rough-cut of the film was posted on the Nissan website, and an edited package followed three hours later.

The newsroom also produces material for the large number of websites that aggregate news about the car industry, which have a huge appetite for video content. The *Financial Times*, in a story headlined "Nissan's PR Mimics the Newsroom", gave this example of how successful such a strategy can be:

> ... the operation recently produced a feature on the Nissan Leaf Nismo RC electric sports car, in which its cameras were given exclusive access to the car and the engineers who built it. When the editors of *Top Gear's* website put the film on their homepage, it went viral and generated more than 60,000 views.[8]

The newsroom also tackles hard news stories in which Nissan is under pressure, producing reports on matters such as, post-earthquake, Japan's nuclear melt-down, radiation checks on cars awaiting export, and a software glitch on a model.

The Simpaticor PR Blog says of the enterprise:

> This in-house team gets under the skin of the company; reveals how its production process works, interviews senior management and talks with its technology and design teams. In effect it reveals the brand in controlled detail to those who are interested and as such presents a compelling and influential picture of itself.[9]

The newsroom operation doesn't replace Nissan's other forms of communication. It only accounts for around 5 per cent of its worldwide public relations budget and a tiny fraction of marketing spending. But it is seen as superseding traditional public relations.

Dan Sloan told the *Financial Times*:

> Traditional public relations is not that sophisticated – it's something that is so heavy-handed that it can be potentially unwatchable or unreadable. In coming to this enterprise, what I said from day one was: "It won't work if it comes off as state television – it's got to be much more interesting than traditional marketing communications attempts have been."

And Simon Sproule, Nissan's head of global marketing communications, said: "It's about killing press releases. We decided that if we've got good stories to tell, we'll tell them ourselves." He also explains that Nissan would never outsource the venture, saying humorously: "The media centre is the first love child from the coupling of marketing and PR."

Simpaticor PR Blog underlines what is needed for such an approach to work:

> Of course there are two critical caveats to this kind of activity. First, it doesn't and shouldn't replace "independent" journalists and the kind of objective reporting and commentary that they will unleash on a daily basis. The second is ... it must be credible and interesting. A brand journalist must have the freedom to generate stuff that a general or specific audience will want to consume. No one will watch the 24/7 Nissan channel, but design students and practitioners may pick up on a YouTube video on the future of aerodynamics. Engineers might be fascinated by electric motor developments or production line automation. Business analysts and yes the press, might catch the latest comments from the CEO.[10]

Imperial Sugar

Imperial Sugar set up its newsroom in response to a crisis. In 2008 an explosion at a US sugar refinery caused a fire that burned for two weeks.[11] Two months later, Imperial Sugar hired a team of independent journalists from an outside PR agency headed by David Henderson, a former CBS Network News correspondent, that together had skills from print, TV and photojournalism. They set up ICS Newsroom.

Newsroom Ink reported that Imperial Sugar had a list of requirements, established by John Sheptor, then president and CEO.[12] They included:

1 Provide an online alternative for media to access credible and unbiased information about Imperial Sugar.

2 Position Imperial Sugar as the new leader in sugar-refining safety.
3 Create awareness for its products and services, acquisition of new customers and growth of business.
4 Restore company integrity with employees and customers.
5 Establish Imperial Sugar as a viable choice for investors, investment firms and customers.

The strategy also included:

- a concise, appealing *USA Today* style
- clear, informative, accurate and balanced stories with eye-catching photos
- stories and photos available for reuse without permission
- online library of high-resolution photos and videos
- media enquiries immediately forwarded to cell phones so that questions can be answered within minutes, not hours
- social media, including Twitter, Facebook, YouTube, Flickr
- rotating RSS (really simple syndication) feed featuring the latest sugar news.

The newsroom published a steady flow of legitimate news stories and high-quality photos shot by a former Associated Press and *People* photographer. David Henderson told *Newsroom Ink*:

> The stories were about the industry, customers, and the communities in which the company does business ... The SC Newsroom positions the Imperial Sugar Company as an authoritative voice in the sugar industry, in the U.S., Mexico and elsewhere. It is a one-stop shop for the best thinking and views on sugar and all of the issues and market forces that surround it.[13]

This means it achieves at least two of the potential business goals behind a brand journalism strategy that we discussed in Chapter 3: it's a news source and a thought leader:

> We're expressing the ICS corporate voice above the noise of the marketplace, where often people much less qualified – but far more vocal – pump out their opinions into mainstream and social media. The sheer speed, volume and rapid dissemination of information – right or wrong – can inundate communications and sway public opinion.

How to integrate your brand journalists within the company

What if you just want one corporate reporter? Some brand journalism operations are far smaller than the case studies above. Some involve hiring just one journalist.

Brian Kardon of Eloqua, an Internet marketing specialist, wanted to do just that. He wrote on the Eloqua blog: "I had a simple problem I needed to fix – to produce more and better content. Our blog was not particularly well read or indexed. The frequency of our postings was too low. Many of the postings were too Eloqua-centric."[14] He hired Jesse Noyes, formerly of *The Boston Herald* and *Boston Business Journal*, as his corporate reporter: "The results have been fantastic, including thousands of new followers to our blog It's All About Revenue, a Stevie Award for the blog, a doubling of unique visitors between Q2 and Q3 of this year, and thousands of new, valuable links. It has become the hub of our content marketing strategy."[15]

Kardon has some excellent insights into how to make bringing a journalist into a company work. They include integrating the journalist within the team:

> The journalist needs to understand the company's strategy, partner ecosystem, and goals if they are to be successful. Some companies don't see the journalist as a "marketer". That's a big mistake. Writing timely, engaging content is at the heart of great marketing. The more your reporter knows about your company, the more valuable he will become.

It's also important to give the journalist room to breathe and, for goodness sake, don't ask the reporter to shill (hide their association with the brand): "We give Jesse plenty of freedom to find the stories that he thinks our readers care most about. We do not overly scrutinize his choices of topics. We try to create a frictionless environment to get content up fast."

How to develop a social media engagement policy within an organization

A social media engagement policy defines who uses social media on behalf of the organization and how they use it. Yet, 76 per cent of companies do not have one, according to research from Mindflash.[16] You need a policy and it should cover the following key areas.

Guidelines for engaging

- In order to avoid the potential for reputational damage you should set clear limitations on what can be discussed, commented on or promoted via social media.
- Will you allow staff to post as individuals as named spokespersons for you or anonymously in a feed that bears your brand name? Anonymity doesn't sit well with the ethos of social media. It feels much more natural for individual representatives of a brand to identify themselves. Your community likes to know who it is tweeting about airport delays or updating on company news, especially if the tone of engagement is friendly and relaxed.

- If staff can tweet and post as individuals, you may want to require them to place a disclaimer on their profiles stating that the views expressed are their own.

Roles and responsibilities

It must be clear who will oversee social media activity and take responsibility for the day-to-day administration of it:

- You must establish who can engage on your behalf.
- Another key question is: who will "own" social media contacts? This is something of a controversial area; but legally, if an employed individual is responsible for an organization's page on a social media site, then the organization owns that content and the contacts. If a person tweets or posts on their own personal page on a social media site, content and contacts belong to them. There have been controversies over individuals who have left for a rival brand, taking their Twitter followers with them.

Management

Who will manage your brand's social media policy and ensure that it is adhered to? Key considerations in this area include:

- Will the policy be written into contracts of employment?
- What processes will apply if the policy is breached?
- What training and support will be given for those who use social media on your behalf?

Consistency

A consistent style and tone is necessary if a corporate account is to accurately reflect the brand, though with individual accounts variations that reflect an individual's personality are inevitable. So training should include style and content guidelines.

Case study: How McDonald's operates on social media

McDonald's is a brand we feature at several points in this book; here I want to look specifically at how its social media strategy works as an example of what a social media team does, and what disciplines it can incorporate.

Rick Wion, director of social media at McDonald's USA, told the Social CMO Blog:

> We have a team in place that [tracks conversations on social media using monitoring tools]. It's a combined team, some folks from our

communications – our PR department – and some from our satisfaction team. These are folks who, a couple of years ago, they were answering 0800 number calls. We did that because we wanted to have a combined experience of dealing with customers but also the communications aspect because, at the end of the day, we are there because people are having conversations about us. A lot of those conversations have a marketing or communications aspect to them, so we need to have combined resources.[17]

McDonald's assembled a group of tweeters who use Twitter both on behalf of the brand on a branded account and also as individuals who are free to talk about themselves and their lives away from work on personal accounts which identify them as McDonald's employees.

Rick Wion told Social CMO:

> None of them started out as solely focused on Twitter. I think the most important skill you need to have is just the ability to communicate. Our best tweeters are the best writers. They are the folks who very easily get comfortable with the medium and have conversations with folks. What's interesting is we've set up a schedule so we have a person who's kind of the lead person on Twitter each day of the week. And so we have people who come and talk with us on Twitter based on those days of the week. So there are people who are fans of George, there are people who are fans of Dana and they'll come on those specific days just to talk with them.

They did that, he says, to humanize the brand. On each tweeter's profile there is a biography, a light-hearted, fun paragraph about themselves and a headshot:

> It should be fun. We're a fun brand. We're a food company but people eat the food because it's fun, a fun experience. I love the ability that Twitter and these other mediums give us to take real people and put those real people and the real faces in front of the brand.

What about the level of resources needed to operate at this level? Wion says:

> There are definitely some steps we are going to need to look at in terms of how we expand globally. The amount of conversations we have on Twitter has quadrupled in the past 18 months [the interview was conducted in spring 2011] We get 2,000 @ replies a week. It's a function of having the people there. So what we are going to need to look at is, over time, if we see more and more engagement there do we want to shift more resources from our call centre?

Also is there the ability – and I'd be very, very careful about this – to automate some things? We get a lot of the same questions. Do we want to have auto replies set up for certain types of questions. I don't know that we do, but if we get to a resource constraint issue then we might need to.

How to train your staff to use social media

If you are going to have a wide range of people within an organization using social media, you'll need to train them to do so. And that training will need to reflect their level of familiarity with the platforms you want them to use. You'll need to determine each individual's level of competence and tailor their training to reflect it. You can, for example, establish the following training modules, then provide just the ones needed in any particular case:

- the basics of using social media for those reluctant to use it
- advanced training in the use of the particular platforms you want them to work with and how to engage audiences
- demonstrations of how business can benefit from skilled social media campaigns, and how social media can help them to do their jobs better and be more effective and successful
- the company's social media goals and how to measure returns.[18]

Assignment

Seek out a brand that will let you study its brand journalism goals and delivery structure in detail. Write an analysis of what they do and how effective it is.

Notes

1 Larry Light and Joan Kiddon (2009) *Six Rules for Brand Revitalization: Learn How Companies Like McDonald's Can Re-Energize Their Brands* (Upper Saddle River, NJ: Prentice Hall).
2 Shel Holtz in a post at *Social Media Today* called "Marketers Keep Your Hands Off Your Company's Brand Journalism": socialmediatoday.com/shelholtz/342466/marketers-keep-your-hands-your-company-s-brand-journalism.
3 Marcus Sheridan in a post at *Social Media Examiner* on achieving social media buy-in: www.socialmediaexaminer.com/5-ways-to-get-your-entire-company-on-board-with-social-media/#more-14363.
4 The Content Marketing Institute on six ways to get employees involved in content creation: www.contentmarketinginstitute.com/2011/08/developing-your-content-marketing-mindset/.
5 Albert Pusch in a Wall Blog post headlined "Brand Journalism – How the Marketing Department of Today Is Tomorrow's Social Media Newsroom": wallblog.co.uk/2011/05/17/brand-journalism-how-the-marketing-department-of-today-is-tomorrows-social-media-newsroom/.

6 David Meerman Scott quoted in the *Ryerson Review of Journalism*: www.rrj.ca/m14057/.
7 Shel Holtz: holtz.com/blog/brands/marketers-keep-your-hands-off-of-your-companys-brand-journalism/3719/#When:23:11:04Z.
8 The *Financial Times*, "Nissan's PR Mimics the Newsroom": www.ft.com/cms/s/0/54d36b2e-92c4-11e0-bd88-00144feab49a.html#axzz2SEayFZQj.
9 The Simpaticor PR Blog: simpaticopr.co.uk/blog/?p=97.
10 Ibid.
11 *Newsroom Ink* on Imperial Sugar's newsroom: newsroomink.com/3141/brand-journalism-corporate-journalism-or-just-good-journalism/.
12 *Newsroom Ink*, Imperial Sugar case study: newsroomink.com/7300/case-study-imperial-sugar-newsroom-having-a-better-story-to-tell-while-improving-google-ability/.
13 David Meerman Scott, Imperial Sugar Company Newsroom, "Brand Journalism Creates an Authoritative Voice": www.webinknow.com/2009/07/imperial-sugar-company-newsroom-brand-journalism-creates-an-authoritative-voice.html.
14 Brian Kardon, "Why Eloqua Hired a Journalist": blog.eloqua.com/why-eloqua-hired-a-journalist/.
15 Jesse Noyes, Eloqua's corporate reporter: twitter.com/noyesjesse.
16 Mindflash on social media engagement policies: www.mindflash.com/blog/2012/03/infographic-how-to-train-your-employees-to-handle-your-social-media/?view=mindflashgraphic.
17 Rick Wion, director of social media at McDonald's USA, on the Social CMO Blog: www.thesocialcmo.com/blog/2011/03/mcdonald%E2%80%99s-scales-to-meet-social-media-demands/.
18 Kerry Bridge on the Direct 2 Dell website, "10 Social Media Tips When Commenting and Responding to Customers Online": en.community.dell.com/dell-blogs/direct2dell/b/direct2dell/archive/2012/05/08/10-social-media-tips-when-commenting-and-responding-to-customers-online-infographic.aspx.

5 Your Brand Is Your Beat

How to Find Stories Within an Organization – and How to Tell Them Compellingly

Goals of this module

- Establish how to make your brand your area of expertise.
- Analyse what kind of stories your brand can tell.
- Demonstrate how to turn your organization's expertise, experience and projects into compelling copy.
- Emphasize the importance of putting people, and personal stories, in place of products and services in your storytelling.
- Show how you can get the media to pick up on your stories.

On the website

Find a primer on covering a journalism beat, essential updates, further resources and links to all the sources referenced here.

The concept of covering a beat – of developing expertise in the reporting of a subject, an industry, an aspect of hard news – is one that is familiar to any journalist. As a brand journalist, you must cultivate a beat that covers the issues that are of concern to your brand, industry, mission, cause or campaign, and which matter to the community you seek to inform or entertain. Some of those stories will be external to your brand, but many will come from within it – or they should, if your brand journalism is serving the interests of the organization you work for.

Larry Light talked about using brand journalism to tell the brand narrative of McDonald's.[1] He realized that the company had many individual stories to tell, and that when all those individual story strands were woven together and told effectively, they added up to a compelling brand narrative. Most brands have such stories, and most big brands have hundreds of them. It's the job of the brand journalist to find them and tell them in a compelling way.

But not all brands are the same. Not all can support a heavy news flow, so we need an approach to story finding and telling that is flexible, that can be applied to any brand, whether big or small, whether a strong generator of news or not.

What kind of stories can your brand tell?

Chris Sietsema on the Convince and Convert blog drew a useful distinction between two types of content: he called them bricks and feathers.[2] Bricks are the heavy stuff: research reports, events, White Papers, video series, mobile apps (we explore each of these in Part II). Chris says: "They typically require decent budget and time to produce but have the potential to make a larger splash when executed and promoted correctly." Such content helps if one of your goals is to establish the brand as a thought leader.

Feathers are simple text and photo content published via popular social media tools such as Facebook, Twitter, LinkedIn, Google+, Pinterest and so on (again, we analyse the use of these platforms in Part II). Chris says: "Less intensive than bricks from a production budget standpoint, feathers are created consistently to maintain an ongoing stream of communication between a brand and its audience." This kind of content helps to establish a brand as a news source.

Chris addresses the benefits of bricks versus feathers, saying:

> Larger productions [bricks] allow you to position your brand as a reliable resource for superb ideas. By continuously sharing small bites of information [feathers], you would likely be considered a news maker by the audience. Both positions are attractive in their own right, but businesses which have the capacity to create and share short, informative posts on a daily basis are more inclined to go the feathers route. Those brands that simply cannot provide entertaining, enlightening and/or educational content on a daily basis (e.g. law firms, insurance companies, some medical facilities) should focus more on building bricks for the purpose of conveying their value to prospects and influencers.

Brick content tends to have a long lifespan and can help with search engine optimization (SEO) because it can attract high-quality and relevant links, a must-have for any organization focused on improving activity from natural search, says Chris. He goes on:

> One potential issue with bricks is that there is really no way to predict what will resonate. Your organization may have research to support that there is a demand for a specific piece of content within a particular medium. However, there are no guarantees that your bricks will generate interest, links, traffic, leads, sales, etc. Thanks to the time and resources needed to create bricks, there is a much higher opportunity cost when compared to feathers.

Feathers such as tweets and Facebook posts can be used as promotional tools linking to that rich content, but they have a short shelf life. The success of feathers "is often gauged by how many audience members saw a post and, more importantly, how many of those people actually took some action (i.e. clicked or shared)".

Which can your company produce: one or both? Developing a successful brand journalism strategy depends on your accurate appraisal of the stories that you can tell and marrying that with the stories your community is interested in reading, and which can benefit your brand.

How to turn an organization's expertise, experience and projects into compelling stories, and how to find those stories

Stories work for everyone – we all want to hear them. But many brands don't realize that they have compelling stories to tell. In fact, they've often been hiding great stories from their community.

In a post at *Platform Magazine*, Rachel Childers said: "Consumers want authenticity and transparency. People want to feel like they identify with a brand. They want to know about the sheep that were sheared for their sweater ... how the inventor of the product they love dreamed it up ... This is where brand journalism comes in."[3] Stories can come from the brand – from the people within the company, from the processes of creating the products, services, causes or whatever that it deals in, and from the people who use the things it makes, the services it provides, the causes it espouses. Your job as a brand journalist is to find those stories and to tell them in the most compelling way you can. Your advantage is that you know what a story is. Your challenge is that those who have stories to tell very often don't realize it.

One particular challenge can be getting material from the senior executives who often have some of the best stories to tell. These can be particularly valuable with business-to-business (B2B) brands. Joe Pulizzi blogged at the Content Marketing Institute on how to get material from senior executives:

> Some CEOs love to write, but most CEOs like to talk. If it's a challenge to get your C-level executive to produce thought leadership content, capture their thoughts in a different format. Interview them using Skype, and record the conversation.[4]

Or if you can get to them in person, interview them using high-quality video and audio, so you can broadcast the talk or turn what they have said into blog posts, White Papers and so on. If they'll type an email, get them to do that, suggesting they just hammer out their thoughts. Use any opportunity to get material from them. At events, get pictures and video of them, even if you can't get a talk – the visuals will come in useful later when a talk is all you have.

Help them tell stories. Often they'll say they don't know where to start or how to structure their story. Talk to them and, from what you now understand, suggest the introduction and a rough structure. Email an outline to them so they can follow it when they write. When you get their effort, polish it and get it approved. Stand your ground if they try to alter it back and you know journalistically you are right. You won't always win, but your job is to make the executive look as good as you can, and you often have to work to reach that goal.

Help them become aware of content opportunities. Joe Pulizzi says:

> In one technology company we worked with, much of the customer service happened through back and forth email ... we realized that a large portion of [potential] blog and article content was happening through direct customer email. It took only one customer service rep to notice this, and now the entire organization looks at the content they create every day as part of their business. Now, customer service reps, as well as sales reps, are more routinely aware if one of their emails should be used as an FAQ on the web site or expanded upon in a blog post.

In a post on *Social Media B2B*, Jeffrey L. Cohen offers four sources for stories that relate particularly to B2B brands, but also have relevance across the board:[5]

- Company history: "Look for compelling events in your company history as sources for individual stories. Consider how any of this content can be added to your B2B company Facebook timeline."
- Customer successes: "Prospects and customers really like to hear from successful customers." Readers look for parallels with their own experiences, solutions to the problems they face and guidance on the issues they are struggling with. Stories about problems solved – particularly after a struggle – are likely to resonate.
- Employee activities: "Customers and prospects want to know more about the face behind the Twitter account or email address. This is especially true with B2B relationship-based sales. We know that people do business with those that they know, like and trust and this is a great way to build up the trust with your team." Help your people tell their stories – through short video profiles, via a blog or whatever works best for them and for your brand.
- Community support: "Many B2B companies are involved in their communities because they care. Show this compassion by sharing a story about your community efforts." A cheesy PR-style press release isn't going to work, but a talk with the person who urged your brand to support a particular charity, and went on to lead an impressive fundraising effort, could. As ever, such stories have to be true, and if your community efforts are paltry, don't draw attention to them. But as a brand journalist you should be looking for opportunities where your

brand could make a difference – initiatives which, as a by-product, will produce good copy.

Cause marketing

Some brands are all about causes and, naturally, their content concerns them. But many other organizations can also include championing a particular cause in their brand journalism, even if that cause has nothing directly to do with the brand's business. An organization that operates in a particular market, or a particular location, can support causes that concern the community they are seeking to engage with.

In a post at Web Marketing Therapy, Jennie Jacobs writes:

> Every product, brand or business saves the world in some way large or small. Discover how your ideas, business, brands or products save the world and then align with a cause that is consistent, aligned and a good partner for those brand values. Choose carefully as you want the association to be long, rewarding for both parties and helpful in completing your brand's story.[6]

Know your audience, the stories that interest them, and the right places to tell them

What are they interested in learning about you and where can particular types of story best be told? These are things you'll need to learn through doing brand journalism, and monitoring the success of particular types of stories on particular platforms.

In the post for *Platform Magazine* quoted from above, Rachel Childers interviewed Boeing communications director Todd Blecher:

> Boeing had to learn which stories their audience wanted, and which ones they didn't. Blecher said that stories about aerospace and aviation, what he calls the 'hardware', tend to be more successful on the Boeing website due to audience expectation. For example, the story of a K-9 [dog] bomb team member didn't work well on the website. Blecher said that it would have been better accepted on Facebook because that is what the social media audience desires.
>
> "You have to know your audience and know your tools," Blecher said.
>
> In this case, Boeing's tool was brand journalism. It was a successful addition to the other tools that Blecher uses every day; however, Blecher said that brand journalism might not be able to be effectively used by every company … He said that culturally, companies need to be attuned to discovering stories that interest their audience and finding out how this content can be interesting.[7]

Putting people in place of products and services in your storytelling

Stories are about people – any trainee journalist learns that in their first week. You need to bring your understanding of that fact to your brand journalism and your skill in finding people through whom you can tell otherwise abstract and perhaps dry and technical stories.

Honda makes cars, motorbikes, all-terrain vehicles, engines for fishing boats, loads of things. But its brand journalism storytelling is not about these objects. Rather, it's about the people who use those things and what they do with them. It makes mini-documentaries of its own which it previews in ad breaks during the UK terrestrial Channel 4 documentaries, which it sponsors. So Honda becomes closely connected with factual storytelling. It also has a branded website that acts as a hub for those documentaries.[8]

The PSFK blog wrote about Honda's documentary storytelling strategy:[9]

> In the UK, Honda has marked its new sponsorship of Channel 4 documentaries by creating its own mini-documentaries featuring real-life Honda customers who use their products in surprising and unusual ways. The first, Alpaca Farming,[10] featured Philippa, an alpaca breeder from Oxfordshire, who tends to the animals on her farm using her Honda ATV. Night Fishing features fishermen who take their boat out at night off the coast of Brixham to catch their fish in the dark with luminous lures.[11] The boat is called "Goldfish" – a Cheetah Marine 9.95m catamaran powered by twin Honda BF135 marine engines.

Honda has invited other users of its products to volunteer to feature in films, and has used a wide range of local websites to get that message out, including one called the People's Republic of South Devon, which wrote:

> I once knew a man with a Honda Civic, out of which he operated a carpet-fitting service. Strange, and sometimes a little cramped, and it's exactly the kind of thing that Honda are looking for as they yet again support documentaries on Channel 4 … on the Honda documentaries site there are stories of Honda motorcyclist Nigel Farquhar, who uses his Honda Transalp to clear the way for cyclists as a motorcycle escort for British cycling.
>
> Or, back on the farm again, there's Adrian Bell, who checks if his sheep are pregnant with his Honda generator-powered scanner. If you've got a Honda which you use in an interesting way, or as part of your interesting life, upload an image or two, or even short film of your own, to the Honda site.
>
> Out of the stories on the site, the filmmakers will chose their favourite to make the final ident about – and they are well-made. Each film

that's made will have its own webpage, along with extra content with more information about the people featured.[12]

How to get the media to pick up on your stories

Even though your brand is a publisher, you still want good relationships with traditional media companies, (a point we cover in depth in Chapter 13). To that end you will need to interest the media in your content and the stories you are telling. Don't do it with a press release. Poorly targeted generic press releases belong, if anywhere, to the days before brand journalism.

Two alternative approaches are via curation or with a personal pitch.

Curation

We look at curation in detail in Chapter 10, but there's one aspect of its use that is worth mentioning at this point. In a post at the Holtz Communication and Technology site on targeted, results-focused uses of curation, Shel Holtz considers the role of collecting content as a means of creating a resource for the media. He writes: "Curating news that the media isn't covering can lead to media coverage. And, by extension, it can improve and expand on stories the media are covering."[13]

He argues that any company news is potentially curatable, including a product launch, a shareholder meeting, corporate social responsibility initiatives, maybe even damage limitation:

> It's not unreasonable to think about curating bad-news stories. The press tends to cover the most lurid dimensions of a company crisis. A collection that provides a more balanced overview of the situation could conceivably lead to some of the more positive aspects of the story finding their way into the public consciousness.

It's essential the curation is balanced and you are transparent about your interest in the subject: "A company needs to be beyond reproach in its effort to be objective, lest the collection be shrugged off as little more than corporate flackery." Shel gives Microsoft as an example: "Look back to the resource Microsoft maintained when it faced federal and state antitrust lawsuits. The media tapped it as one of the most comprehensive archives of documents related to the suits. Companies curating news should keep that example in mind."

We could also cite the Imperial Sugar newsroom, which we looked at in Chapter 4. Imperial Sugar set up a newsroom, following a disastrous fire at a plant, and it quickly became an integral communications component for the company. Within six weeks, it was the most popular online sugar site in the sugar industry.

A personal pitch to a reporter

In the Covering Health blog, Andrew Van Dam offered this useful template for how to identify appropriate journalists, pitching your story to them personally, rather than using a generic approach.[14] I summarize here.

An email pitch

Pitch your story to them, as you would to your own editor, in an email. Use bullet points to list the most important details.

Research the right reporters to send it to. Google them, confirm they still work for the organization, read their recent articles to make sure what you pitch is within their beat. Van Dam says: "If you are pitching a health-care story, make sure she covers health care." Personalize the opening of each email with a paragraph such as: "I read your series on healthcare abuses in the nursing home industry ... ." Make sure the email's subject line sells the story.

A tweet pitch

Turn your key idea into a tweet, ideally as a direct message, failing that as an @. If they don't respond, follow up with an email pitch.

A Facebook pitch

Even if you aren't Facebook friends, you can still send them a message. Include your pitch in it.

A phone pitch

Van Dam says: "Sometimes a quick conversation to gauge a reporter's interest can save you a lot of time ... If they don't answer or are on deadline, follow up with a pitch email."

A face-to-face pitch

If what your brand does is covered by the reporter's beat, there's a mutual benefit in them considering your story suggestions. So, if you are in the same city, see if you can fix a chat over coffee.

Assignment

Analyse how one brand tells stories. Look at where those stories originate. If you can, interview a brand journalism editor-in-chief about their story finding, telling and publishing strategy.

Notes

1 Larry Light and Joan Kiddon (2009) *Six Rules for Brand Revitalization: Learn How Companies Like McDonald's Can Re-Energize Their Brands* (Upper Saddle River, NJ: Prentice Hall).

2 Chris Sietsema on the Convince and Convert blog: www.convinceandconvert. com/social-media-strategy/planning-your-content-marketing-bricks-vs-feathers/.

3 Rachel Childers in a post at *Platform Magazine*: platformmagazine.org/2012/03/ brand-journalism-pr-storytelling/.

4 Joe Pulizzi at the Content Marketing Institute on how to get material from senior executives: blog.junta42.com/2012/04/brand-stories/.

5 Jeffrey L. Cohen on *Social Media B2B*, "4 Ways to Use Storytelling for B2B Social Media": socialmediab2b.com/2012/05/b2b-social-media-storytelling/.

6 Jennie Jacobs at Web Marketing Therapy: www.webmarketingtherapy.com/blog/ web-marketing-best-practices/design-education-session-brand-style-guide/.

7 Rachel Childers in a post at *Platform Magazine*: platformmagazine.org/2012/03/ brand-journalism-pr-storytelling/.

8 Honda's documentaries hub: hub.honda.co.uk/?s3campaign=HN_SEM_UK_ EN_Brand_+_Generic&s3advertiser=Google_PPC&s3banner=honda_ documentaries.

9 Honda's documentary storytelling strategy from the PSFK blog: www.psfk.com/2011/ 07/honda-documentaries-reveal-unusual-uses-for-their-products-video.html.

10 Honda's alpaca farming mini-documentary: youtu.be/6aRmAPMLAcw.

11 Honda's night-fishing mini-documentary: youtu.be/fOmwo_ofi88.

12 People's Republic of South Devon blog on Honda documentaries: www.people-srepublicofsouthdevon.co.uk/2011/06/13/real-life-stories-in-honda-mini-documentaries/.

13 Shel Holtz on targeted, results-focused uses of curation at the Holtz Communication and Technology site: holtz.com/blog/business/curating-company-news-time-for-company-content-curation-to-grow-up/3796/.

14 Andrew Van Dam, writing on covering health: www.healthjournalism.org/blog/ 2012/02/study-good-press-releases-contribute-to-good-health-journalism/.

6 The Ethics of Brand Journalism

Goals of this module

- Outline a code of ethics for brand journalism.
- Establish transparency as the essential underpinning of ethical brand journalism.
- Look at questions of balance and independence in relation to brand journalism.
- Identify unacceptable practices such as astroturfing and sockpuppetry.
- Consider in what context sponsored conversations might be acceptable.
- Show that poor ethical standards damage a brand's credibility.

On the website

Find updates on developments in the emerging code of ethics for brand journalism, further resources and links to the sources cited here.

"Journalism is conducted at arm's length, and brands have grasping hands."[1] The advertising, marketing and media reporter Bob Garfield encapsulated the concerns many have about the ethics of brand journalism in that pithy phrase. Underlying the statement is the view that traditional "independent" journalism is objective, balanced, unbiased, serves no agenda – hidden or otherwise – and is conducted by practitioners who have no vested interest in the information they are revealing and the story they are telling. By contrast, the theory goes, when journalism is conducted on behalf of brands, it is not objective, balanced, unbiased or independent. Indeed, if brands use journalists, or journalistic means, to tell stories in which they have a strong vested interest, what they produce will not be journalism. So the very idea of calling something brand journalism is a misnomer: "Obviously", Garfield says, "the nouns are incompatible."

Is he right? No. Or, at least, he doesn't have to be if brand journalists behave ethically. But you can understand why the concept of brand journalism raises some very fundamental concerns. There are three things we should note here before we look at how, and why, brand journalism should be conducted ethically.

One, this pure-as-the-driven-snow vision of traditional journalism is illusory in very many cases. That's not to say that traditional journalism should not be conducted at this high ethical standard; it's rather that, in reality, it often isn't. Two, brand journalism is not killing traditional journalism. If traditional journalism is under threat, it's because of a growing reluctance to pay for it. Three, brands are going to do journalism, whether we like it or not. So the only practical course of action is to address the question of how ethical standards can be brought to brand journalism.

When we consider what those ethical standards should be, we ought also to look at the broader picture of how we make all journalism ethical. Those who see brand journalism as a threat, as the pernicious advance of marketing content masquerading as journalism, rarely understand that ethics in brand journalism are not just an added option like one of the optional extras on a new car. As I hope we've seen in much of what we have discussed so far, and will find reinforced in the rest of this book, brand journalism won't work if it is in any way false or suspected of being false. The power of social and online media, and the great check on brands and other entities that seek to manipulate the facts, is the wisdom and knowledge of the crowd. Be anything less than completely transparent and you'll be found out.

First, let's consider the question of how close brand journalism can get – in terms of conduct and ethics – to the ideal version of traditional journalism. In doing that, let's look at the ethical debate there is around traditional journalism and outline tenets of journalism that is practised to high ethical standards.

The ethics of traditional journalism

Of course, journalism codes vary from industry to industry and from country to country, but we can draw up a shortlist of what they have in common. The big issues include:

- truthfulness
- transparency
- accuracy
- objectivity
- impartiality
- balance
- fairness; and
- public accountability.

These guiding principles are codified, industry by industry, country by country, into standards of practice that also cover specifics such as the local laws of defamation and contempt of court, as well as questions of privacy, public interest and freedom of expression (including freedom of the media) and how to balance those conflicting principles.

In the US, bodies including the Society of Professional Journalists (SPJ)[2] and the American Society of News Editors[3] outline the ethical standards they expect from members. Individual publishers also have their ethical codes. The *New York Times* publishes an *Ethical Journalism Handbook*[4] and the Poynter Institute ("a school for journalism that also practises journalism") adheres to seven core values:

- accuracy
- independence
- interdependence (revealing relationships with other entities that might cause a perceived conflict of interest)
- fairness
- transparency
- professional responsibility; and
- helpfulness.[5]

The SPJ's definition of journalism's core ethical values covers similar ground:

- Seek the truth as fully as possible.
- Act independently.
- Seek to minimize harm.
- Be accountable.

It also states that news must always be clearly distinguished from opinion.

The *New York Times*'s ethical handbook demands transparency when a reporter's background or relationships might pose a conflict of interest.

In the UK, there has not been the same concern with establishing ethical standards for journalism. The Leveson Committee's recommendations, following its 2012 enquiry into the conduct of the press, were for the creation of a regulatory body that set a code of professional practice, with sanctions for publications that break the rules and a means of redress for those who believe they have been wronged. As this book went to press, what form legislation should take was still being debated. It appeared there would be a beefed-up code of conduct, but no overt ethical code. You'll find an update on this on the *Brand Journalism* website.

Ofcom, which regulates UK broadcasters,[6] publishes a broadcasting code that covers such requirements as: news should be accurate and impartial.[7] Ofcom's website offers a lengthy, legalistic tangle of instructions on how to interpret and follow the broadcasting code, but has few if any references to ethics. Certainly, I couldn't find any succinct ethical code which broadcasters should follow, and a search for "ethics" on the website does not bring up anything meaningful.

The ethics of brand journalism

How many of the items on the ethical lists above can brand journalism be said to abide by? And who will judge whether they do?

Shane Snow wrote on Poynter.org: "the brand publishing world has no universal set of ethical standards. There's no Society of Professional Journalists for content marketing. Brands have motivations that sometimes conflict with the values of traditional journalism, putting reporters who work for them in a pickle."[8] He poses this question to both traditional and brand journalists: "Ask yourself: What would you do if a client asked you to scrub mentions of a competitor from a story? Or what if a brand wanted to hide the fact that it's behind a piece of content it hired you to produce?" He's inviting the traditional journalist to say that they would refuse. He then asks: "Could your answer to either of those change if you worked on behalf of a corporation rather than a 'neutral' news organisation?"

The response to that second question gets to the heart of the debate over brand journalism ethics. If you are working for an ethically organized brand journalism operation, your answer would not change. Like traditional journalists, brand journalists must strive to act ethically. The strongest force for openness and transparency, balance and truthfulness in brand journalism, as in traditional journalism, is the power of the Internet.

As Shane Snow says: "Fortunately, social media seems to ferret out and publicize the sketchiest publishing behavior, which encourages content purveyors to act with integrity. But best practices are not the same thing as ethics, and often the gray line is blurry."[9] In a less than perfect world, this may be the most we can hope for.

Most people assume standards must be lower for brand journalism, but not everyone agrees. Shane Snow is founder of Contently, an agency that brings brands seeking professionally created content and journalists together, and where they practise both traditional journalism and what they call content marketing. He says that they insist on higher ethical standards for the latter. In their code of ethics, Contently states:

> Content marketing should seek to adhere to stricter standards of reporting than traditional journalism, due to its different legal position and increased commercial motivations. Content marketers should take care to disclose the sponsorship and intent of their work while abiding by the following practices:
>
> - Adhere to journalism's core values of honesty, integrity, accountability, and responsibility.
> - Acknowledge facts that may compromise the integrity of a story or opinion.
> - Minimize potential harm to sources or subjects of stories.
> - Expose truth as fully as possible.

- Always credit sources of content or ideas, never plagiarizing or repurposing stories or prose, whether one's own or another's, whether written content, photography, or other media, whether the original source is known or not.
- Fulfil promises made to contributors and sources in the course of reporting.
- Ensure that the reader understands the source, sponsor, and intent of the content.
- Disclose all potential conflicts of interest or appearance of conflict.[10]

It should be clearly stated that much of what is practised under content marketing or brand journalism cannot be said to follow the principles of balance, impartiality and transparency. The same can be said for traditional journalism. But there are examples of companies that seek to emulate the transparency of ethical traditional journalism in their brand journalism. Caitlyn Coverly, writing at the *Ryerson Review of Journalism*, interviewed Bill Calder, who took Intel into the brand journalism business.[11] He told her the brand did so because of the dearth of good, solid technology reporting from traditional publishers. So he launched a website called (perhaps provocatively) Free Press. Coverly reports:

> Its goal according to the website's mission statement: to cover "technology and innovation stories that are often overlooked or warrant more context and deeper reporting." ... Calder insists the Free Press be transparent. He explains that all published articles are reported and produced by identified company writers and their work can be republished, edited and re-used by anyone. To address the obvious question of corporate bias, the site's mission statement says the writers, "are all Intel geeks at heart, taking an editorial approach to producing stories with journalistic style and integrity, and doing it as objectively as possible while being transparent about who [they] work for."

He believes he has achieved this and gives Coverly this example:

> ... the Free Press published an article titled "Caught in the Crossfire: Intel's Investor Relations Chief." The article provided a behind-the-scenes look at the struggles of Kevin Sellers as he explains to Intel investors why the company's stock price continues to spiral downward while the company is making a large profit. The following day, the article appeared in its entirety on the *Silicon Valley Watcher* website – an independent technology news website operated by former *Financial Times* writer Tom Foremski. That in turn led to a short blurb on National Public Radio's website, with a link directing readers to the full article on the *Watcher*'s website. "It's still early and we are testing various things," says Calder. "But this is an interesting example of how it could work."

Establishing an ethical framework for brand journalism is certainly a work in progress. Shane Snow admits as much of his code, discussed above, but says that the abiding and well-established principle underlying any ethical framework is clear: that the reader must never be conned:[12]

> It's all about not deceiving readers. Brand publishers should make clear who is behind a piece of content and why. Journalists who write for brands need to ensure their clients understand the ethical reasons for such disclosure ... New players and new forms are coming to the content industry. As journalists, we need to promote a framework for ethics in these new industries if we want to maintain the integrity of our craft.

There are plenty of examples of brand journalism practices that fail the reader. Let's look at some of the main ones and then consider why brand journalism that seeks to deceive will fail.

Unacceptable practices

Astroturfing

Wikipedia defines astroturfing as: "a form of advocacy in support of a political, organizational, or corporate agenda, designed to give the appearance of a 'grassroots' movement. The goal of such campaigns is to disguise the efforts of a political or commercial entity as an independent public reaction to another political entity – a politician, political group, product, service or event."[13]

American political campaigners use the term astroturfing to describe campaigns that are created to look like spontaneous grassroots protests but that are, in fact, highly orchestrated, usually with significant financial backing. The practice is thought to be quite common, though it's prohibited by the Public Relations Society of America's code of ethics. Campaigners use social media tools to give the impression that the public have created a campaign themselves.

Sockpuppetry

Wikipedia defines a sockpuppet as "an online identity used for purposes of deception".[14] A brand journalist who promotes a brand without revealing their connection to that brand is guilty of sockpuppetry.

Sponsored conversations

One key threat to independence is the area of sponsored conversations. Some brands seek to turn the newfound power of bloggers and celebrity influencers to their advantage. As Brian Solis writes, they aim to do this by "showering them with endorsement deals rich with products, cash, trips, exclusive access to information, and VIP treatment each and every day, creating a new genre of star spokespersons."[15]

He goes on:

> These new brand ambassadors are almost the perfect instruments for surreptitiously sparking and cultivating groundswell within desired and vital target markets. Consumers look to experts and trusted peers for guidance and insight when making decisions. Who's to say that the information they're receiving from their trusted sources is indeed truthful and honest, if they're unaware that these authorities are actually directly or indirectly compensated for their opinions and insights.

But some conversations are more subtly sponsored. Let's take as an example Ford's Fiesta Movement, used to launch the compact car in the US. Ford raised concerns with this campaign, as reported on the Centre Networks blog, when it "gave 100 special 'digital influencers' a European-spec version of the new Ford Fiesta for six months and seek their feedback. Unlike your normal test drive and feedback form type deal, here they have decided to get these so-called digital influencers to complete missions each month."[16]

The key question is could those influencer/reviewers say what they liked about the car? And would they be inclined to do so as they enjoyed Ford's generosity? Ford insisted that reviewers were free to say what they liked and were required to disclose in their posts that they were taking part in the Ford-sponsored scheme. However, says Brian Solis: "Ford is buying media mentions – if all they wanted was feedback, they would give the people a form and have them submit it. This is more of a PR campaign than it will ever be a social media campaign." We look in detail at Ford's Fiesta Movement campaign in Chapter 14. You might like to refer to that chapter before you consider the next point.

So what do we think? Does the Fiesta Movement pass the ethical brand journalism test? I believe it does, as long as we have transparency – as long as the reader can decide for themselves, given all the evidence, whether the content created by reviewers is tainted by their association with Ford. As so often when discussing ethical brand journalism, transparency is the key.

Consumer legislation can provide one check on hidden endorsements. UK regulators made clear, when Wayne Rooney's sponsored tweets on behalf of Nike were not identified as such, that such content must be clearly identified as marketing.[17] In order to act ethically, brands should apply the same principle to any source of rewarded brand endorsement. But Brian Solis argues that it shouldn't be down to legislation to halt clandestine endorsements:

> This is about building credibility and earned relationships through engagement and empowerment for both company/product brands and personal brands ... the practice of paying bloggers and influencers or

providing them with free products not only clouds their ability to share an impartial story, but also risks credibility and trust of brands and influencers among the very people they're trying to inspire and galvanize ... the practice of disclosure is not an option when the potential for significantly damaging customer relationships in a very public spotlight is at stake. Unfortunately, it's not at the forefront of many of our marketing programs.[18]

Be ethical in your brand journalism or lose your brand its credibility

As Tony Burman, ex-editor-in-chief of CBC News, *The Globe and Mail*, said: "Every news organisation has only its credibility and reputation to rely on."[19] The same applies to any brand engaging in brand journalism. To fail to act ethically when conducting brand journalism will be to risk damaging a brand's credibility and reputation. But will they be found out? Without a significant risk that they will be held to account for unethical journalism, brands will be tempted to flout ethical standards. As we will see in the discussion in Chapter 11 of Mumsnet, the modern online consumer is highly attuned to being marketed to covertly and reacts angrily when they sense it happening.

But can relatively powerless individuals or pressure groups really counter – and counter-balance – biased coverage from brands? An SXSW panel debate on brand journalism[20] discussed the question. One view was that brands have "signal strength", which gives them an advantage in the publishing arena, and enables them to manipulate, rather than inform, information seekers. But the counter-argument was that audiences have the ability to identify such attempts at manipulation:

> "Signal strength of brands is a problem", noted Gary Kim [of Carrier Evolution], "But an active citizenry with tools can defeat it." He pointed to the fact that people still hold BP responsible [for the damage caused by the catastrophic 2010 oil spill in the Gulf of Mexico] despite spending on clean up and reimbursement of damages by the company. And a great comment on the Twitter backchannel during the discussion underscored the power of social media: "With regimes falling around us [this was at the time of the Arab Spring], why would journalists think a social internet can't call b.s. on brands!"

Why unethical brand journalism will fail

How "good" can we realistically expect brands to be? Can brand journalism ever be as independent and arm's-length as traditional, ideal, independent journalism?

There are those who believe it can and should be. Digital strategist Adam Schweigert explained:

> ... consumers increasingly see through PR spin and marketing hype anyway, so it's to your benefit, if you proceed down this [brand journalism] path, to not just co-opt journalism's name, but to adopt its standards and practices as well. You know what could work? Telling true stories – the good, the not so good, and, yes, the ugly – about your brand and your industry in a journalistic manner, informing consumers and letting them make up their own minds.[21]

We can't expect all brands to do this just because it's right. It needs to be in their own interests to be that open. There is evidence of some brands deciding it is. PR professional Derek DeVries states:

> Ironically, one of the best visible models for Brand Journalism is "Howard 100 News" – the entity created by Howard Stern for his programming on Sirius/XM satellite radio. The team is stocked with investigative news veterans who have free rein to cover the good and the bad (often to Stern's chagrin), which gives them credibility with their audience.[22]

Brian Clark of GMD Studios, speaking at the SXSW discussion on brand journalism mentioned above, talked of:

> ... how brave and unvarnished stories from Ford helped the company weather its darkest days during the 2008–10 recession. He described how the company reported the stories from within, providing visibility into the tough conversations happening at the company. Using a variety of media, including video, images and text, Ford stripped away its corporate veneer, using what Clark called "real language and real people" to tell the stories of the company's struggles and successes. One key outcome Clark noted was the attention professional media paid to the stories coming out of Ford at the time.[23]

Let's face it, not all brand journalism is going to keep up to the ethical standards we expect of it, just as not all traditional journalism does.

Assignment

Draw up an ethical brand journalism policy for a brand.

Notes

1 Bob Garfield writing on AdAge: adage.com/article/bob-garfield/chrysler-tweet-controversy-shows-brand-journalism-a-lie/149489/.

2 Society of Professional Journalists: www.spj.org/.
3 American Society of News Editors: asne.org/.
4 *The New York Times Ethical Journalism Handbook*: www.nytco.com/pdf/NYT_Ethical_Journalism_0904.pdf.
5 Poynter Institute's seven core values: www.poynter.org/archived/about-poynter/20209/ethics-guidelines-for-poynter-publishing/.
6 Ofcom: www.ofcom.org.uk/.
7 Ofcom broadcasting code: stakeholders.ofcom.org.uk/broadcasting/broadcast-codes/broadcast-code/.
8 Shane Snow writing on Poynter.org: www.poynter.org/how-tos/digital-strategies/187229/what-journalists-need-to-know-about-content-marketing/.
9 Ibid.
10 Contently's code of ethics: contently.com/blog/2012/08/01/ethics/.
11 Caitlyn Coverly, *Ryerson Review of Journalism*: www.rrj.ca/m14057/.
12 Shane Snow writing on Poynter.org: www.poynter.org/how-tos/digital-strategies/187229/what-journalists-need-to-know-about-content-marketing/.
13 Astroturfing as defined by Wikipedia: en.wikipedia.org/wiki/Astroturfing.
14 Sockpuppetry as defined by Wikipedia: en.wikipedia.org/wiki/Sockpuppet_(Internet).
15 Brian Solis on sponsored conversations: www.briansolis.com/2009/05/this-is-not-a-sponsored-post-what-you-need-to-know-about-sponsored-conversations-the-ftc/.
16 Centre Networks blog on the ethics of Ford's Fiesta Movement campaign: www.centernetworks.com/ford-fiesta-movement/.
17 PaidContent on Wayne Rooney's sponsored tweets on behalf of Nike: paidcontent.org/2012/06/20/celebs-must-clearly-identify-sponsored-tweets-uk-body-says/.
18 Brian Solis on sponsored conversations: www.briansolis.com/2009/05/this-is-not-a-sponsored-post-what-you-need-to-know-about-sponsored-conversations-the-ftc/.
19 Tony Burman on ethics: www.theglobeandmail.com/news/national/media-cant-sate-news-hunger/article562795/.
20 SXSW panel debate on ethics in brand journalism: blog.prnewswire.com/2011/03/13/brand-journalism-ethics-opprtunities-outcomes/.
21 Adam Schweigert: adamschweigert.com/brand-journalism-has-a-lot-to-learn-from-real-journalism/.
22 Derek DeVries: prsay.prsa.org/index.php/2012/01/19/brand-journalism-takes-advantage-of-mass-media-fragmentation.
23 Brian Clark of GMD Studios, speaking at an SXSW discussion on brand journalism: blog.prnewswire.com/2011/03/13/brand-journalism-ethics-opprtunities-outcomes/#.

Part II

The Publishing Platforms to Use

In Part I we looked at establishing, implementing and managing a brand journalism strategy. Here, in Part II, we focus on content creation and distribution. We begin with a look at one brand that has demonstrated a huge aptitude for brand journalism, content creation and content marketing. That company is Red Bull, and it has moved into brand journalism with such vigour and on such a scale that it is as much a media company as it is a manufacturer of energy drinks. Red Bull uses the full range of available platforms – from print to the web, social media to video, audio, music and games. We look at what it does on each.

We continue with a detailed, platform-by-platform look at what other brands are doing. Other chapters in Part II cover:

- social media platforms – where many of the visitors to your websites and other branded presences will begin their journey to you – including Twitter, Facebook, Google+, YouTube, Instagram, Pinterest, Flickr and AudioBoo
- mobile platforms, including Foursquare
- platforms on which you can create substantial brand journalism content, including blogs, White Papers and e-books
- specialist online forums – for when the audience you want to reach is not on the big-name social platforms
- branded websites: the place we seek to bring those who find us through the means outlined above in order to deepen our relationship with them
- how all the new media entities discussed above mesh with our presences on traditional media, and the brand journalism staple of a customer magazine.

7   How Brand Journalism Gives Red Bull Wings

Goals of this module

- Demonstrate how Red Bull has become a powerful media company.
- Outline its corporate strategy.
- Analyse its brand journalism strategy.
- Explore, platform by platform, what content Red Bull publishes.
- Consider what brands and brand journalists can learn from Red Bull's success.

On the website

Find further examples of Red Bull brand journalism, videos and links to all the sources mentioned here.

Red Bull is an energy drink. It's also a giant media network spanning web TV, audio, print, online, social, mobile, music and games, and with a presence in 160 countries. When it comes to looking at how a brand creates, manages and coordinates brand journalism across all media, and in many channels within each medium, Red Bull offers an unparalleled case study. It doesn't build content around the sweet fizzy drink that is the foundation of the empire. Indeed, go to any of its media presences and, if you didn't know it was a drinks brand, you might not find out. Instead, it creates content around sports and cultural events – both for its own branded presences across all media and to sell to others.

So how was this empire built? What is its goal and what strategies does it use in pursuit of that goal? Red Bull was founded in Austria in 1987. It has been creating content for over 25 years, but it wasn't until 2007 that it launched the Red Bull Media House.[1] Today that media house runs a web TV station; prints a magazine with a circulation of 5 million, making it one of the biggest magazines in the world; produces documentaries, movies and music; and has a comprehensive digital strategy. It has over 900 web domains in 36 languages under the umbrella of RedBull.com. It creates newsfeeds and digital databases. It builds smartphone and tablet apps. And whereas you might expect to find traditional media companies offering content to Red Bull, the relationship is actually reversed. It sells and licenses content to media organizations and to other brands.

How exactly has Red Bull achieved all this off the back of a soft drink, when Coca-Cola, for example, has chosen not to? To answer this question, we'll look first at the big picture – the overall corporate strategy of Red Bull; then at how its media strategy fits into that; and move on to survey the brand journalism it produces. Finally, we'll consider what other brands – and we as brand journalists – can learn from Red Bull's success.

Red Bull's corporate strategy

Lisa Kimmel of Edelman Canada succinctly nails the corporate strategy – what Red Bull is about – when she says:

> Red Bull is a lifestyle brand that, through its positioning that it "gives you wings", is centred on a philosophy that any person can get on to the world stage to excel in the field of sports or entertainment that Red Bull has created for him/her. And, over time, it has leveraged that positioning to become a media company ... that produces and distributes content that will appeal to a cross-section of demographics and psychographics.[2]

Red Bull's sponsorship efforts, and the brand journalism it creates around those it sponsors, are that philosophy in action. As Hal Halpin wrote on iMedia Connection:

> Red Bull identifies a target demographic, examines who could build a career from that segment, hones in on those professionals, and supports them to the fullest – thereby creating very popular and influential pros in the process. The company then builds from there, adding support for multiple professionals and teams and follows it up with live events.[3]

The success of these individuals and teams, the excitement of the live events – and the brand journalism created around them – inspires Red Bull's primary audience of males aged 12 to 34 and results in great engagement with them.

Why does Red Bull engage so successfully? As Karlene Lukovitz writes on *Mediapost*: "The key factor is that their messaging across all contact points consistently reflects and conveys an 'idealized self' or 'Me Statement' embodied by the brand – the reason that users want to be associated with it."[4] Red Bull's Me Statement is: "I'm cool under pressure and can conquer any challenge."

We'll look at other brands that create brand journalism around a lifestyle – sometimes an aspirational lifestyle – which appeals to the community they want to engage with. Red Bull does that, but it also creates content around that Me Statement, that attitude to life.

Red Bull's brand journalism strategy

From that brand philosophy flows Red Bull's media and brand journalism strategy, goals and ambitions. Lisa Kimmel says: "Red Bull's goal is clear: to become a global media player across all media types by creating and distributing high quality media assets via owned and external channels."[5]

Let's look at what Red Bull does across those media types and channels. Edelman likes to talk about something it calls the media cloverleaf – that is, four overlapping areas of media which they represent as being like the leaves of a four-leaf clover. The media areas are:

- traditional media – radio, TV, print
- hybrid (or tradigital) media – digitally native media companies that are largely blogs, sometimes niche focused, sometimes broadly focused
- owned media – the "every company is a media company" concept whereby any brand can create valuable content of its own
- social media – platforms such as Facebook and Twitter that are driving increased engagement with brands and increased traffic to the other media spheres.

As Edelman sees it, those four leaves all overlap, both with each other and also with a central hub of "public engagement". Red Bull creates owned media that it distributes across the other three areas – traditional, hybrid and social – on platforms it owns, on platforms owned by other media and brand entities, and on the major social networks.

Steve Rubel, executive vice president of global strategy and insights for Edelman, says that the four distinct spheres of media should all be used regularly to engage the public.[6] This is the idea of transmedia storytelling: the technique of telling a single story across multiple platforms and formats.

Nate Warner, Red Bull's digital marketing director, gave an audience at the University of Montana's school of business administration an overview of the new media model developed by the Red Bull Media House.[7] He said that the division is responsible for the brand's overall lifestyle marketing strategy, which is to create and syndicate digital content that engages consumers while interacting with them through social media platforms, such as YouTube, Facebook and Twitter. He outlined the approach to creating cross-media and largely event-driven brand journalism that is "social by design", which means finding the right story and making it meaningful – giving people what they want to see and experience – so they will talk about it and want to share it with others. Examples of such proprietary digital content include the snowboarding movie *The Art of Flight*[8] and the Red Bull Signature Series, an action sports TV initiative created with NBC.[9]

By creating such content, Nate said, Red Bull demonstrates its commitment to its consumers and their lifestyles – specifically within the domains of action sports, gaming and music. It also showed that commitment by authentically engaging with their consumers, fans and followers on social media.

Surveying Red Bull's brand journalism output

Red Bull on social media

Red Bull has social presences on:

- Twitter: twitter.com/#!/redbull plus individual accounts for racing, gaming and other divisions
- Foursquare: foursquare.com/redbull
- Instagram: instagram.heroku.com/users/redbull
- YouTube: www.youtube.com/user/redbull
- Facebook: www.facebook.com/redbull
- Pinterest: pinterest.com/redbull/, plus as Red Bull Racing: pinterest.com/redbull/infiniti-red-bull-racing.

It as well as its staff have presences, some experimental, on many other platforms. In fact, Red Bull is highly engaged on the social media channels it uses. Its goal on each is to do them as well as possible. So, on YouTube, the offering is "the best action sports clips on the web and YouTube exclusive series". It also checks in on Foursquare to venues relevant to its brand interests, and it leaves tips – just as an individual who fitted the brand profile might. Above all, Red Bull engages with its community.

Red Bull on Twitter

On Twitter (600,000 followers) it tweets, re-tweets, replies @ and generally runs the account like an individual with this profile: "Likes: F1, racing, skate, surf, snow, moto, BMX, MTB, X Games, wake, music, art, culture, gaming. Fun."

In a post on *Socialize with Us* called "How Red Bull Is Dominating Social Media", Morgan Barnhart wrote: "No matter how large their audience grows, they are constantly engaging. Every time I send a tweet to Red Bull, they almost instantly reply. It's quite impressive. A Twitter search shows that mentions of Red Bull on a daily basis reaches up in the hundreds."[10]

Red Bull on Facebook

On Facebook (29 million likes), Red Bull profiles itself like this: "Red Bull Energy Drink is a functional beverage vitalizing body & mind. Red Bull gives wings to people who want to be mentally and physically active and have a zest for life."

In a post on *Mashable* headlined "Killer Facebook Fan Pages", Callan Green wrote: "The Red Bull fan page is easily one of the best on Facebook simply because it has been able to break out of the typical fan page mould by providing fun content that encourages fans to interact with and ultimately connect with the brand."[11] It uses an app entitled "Athletes" to pull in the Twitter feeds, Facebook pages and official websites of its sponsored athletes.

Callan writes:

> Integrating a Twitter stream is not special on its own, but Red Bull doesn't just pull in tweets from their official corporate account, as you might expect most brands do. Instead, Red Bull has aggregated tweets from sponsored athletes like skateboarder Ryan Sheckler and snowboarder Shaun White and included them directly in their Facebook presence. Associating themselves with popular athletes, and letting fans connect to those athletes on a separate social network (i.e., not boxing them in) gives Red Bull some instant cool points.

Morgan Barnhart wrote:

> Their engagement on their Facebook is astronomical. They're highly into their audience and their audience is highly into them. They've created a cool, collected and engaging environment which makes anyone feel welcome to contact them and know that Red Bull will be more than happy to contact them in return.
>
> Red Bull is setting a prime example for all other beverage companies [you could delete the "beverage"]. No matter how large they may be, they're not ignoring their fans – they're embracing them. They are the epitome of what all other brands, both big and small, need to be doing.
>
> You don't have to be sponsoring big time sports stars or creating crazy commercials just to get to the stature that Red Bull is at now – you simply need to enjoy, listen and engage your audience.[12]

Red Bull on YouTube

On YouTube there are mini-documentaries on action sports, such as one on high Alpine single-track mountain biking. You won't know it's Red Bull brand journalism unless you notice the Red Bull Media House credit, which follows two for-cycle brands – Shimano and Trek. You can see the video on the Brand Journalism website. There are other videos on surfing, skateboarding, football and other sports.

Erica Swallow, writing at the Content Strategist blog in a post headlined "How Red Bull's Content Strategy Got Its Wings" says:

YouTube is perhaps Red Bull's biggest social strong suit. It joined as one of YouTube's inaugural action sports content producers. And to date, nearly 300 million YouTube views have been generated from Red Bull content, making Red Bull Media House one of the top five sports content producers on YouTube globally.[13]

It has stretched the parameters of YouTube by creating an action sports video series: "These shows chronicle the day-to-day lives and competitions of some of the world's most popular athletes from a variety of sports, including skateboarder Ryan Sheckler, motorcross star Travis Pastrana, surfer Jamie O'Brien and trials cyclist Danny MacAskill." There's a video introduction to the series on the Brand Journalism website.

Red Bull on Instagram

In a *Fortune* report about how brands, including Red Bull, are using image-focused social media platforms, Anthonia Akitunde writes that, in using Instagram:

> It's also following one of the first rules in business: go to where your audience is. "Ubiquitous camera phones and connected mobile devices have exponentially boosted social sharing of digital images," says Nate Warner, Red Bull's digital marketing director. "We saw a constant stream of people sharing their own images from our events as well as images pulled from [our] properties, or re-sharing images from Red Bull's social media accounts," he continues. "The ongoing growth validates this type of positive connection our fans feel with the brand." Red Bull – one of the first and more popular brands on Instagram – has more than 230,000 followers and more than 87,000 user-submitted images tagged #redbull on the app.[14]

On his Pinterest Red Bull Social + Digital Media board, Andrew Nystrom, social media lead for Red Bull Media House and Red Bull North America, pins the above story and comments: "Unlike other brands quoted by *Fortune*, we're not focused on ecommerce on Instagram. We're focused on the Daily Awesome."[15] Red Bull posts a Daily Awesome photo and is active on the platform. According to *Business Insider*, it often likes other users' photos "that illustrate people's ideas of getting wings".[16]

Red Bull on Pinterest

As we'll discuss in detail in Chapter 8, Pinterest is a lifestyle platform, and as Red Bull is the ultimate lifestyle brand, the two are a good match. On Pinterest the Red Bull profile comment is "The only Energy Drink that

#GivesYouWings." Under the main Red Bull account it has boards for variants on the "gives you wings" theme. There is a separate Red Bull Racing account.

In a post at *MissCommunication*, Megan Farmer writes:

> It is important to create "moodboards" organized by theme or topic of what makes the brand work, focusing on what inspires the organization and aimed at having the same mindset as their demographic. These boards give value to followers and resonate with their lifestyles ... [Red Bull] don't simply promote their product, but also the wild, carefree lifestyle of those who drink their product (or the lifestyle their customers *wish* they had). They have a board called Give Wings to Your Body promoting working out and staying fit, and even one called "Holy Sh!t" that embodies the wild, crazy spirit that Red Bull celebrates [and] showcases motorcycle jumps, snowboarding tricks, and other extreme sports.[17]

The Red Bull Social + Digital Media Pinterest board run by Andrew Nystrom is a pretty comprehensive curation of articles about the brand.[18]

Red Bull and gaming

Red Bull's gaming operation has its own presences on the full range of media platforms that the company uses. You can play games on the web, on social platforms, and via apps and mobile devices. There is, for example, a Red Bull Arcade of games on Facebook.[19]

According to iMedia Connection:

> Red Bull uses social media to play with its fans. Rather than offering one marginally entertaining casual game, Red Bull adheres to entertainment standards you might find at a gaming company. In total, Red Bull offers users seven branded games to choose from. Each game is fun and totally on target for the audience. But most importantly, the games afford Red Bull the opportunity to serve as a forum for players to compete and share their achievements with each other.[20]

I quoted Hal Halpin on iMedia Connection earlier about how Red Bull identifies promising sports people and builds their careers, using them as the subjects of brand journalism. Here's Hal on that approach in relation to gaming: "In the case of gaming, that meant recruiting Dave 'Walshy' Walsh, the No. 1 'Halo' franchise gamer in the world at the time. This was a wise choice since Walsh – at the ripe old age of 26 – retired and became the John Madden of pro gaming. Talk about a return on investment for the brand! Taking to heart the valuable feedback of its pros, Red Bull partners with organizations that reflect the company's philosophy."[21]

Red Bull also brings gaming elements to other enterprises, such as a partnership with a start-up called Fitocracy, a one-year fitness tracking platform.[22] As *Mashable* reported:

> Users earn points to "level up" and rank on a leaderboard by reporting any fitness activity. They earn extra points for completing specific groups of fitness tasks or "quests". The "Paperboy" quest, for instance, suggests this: "Take a ride around your neighbourhood. If you hit a trashcan make sure you sprint away from that lady with the knife and rabid dog." That's 20 minutes of biking and 0.5 miles of sprinting, according to Fitocracy.[23]

Red Bull mobile apps

There are mobile apps for many games, as well as for Red Bull TV, the magazine *Red Bulletin* and Red Bull Music Academy Radio. Other apps venture into areas, including geo-located venue-finding with Hot Spot Viewer, sports performance and personal training with Coach, and the ability to upload photos, text and videos to Facebook, Flickr, Twitter and YouTube with Red Bull Community.

Red Bull TV

Red Bull's web TV is described by the company as being "your exclusive wingman to the best seats at spectacular sporting and culture experiences worldwide – all without having to leave your location or put down your mobile phone". You can watch it live or select from recorded shows.[24] Content includes the sports and live events in which Red Bull has sponsorship, and there is a strong travel element. Other shows are about the lifestyles of sports stars: "It's safe to say that Danny MacAskill might not be human. Don't believe us? See for yourself as the intrepid BMX rider travels back to his hometown of Edinburgh, Scotland, where his passion for innovation creates something truly spectacular." You can see that video on the *Brand Journalism* website.

Red Bull Music Academy Radio

They say it is: "one of the largest sources for cutting-edge music on the web … it offers thousands of interviews, features, DJ mixes and live recordings from the best clubs and festivals across the globe – all available on-demand".[25] Red Bull Music Academy Radio showcases live recordings, interviews and features, mixes, local spotlights and genre channels.

Music – Red Bull Records

Red Bull Records is an independent label focusing mainly on indie rock; it has a recording studio and a distribution arm.[26] As with other Red Bull entities, it has dedicated social network presences and a strong ethos of interaction with its community. On Facebook and elsewhere, for example, it will invite unsigned bands to send in demo tapes with the carrot: "who knows, maybe you can be the next Red Bull Records artist!"

Print – **Red Bulletin**

Red Bulletin,[27] "The magazine of the world of Red Bull", started out as Formula One's magazine and has become one of the few global monthly magazines, with 5 million distributed. Its production values match most consumer magazines and it features many articles about sports and other stars that it is connected with. Its tag line describes it as "almost independent".

Red Bulletin is distributed as a supplement in leading newspapers in Austria, where it was established in 2007, the UK and Republic of Ireland, the US, Germany, New Zealand, South Africa, Poland and Kuwait. It's also available via subscription, on newsstands in some countries, and as a website and an app.

In a piece to mark the first US edition, Nat Ives wrote in *AdAge*:

> Marketers have long paid custom publishers to produce branded magazines for their customers, but Red Bull publishes *Red Bulletin* through its Red Bull Media House unit. "We're entering a new age of media in terms of what consumers of content want and expect," said Associate Publisher Raymond Roker. "We really feel [we are] ... uniquely positioned to fulfil the promise of the brand that's been in place for years. Now through the web, the app and print we really feel we can have that conversation in ways that are really unparalleled in the brand space."[28]

Andreas Tzortzis, its US editor, told Ives:

> It really begins with the people you involve, people who are committed to the journalistic product and storytelling. It's being willing to go to the Atacama desert for a story on scientists who stare up at the heavens or head into New Orleans to talk about brass band culture years after [Hurricane] Katrina, as well as more obvious stories about Red Bull-sponsored athletes or events.

Red Bull as a producer of media for third parties – the Red Bull Content Pool

Here's what Red Bull says about its content offering for other brands:

> The Red Bull Content Pool is an advanced media asset management system for everyone who is interested in broadcasting or making use of Red Bull-produced content. The portfolio offers quality-driven moving images with relevant stories of lifestyle, action sport and fun. It's

relevant for all media channels that aim to reach a young and dynamic target group.

The unique asset of the Red Bull Content Pool is the fully automatic delivery process of available content: at any time, in any format and in any specification the content is needed. The Red Bull Content Pool offers what a modern media partner demands nowadays: a fast, easy-to-use and target-orientated tool for content supply – almost all at no charge ... [Content covers] a unique variety of media content in lifestyle, fun and sports ... [and] it has access to the whole Red Bull network, including more than 500 athletes, numerous artists and opinion leaders.[29]

What brands and brand journalists can learn from Red Bull

You might remember we mentioned a phrase earlier: "every company is a media company". Red Bull is an embodiment of that claim. It's also an example of how brand journalism can be made to work for a brand and a model for any organization that wants to get brand journalism right.

Lisa Kimmel, writing in a post headlined "What Brands Can Learn from Red Bull's Evolution to a Media Company" on Edelman Canada, said:

> The more a company engages with customers and prospects, the more likely they are to gain awareness, insight and ideas into the needs of their target audience. Through the act of creating, leading and engaging, companies can take a much more participatory role in shaping their destiny. Red Bull has done, and continues to do, just that.[30]

She draws up a list of things we can learn from Red Bull's success, and comes up with a formula for building a brand journalism content strategy. I'm summarizing her suggestions here because I think she has a great deal of good advice, although she does sort of assume all brands are like Red Bull and can engage in the same ways. But – as we'll see in the rest of Part II – that isn't so. There are many brands, many communities with many needs, interests and concerns, and many ways of engaging with them.

Anyway, here are Lisa Kimmel's key points, with her explanations in quotes and my subsequent comments:

- *Find a niche for your brand: "Put a stake in the ground. Become a definitive source on a particular topic, and own it. Focus on a topic that will be of interest to your target audience."* I want to challenge that word "own". In the modern media world, no one can own a topic. What you can do is create content around a topic that successfully engages with a particular audience. If your content becomes definitive, that's fantastic, but you can never think you own a subject because of that. Nevertheless, finding a subject around which to create content is a vital first step for any brand seeking to do brand journalism

- *It all starts with an idea. A story that entertains:* "*Once you've identified an ownable topic for your company/brand, create a compelling idea – and story – to support that topic. And remember, it's critical that this story entertains.*" We can widen that out from "entertains" to other key goals of brand journalism, such as "informs", "educates", perhaps "empowers".

- *It's not just about putting on a great event. It's about a content proposition:* "*From your idea, your story, don't just think about creating an awesome event. Rather, think about all the ways by which you can extend and amplify that story, and through all of the various aspects of the media cloverleaf. And, make sure that your fans can access and share that content.*" Your event might not be awesome – it might be a conference or a seminar – but the important point is that you have to spread the word about the event across all the media you use.

- *Consider incubating an idea. Start small. Refine. And then go big:* "*There's no question that the events put on by Red Bull are large-scale, full-blown productions. But not all of those events started that way. During any given month, Red Bull is experimenting, piloting programs in smaller markets, and seeing what ideas seem to 'stick' with fans. So, start small, and see how your idea evolves from there.*"

- *Determine what's engaging for your fans vs. what's interesting to the media:* "*PR practitioners often think first about what will be of most interest to traditional media. You don't need to start with them. Create an engaging event, story, content for your fans, and then that story may ultimately result in traditional media interest and coverage.*"

But what if your brand is not a major business-to-customer (B2C) one? Does Red Bull have lessons for very different businesses – for example, for business-to-business (B2B) brands?

Matt Wesson wrote on the Pardot blog, in a post headlined "3 Content Lessons Learned from the Red Bull Soapbox Race in Atlanta": "Red Bull has a few great lessons to teach B2B marketers about crafting content that generates crowds of excited fans and devout followers."[31] He comes up with three lessons from the way in which Red Bull uses events, which I summarize here:

1 Make sure you fully understand your audience, and their interests, and target the content you create at them.
2 Make your content stand out from the rest of the pack. Don't abandon your case studies or White Papers, but do explore more visual channels, such as infographics or video.
3 Promote your content wherever you can: on social media, via industry influencers and thought-leading blogs in your industry.

Assignments

1 Carry out your own audit of Red Bull's brand journalism.
2 Choose a suitable brand and draw up a multiplatform brand journalism strategy for it based on what Red Bull does.
3 Consider this question: if one of the stars whom Red Bull sponsors was involved in a story that was damaging to the brand, should they report it? Reflecting on what we discussed on ethics in Chapter 6, what is the right way for an ethical brand journalism outfit to handle bad publicity? Use this question to explore the differences, as you see them, between how traditional journalism and brand journalism are practised.

Notes

1 Red Bull Media House: www.redbullmediahouse.com/.
2 Lisa Kimmel writing on what brands can learn from Red Bull's evolution to a media company: edelman.ca/2012/06/07/what-brands-can-learn-from-red-bulls-evolution-to-a-media-company/.
3 Hal Halpin writing on iMedia Connection: www.imediaconnection.com/article_full.aspx?id=32168.
4 Karlene Lukovitz writing on *Mediapost*: www.mediapost.com/publications/article/171130/top-social-engagement-brands-make-me-statements.html.
5 Lisa Kimmel writing on Edelman: edelman.ca/2012/06/07/what-brands-can-learn-from-red-bulls-evolution-to-a-media-company/.
6 Steve Rubel writing on *Mashable*: mashable.com/2011/05/14/steve-rubel-authority/.
7 Nate Warner, Red Bull's digital marketing director, quoted on the University of Montana's School of Business Administration's website: www.business.umt.edu/Soba/featureStories/redbullmarketing.aspx.
8 *The Art of Flight* video: artofflightmovie.com/; or on the *Brand Journalism* website: www.brand-journalism.co.uk.
9 Red Bull Signature Series: www.redbullsignatureseries.com/.
10 Morgan Barnhart writing on *Socialize with Us*: www.blogengage.com/story.php?title=how-red-bull-is-dominating-social-media.
11 Callan Green writing on *Mashable*: mashable.com/2009/06/16/killer-facebook-fan-pages/.
12 Morgan Barnhart writing on *Socialize with Us*: www.blogengage.com/story.php?title=how-red-bull-is-dominating-social-media.
13 Erica Swallow writing on the Content Strategist blog: contently.com/blog/red-bull-media-house/.
14 Anthonia Akitunde writing in *Fortune*: tech.fortune.cnn.com/2012/05/30/brands-are-learning-to-say-cheese/.
15 Andrew Nystrom on his Pinterest account: pinterest.com/adnys/red-bull-social-digital-media/.
16 *Business Insider*: www.businessinsider.com/these-brands-are-doing-amazing-things-with-instagram-2012-6#red-bull-2.
17 Megan Farmer writing on *MissCommunication*: megfarmer.blogspot.co.uk/2012/05/4-best-ways-to-use-pinterest-for-your.html.
18 Red Bull Social + Digital Media board: pinterest.com/adnys/red-bull-social-digital-media/.
19 Red Bull Arcade of games on Facebook: www.facebook.com/redbull?v=app_9279253524.

20 iMedia Connection on Red Bull gaming: www.imediaconnection.com/iMedia25/ 2011/brands-redefining-social-media/Red-Bull/PrintView/.
21 Hal Halpin writing on iMedia Connection: www.imediaconnection.com/article_ full.aspx?id=32168.
22 Fitocracy: www.fitocracy.com/accounts/login/?next=/home/.
23 *Mashable* on Fitocracy: mashable.com/2012/02/03/red-bull-fitocracy/.
24 Red Bull TV: live.redbull.tv/.
25 Red Bull Music Academy Radio: www.rbmaradio.com/.
26 Red Bull Records: redbullrecords.com/.
27 *Red Bulletin*: www.redbullusa.com/cs/Satellite/en_US/Red-Bulletin-Magazine/ 001243140905767.
28 Nat Ives writing in *AdAge*: adage.com/article/media/red-bull-brings-red-bulletin-magazine-u-s/227441/.
29 Red Bull Content Pool: www.redbullmediahouse.com/content/red-bullcontent-pool.html.
30 Lisa Kimmel writing on Edelman Canada: edelman.ca/2012/06/07/what-brands-can-learn-from-red-bulls-evolution-to-a-media-company/.
31 Matt Wesson writing on the Pardot blog: www.pardot.com/ideas/3-content-lessons-learned-red-bull-soapbox-race-atlanta.

8 Using Social Media Channels for Brand Journalism

Goals of this module

- Survey a wide range of social media channels including Twitter, Facebook, Google+, YouTube, Pinterest, Instagram, Flickr and AudioBoo.
- Identify what each channel could add to your brand journalism strategy.
- Demonstrate, through case studies, what a wide range of brands are doing on these channels.

On the website

Find links to primers on the basics of using the social platforms we look at here, further case studies, videos and other resources referred to in the text, as well as links to all the source materials referred to.

How well do social media platforms work for brands? And how well are brands using them? The evidence is mixed. Facebook marketing company Pagemodo examined research into how much faith marketers have in social media. *Mashable Business* reported that the results show "a sense of conservative optimism".[1] *Mashable* goes on:

> Sixty-four per cent of business owners say social media marketing is a promising tactic and they believe it provides returns – but they aren't willing to go all in with it just yet and favour a more cautious approach. Another 20 per cent are more bullish on its potential, according to the same study, while just 6 per cent are hardcore sceptics.

There is variation, too, in how brands choose to measure their success on social media:

> Most do so by measuring the accumulation of friends, likes, followers and other online connections. Thirty-nine per cent look at shares of brand content, while 35 per cent measure actual leads from social media. Just 18 per cent measure success by overall brand awareness and favourability as gauged by consumer surveys.

So, the evidence from Pagemodo is generally upbeat, but not all assessments are as positive. Kaleel Sakakeeny on *Go Travel*, which looks at brand journalism in relation to the travel industry, discussed the more critical measure of brand recommendations:

> There's no doubt marketers and brand managers are spending lots of human and real capital to leverage the power of social sites, especially Facebook and Twitter. But does it do them any good? Meaning, do consumers promote brands via social media?[2]

Sakakeeny notes that an eMarketer report found that: "Consumers occasionally post about brands on Facebook and Twitter, but offline and non-social online methods keep them informed".[3] The stats, says eMarketer, are that "57.8 per cent of US Facebook users had not mentioned a brand in their status updates." Sakakeeny says: "This has to be disappointing to all those companies and corporations counting on the powerful social network sites to power their brand to more recognition."

That's why the brand journalist must be wary of relying too heavily on social media, and why in Part II of *Brand Journalism* we give equal weight to all the other non-social and off-line media platforms we can use. On a more positive note, if brand mentions are low, the vast majority of them are positive, so fears of opening a brand to a firestorm of negative comment on social media may be exaggerated.

The eMarketer survey discovered that of those who mentioned a brand, only 0.5 per cent of Facebook users posted negative mentions, 25.3 per cent made positive brand mentions, and 16.4 per cent a mix of positive and negative. On Twitter, we get the same story: 61.3 per cent of Twitter users say they have not mentioned a brand in their Tweets; 25.4 per cent say they mentioned brands in a positive way; and just 0.4 per cent state that they tweeted negative comments. The report also reveals that brand discovery is not taking place nearly as frequently on social platforms as via other media. The figures for discovery are:

- TV, radio, print and other offline sources: 16 per cent
- word of mouth: 14 per cent
- online media such as blogs and websites: 9 per cent
- social media sites (Facebook and Twitter): 6.5 per cent
- online advertising: 5.7 per cent.

eMarketer's conclusion:

> Consumers are using social media more and more, and brands are on these social networks and willing to interact there. Getting consumers to discuss brands and products in their status updates and tweets is a challenge, but if they start to do so, it could continue to increase the

influence that social media has in learning about new products and services.

Could this failure to engage be down to the way in which brands, in general, are using social media? In a post revealing that 90 per cent of marketers are using social media, Marketing Pilgrim says that:

> ... while social networks may have attracted most businesses there has been nominal progress in the true growth of the use of social networks from a marketing point of view. We are in the "trial and error as the norm" phase of social media and its use as a marketing tool. Something this new has no hard and fast rules and, as a result, some are cautious to truly jump in. As the comfort level grows so will the real use of social networks to help marketers meet their goals.[4]

Our goal in this chapter is to identify successful social media strategies. We look in detail at measuring our success in Part IV.

How to use Twitter for brand journalism

The Ultimate Twitter Study organization has researched what people want from Twitter and found these main wants:

> Honesty, interaction and helping seem to be the most common expectations. Tweeters expect brands to listen to their questions/problems and help find quick solutions. They expect a great deal of interaction! Especially DM response. Authenticity also seems to be very appreciated. Consumers want to experience a real connection ... Treat your followers as equals. They want relevant information. No broadcasting. No peptalk. And definitely no spamming. Overall, consumers expect brands to be active and interactive. So, if brands want to gain (happy) followers they need to adapt to consumers. All you have to do is help and inspire them. And, once in a while ... make them smile.[5]

Case studies: Brands that are doing a good job on Twitter

Whole Foods Market

Sprout Social identified Whole Foods Market – a chain of health food stores in North America and the UK – as one of five national US brands using Twitter in interesting ways.[6] Whole Foods Market has a main account @wholefoods, twitter.com/#!/wholefoods, where it is ready to answer questions: "Fresh organic tweets from Whole Foods Market HQ in Austin, TX. Ready to answer your questions Mon-Fri 9am-5pm CST!" It engages in conversation with individuals who have had a bad experience with the brand. For example: "@langsung17 Sorry to hear about this. Please let your store know and they'll love the opportunity to make it up to you!"

It also offers useful information not connected with its brand – for example, recommending a meal at a restaurant that fits with the tastes of its community: "Spicy Japchei with Shitakes and Fried egg at Koriente Restaurant – fork.ly/CbZLN3." Recipes are provided, and a way to add the ingredients needed to a shopping list. For example: "Here's a #vegan breakfast for mom with quinoa, hemp seeds & hemp milk COCOA – ALMOND BAKED BREAKFAST QUINOA: bit.ly/k3M8q3 #WFMdish." And it responds to queries: "@1lrussell Our new location in Charlotte is currently scheduled to open on August 29."

According to Sprout Social: "Based on some tweets in the Whole Foods timeline, it's obvious that the company monitors keywords related to its business and jumps into relevant conversations when opportunities arise." There are automated feeds for recipes (@WholeRecipes) and Twitter accounts for some specialists @WFMCheese – "our global cheese specialist, Cathy Strange"; @WFMWineGuys – "our wine & beer experts, Doug & Geof".

Whole Foods Market has tweet accounts for each of its 300-odd stores, listed here: www.wholefoodsmarket.com/twitter/ (e.g., the one for Laguna Beach, California: twitter.com/#!/wholefoodsLAG). And there are tweets about local offers, events at the store and links to issues of importance. This tweet goes to a post on the company's blog opposing the easing of regulations on the growth of genetically modified alfafa: "Support farmers in growing foods w/o contamination from genetically engineered crops! READ HERE: cot.ag/hWBWrZ #noGMO."

Poppy Legion

Poppy Legion (twitter.com/PoppyLegion) is the official Twitter account for the Royal British Legion, which looks after ex-service personnel and runs the annual poppy sale to mark Remembrance Sunday. The profile image is an avatar of a young woman, quite different from the simple poppy logo you might expect, and reads: "Follow me, the official voice of The Royal British Legion, and show your support of our brave Armed Forces family."

Poppy Legion tells powerful stories. For example, one tweet read: "To celebrate the anniversary of VE DAY, we've revisited one of our favourite stories from someone who was there. Bit.ly/JPxghG." This link goes to the story of one soldier who was in London's Trafalgar Square on the day that World War II ended in Europe. There is a picture of him sitting on the head of one of the bronze lions that guard the base of Nelson's column and waving the flags of the three victors in an effort to conduct the singing.

Poppy Legion engages with enquiries about information and it's clear from these answers that they distribute many information packs and do thousands of personal presentations. It re-tweets on issues that affect its community, such as this tweet linking to a BBC radio item on the need for more support for service families: "'Unsung heroes' report arguing for more support for Service families now on Woman's Hour @TTDYB @CombatStress bbc.in/JxCbWI."

JetBlue

The US budget airline JetBlue (twitter.com/JetBlue) features in many short-lists of brands using Twitter well. It uses Twitter for updating passengers on flight status/delays, and sharing photos, experiences (both good and bad) and general news that may affect flights, such as weather warnings. It has developed a reputation for responding quickly to issues that followers post, such as questions about ticketing or online check-ins. JetBlue stresses in its profile that it "doesn't respond to formal complaints on Twitter. For official customer concerns go to jetblue.com/speakup or call 1–800-jetblue." It has a separate account for offers, but also tweets them on its main account.

Kyle Lacey, author of *Twitter Marketing for Dummies*, said this in a case study of JetBlue's use of the platform:

> Its goal when joining Twitter was to simply, help customers. They eventually found out what the dos and don'ts were for their customers. How did they do this? By asking. The company found that customer service tweets generated more followers and replies. When tweeting about a press release they found no response. JetBlue then began asking questions in order to find out what the customers wanted. This approach has made them quite successful. JetBlue tore down the wall between the customer and the brand by implementing what was to be just an experiment, Twitter.[7]

As Kissmetrics noted: "JetBlue's brand page on Twitter shows that they use Twitter as a customer service platform. Almost every tweet is an @ reply." For example: "@andrewchen Air traffic control delays in SFO causing grief today. Sorry for the inconvenience, we understand your frustration."[8]

Customer information features regularly: "Thunderstorms in the Northeast may cause delays or cancellations. Check the status of your flight at bit.ly/jbstatus." JetBlue also uses Twitter as a gateway into a closer connection with the company, such as: "Meet Kristi from our Customer Support team, the voice on the other end of the phone, in A Day in the Life! blog.jetblue.com/?p=22302." They link to blog posts that offer features of interest to flyers – for example: "Learn how summer thunderstorms rain on our parade (and your flight) in the next Unpacked cot.ag/MLB7U5."

They do some promotion: "Getaways Cheeps! $299 pp/dbl occ limited avail 2nt pkgs to Nassau, Bahamas w/air from JFK or HPN. Terms apply. cot.ag/J8yBkB." And they re-tweet material from customers that they think will appeal to other customers, such as Instagram pictures. JetBlue's Twitter stream is not hyperactive – it averages one to three tweets a day, unless there are important issues they need to address; but every tweet counts.

Assignment

1 Identify two closely related organizations and compare their use of Twitter. These could be two competing corporations, two charities working in the same area, or any other two brands or organizations that can be expected to have comparable communities or areas of interest.
2 Monitor their use of the platform. Assess their level of engagement with their community through their response to individual enquiries, their re-tweets and internal and external links to material of interest to their community. What do they do well, what less well?

How to use Facebook for brand journalism

How does Facebook work for brands, and will it work for your brand? The BrandGym blog suggests this distinction between brands that work on Facebook and those that don't: "the brands Facebook works best for are ones you could imagine having as friends to hang out with and stay in touch with. So, Red Bull, yes. Pepto Bismol or Vicks, less so."[9]

Is that entirely correct? I think it's worth adding that people also interact with causes and issues that they care about on Facebook. While Coca-Cola is a giant on Facebook, campaigns, protests and causes can also be very big on the platform. In fact, there is a company called Causes, set up by former Napster and Facebook staff, which says that it is "the world's largest platform for activism and philanthropy. We empower individuals to create grassroots communities called 'causes' that take action on behalf of a specific issue or non-profit organization."[10] You can follow a cause or set one up. Causes' Facebook page had 8.9 million likes at the time of writing. It uses its Facebook page to highlight particular causes, interact with them, and to inspire those who might create or follow – and part with money for – a cause.

The evidence shows that it's not just fun brands and causes that work on Facebook. There are many more mundane brands that make Facebook work for them: real-estate agents, accountants, suppliers of components to industry. We'll look at some examples later in Part II and elsewhere in this book.

Whatever the nature of your brand or organization, effective interaction is the key to success on Facebook. Research by BrandGlue showed that the majority of visitors never return to a fan page after clicking "like" on it.[11] So you have to interact with fans and invite them to interact with you via status updates. But getting them to like your page is the essential starting point. You can do that in various ways: run tweets on Twitter that link to richer content on your Facebook page, have a like button on your blog and website, and links to your Facebook page on advertising, products and marketing and promotional tools.

Staffhacker explains what a "like" can lead to: "Once they've liked your page, your page's status updates have a chance – not a guarantee – to inch onto their news feeds."[12] Gathering "likes" is one thing, but it's the "talking about this" count that measures active engagements. Fluctuations in "talking about this" can be dramatic, and their cause is key. They go up when important stuff happens. If your brand is involved in newsworthy events, such as a sports team at the time of a really important match, "talking about this" naturally goes up.

In football, Manchester United is a major Facebook presence. At the time of its final game in the 2011 to 2012 Premier League season, when it was neck-and-neck with its great local rival Manchester City in the battle to win the league, and failed, its stats looked like this: 24,822,725 likes to 963,617 talking about this. Once the season had ended, the talking about this total dropped to 853,474.

So if your brand is making news, that will be reflected in your "talking about" stat – or it should be, if your Facebook brand journalism is effective. We'll look at how to monitor and improve your Facebook performance in Part IV.

Case studies: Brands that are doing a good job on Facebook

Duck Tape

Duck Tape (www.facebook.com/ducktape), a manufacturer of colourful tapes that can be used in crafts, has over 5 million "likes" on Facebook. In contrast, the brand has only a few thousand followers on Twitter (twitter.com/theduckbrand/). Clearly, this is a brand for which Facebook works brilliantly, but for which Twitter is almost irrelevant.

Success.com used Duck Tape as a case study for building your brand on Facebook and found that it had a customer base that was highly active on the platform.[13] David Rodgers, Duck Tape's digital marketing manager, told them:

> It is really people age 14 to 24 who drive our growth. This group uses Duck Tape for crafts – they make wallets and flowers and really amazing things. Our Facebook page plays a huge role in our annual prom dress competition, in which high school students submit photos of prom attire they made from Duck Tape.

Our best-received posts are those that announce new prints [tape designs] – people love to hear about new products and innovations. They also love to participate, and surveys asking people to help choose the next print are very popular. People want to be part of the product.

Today our Facebook fan page is the centre of our media messaging. There is real value in having a massive fan base – it starts to grow organically. But you can never stop being relevant and interesting. We honed our message by culling Google Reader alerts to see what bloggers and other media were already saying about our product. Today I read through each and every post, checking the site at least three times a day. It gives me a real sense of who our customer is and who we should be focusing on. But if we don't have something relevant to say, we don't post. If a week goes by without a post, that is OK.

American Idol

Social marketing director Steve Goldner says:

If I were to give one suggestion how to go about a winning Facebook mentality it would be to think like the producers of *American Idol*. Why is *American Idol* so appealing? I think it really comes down to three factors:

1 *American Idol* has really good, compelling owned media. The contestants they present are talented and provide something that most people enjoy.
2 They make the audience part of their product. You, as a viewer, have an active and important role in their product offering.
3 Even if you are not one that votes on contestants … the fact that so many do interact adds validity and value to the product. The American Idol is selected by the target audience. Not some executives that are removed from pop culture.[14]

But it takes good brand journalism to maximize *American Idol*'s success on Facebook. Let's take a quick look at *American Idol*'s Facebook page (and, by the way, we could be looking at any of the shows aired around the world that follow this or a similar audience-participation format). The page's profile picture (as I write) emphasizes the importance of your (as a viewer's) involvement with a call to action: it is dominated by the word "VOTE!" The visible apps include the vote interface and Idolizer – an app that lets you "follow and respond to your favourite idol's posts and share your support on your timeline." You can also share with your friends.

Other apps you can click to see (there are seven) include Events and Backstage. So the whole set-up of the *American Idol* Facebook page is to encourage interaction and sharing. Here's a typical status update: "Your

Idols are up to the challenge! A fan on Twitter asked: 'Can you knot a cherry stem in your mouth?' See the results in this week's Idol Answers video."

That's a good example of boundary-breaking brand journalism. The content must be first class – that's where your journalism skills come in – in order to promote engagement and effectively market your product, service or cause. Asking for your community's opinions regularly is like an open-ended market research project, and constantly seeing how your brand is perceived gives your organization regular opportunities to improve on that perception.

Assignment

1 Identify two closely related organizations and compare their use of Facebook. These could be two competing corporations, two charities working in the same area, or any other pair of brands or organizations that can be expected to have comparable communities or areas of interest. You could look at the same two organizations that you analysed in the Twitter chapter project.
2 Assess the effectiveness of their use of cover picture, timeline, apps, status updates and calls to action. Assess their level of engagement with their community through their responses to that community's interactions with them. What do they do well, what less well?

How to use YouTube for brand journalism

Video doesn't fit into every brand's strategy. To do it well – and it must be done well – takes time, resources and money. But with YouTube being the second biggest search engine in the world, there are great opportunities to connect there with consumers who are researching prior to purchasing goods or services.

YouTube offers a place to present useful and valued content for your community. It's a place where you can demonstrate and illustrate. So let's take a look at what it can add to your brand journalism content strategy, and take in some examples of brands using the platform well along the way.

In a *Mashable* post, Catherine-Gail Reinhard, creative director at video infotainment company Videsa, says:

> YouTube does represent a great opportunity for marketers to reach consumers who are searching for information about a brand or related products and services. One thing is becoming apparent: The brands that achieve long-term success on YouTube are the ones that consistently and frequently publish refreshing content that has intrinsic value for audiences online.[15]

Case studies: Brands doing a good job on YouTube

Home Depot: Using YouTube for instructional videos

Home Depot (www.youtube.com/user/HomeDepot) uses YouTube to pub-lish free instructional content that is relevant to the brand but which avoids promoting specific products that they sell. This content, says Reinhard, does three things:

- establishes Home Depot as a trusted expert resource for DIY projects
- promotes the products and tools that they sell via product placement rather than outright advertising
- humanizes Home Depot by using shop-floor employees as presenters.

Harley Davidson and Intel: Using YouTube for storytelling

You probably think of YouTube as a free-to-use site, but brands can buy customized YouTube channels on which they own the videos and can control the advertising that viewers see. Russell Working posted on Ragan.com about brands using YouTube to create a storytelling pre-sence.[16] YouTube spokeswoman Kate Rose is quoted as saying: "The benefit to ... Harley Davidson is that they're creating this destination page on YouTube that they can point either prospective customers to or drive people that are just kind of perusing YouTube to see the videos that they want uploaded."

So let's take a look at what Harley does on YouTube (www.youtube.com/user/HarleyDavidson). The videos referred to are available on the *Brand Journalism* website. Working picks out as an example "a video that details the brand devotion of the Latino bikers who call themselves Harlistas". Harlistas (youtu.be/RfHxa_kqL-8) is a high-production value, mini-documentary road trip, and actually a trailer to a longer film. Here's what Harley says about it: "*Harlistas: An American Journey* is an authentic look into Latino motorcy-cling culture in the United States told through four pivotal stories of real-life characters who proudly call themselves Harlistas – Harley riders of Latino heritage." The video links to a range of related media, including a schedule of screenings for the full movie, rider backgrounds and director's commen-tary. Another video series is on the clothes that bear the Harley Davidson name and those who design them (harley-davidson.com/motorclothes).

Intel

The microchip manufacturer Intel uses its YouTube channel partly for instructional guides, but also to tell stories about how its technology is helping people. So instead of talking about the things it makes, it shows the people who use the things it makes. For example, it tells the story of two photographers called Killy and Lala. The film, called *80 Impression* (youtu.be/JFbUbAWbB-s), "illustrates the diverse, personal, and emotional role that technology plays in the everyday visual life of two young Chinese wedding photographers". Intel also uses video to tell the stories of those who create its products, saying: "Inside Intel there are many inspiring and informative stories about people collaborating to make great technologies."

Becky Brown, Intel's director of social media, told Working: "We've really transitioned to that branded journalistic approach, where we've got really great stories that we're producing ourselves."

Assignment

Take a couple of comparable brands in a particular sector and compare their use of video – for example, brands where instructional videos would help their community. Assess what they do and how they do it. Do they, to use a phrase quoted above, "consistently and frequently publish refreshing content that has intrinsic value for audiences online"? Try and find one brand that works relatively well, another that doesn't exploit the opportunity that video offers. Develop a video brand journalism strategy for the brand that could improve.

How to use Google+ for brand journalism

Has Google+ failed as a social network? The jury's still out. It seems hard to believe that Google will let this heroic effort to create a rival to Facebook die, but so far the take-up of the platform has been decidedly limited. ComScore, the web analytics company, found that Google+ users spend only three minutes on the platform every month, on average, compared to 405 minutes for Facebook users. However, it works for some brands, so let's take a look at a couple.[17]

Case studies: Brands that are doing a good job on Google+

H&M

Search Engine Watch argued in a post called "Social Media Insight from 6 Successful Brands on Google+" that there are brands making headway on the platform.[18] Among the successes, they cite the fashion chain H&M:

> Over half a million users have this brand circled on Google+. If you circle H&M you'll see their fashion picks of the day, get access to style guides [such as a guide to denim] and engage with other fans of the brand by discussing questions like 'What's the first sign of spring? Caps, sneakers, sunglasses?' Engagement isn't quite what you'd expect if you

had this many fans on Facebook – under 100 shares and around 100 +1s is common for their daily status updates.

Business 2 Community puts this relative success down to the fact that H&M has been the most active of any brand on the network.[19] Search Engine Watch says that H&M offers a great model for other brands:

> Don't expect Google+ to perform exactly how Facebook or Twitter brand pages do. It's a new platform and all of us are still waiting to see how the community shapes up. Take the lead from H&M and start interacting. Find an anchor topic, like H&Ms fashion picks of the day, and stay consistent with your messaging. If it's not working then switch it up, but at the very least try![20]

However, at least when I looked, H&M's Google+ content was pretty much identical to that on its Facebook page.

Marvel comics

The Search Engine Watch post also singles out Marvel comics. It says: "Marvel is using their brand page to promote upcoming liveblog sessions and even held a Google+ Hangout to announce 'Avengers vs. X-Men' … They've done a great job of promoting their brand across many social platforms."

Cadbury

Business 2 Community praises the confectioner's Google+ strategy:

> They are even running a Hangout event live from the Royal Albert Hall during which you can talk with their special guest at the Olympic team GB event [Cadbury was a sponsor of the 2012 London Olympics]. Cadbury's have over 1 million +1's and are circling nearly 1500 users themselves.[21]

Again, when I looked, posts on the Cadbury's UK Google+ page and status updates on Facebook were almost identical.

Assignment

1 Compare a number of brands that are on both Facebook and Google+. Compare the size of the community they have on each. Compare their brand journalism on both. Are they doing anything different on Google+?
2 Watch out for brands using the Hangout feature and take part in one or more. What's the experience like? Does it build your links with the brand?

How to use LinkedIn for brand journalism

LinkedIn is best known as a place for individuals to connect with others in their profession or business. It requires the most personal contact of any of the major social networks. To connect, you must know people or have done business with them, and they must accept your request to link up. It's most commonly thought of as a place to post your CV/résumé, build your professional reputation by getting others to recommend you, and join or create groups where focused discussions take place.

But LinkedIn also has an option for organizations to create company pages. This is particularly useful for business-to-business (B2B) companies to target business consumers. It seems particularly effective in doing that, when compared with other more general social platforms.

In a post on Hubspot, Pamela Vaughan says:

> In a study of over 5,000 inbound marketers [who market by creating content, and who we can equate with brand journalists] where we pitted LinkedIn against Facebook and Twitter, LinkedIn proved to be the most effective social media channel for lead generation – 277 per cent more effective, in fact.[22]

As Inc.com explains: "Your LinkedIn company page gets listed in Google's and LinkedIn's search engines, allows others to follow your company's updates, gives you a place to promote services and products and even reports analytics."[23] Individuals can follow companies on LinkedIn, just as they can on other platforms. Create a company page with material that is of benefit to your business community and you can establish your brand as an authoritative organization – as a thought leader with many knowledgeable individuals working within it. Its contribution to your brand journalism strategy, if you are in the B2B sector, is to enable you to build authority and influence with your core community. If you aren't in the B2B sector, you can still use it as a professional social network for your employees and others in your sector. Clearly, it will be quite separate from your customer-facing social engagement.

You can aid effective interaction on LinkedIn, and build your brand's – and its employees' – status as influencers and authoritative sources of information by getting involved with LinkedIn Groups. You should join, and consider creating, groups that are specific to your brand's areas of expertise, to the industry you are a part of, and the profession(s) your employees follow.

According to LinkedIn's own marketing: "Philips enabled over 4,400 discussions on healthcare innovation." It quotes Hans Notenboom, Philips's global director of B2B online, saying that LinkedIn "enabled us to create active communities that have become online destinations for medical and lighting professionals worldwide".[24]

Case studies: Brands that are doing a good job on LinkedIn

LinkedIn company pages are an underused resource, but Hubspot came up with companies demonstrating best practice.[25]

PR 20/20

Hubspot says:

> PR 20/20's company page is a great example of one that is effectively making use of company status updates, regularly sharing blog posts and reports they've created as well as third-party coverage of their brand. This drives traffic from LinkedIn back to PR 20/20's website and positions them as a thought leader within the LinkedIn community.[26]

The company's status updates cover careers advice: "4 Tips to Ace Your Next Marketing Agency Job Interview"; links to their latest *Inbound Industry* reports: "See the inbound marketing news you may have missed. This week, we talk social business, lead nurturing, share some great SEO resources, and more"; and an analysis of why "80% of CEOs [chief executive officers] do not really trust, and are not very impressed, by their CMOs [chief marketing officers]" and what to do about it.

It's all highly targeted and valuable to the community they are a part of.

Voices.com

Hubspot praises Voices, an online marketplace for businesses to connect with voiceover professionals, for its use of the product/services tab:[27]

> Its products/services tab clearly identifies the main markets for its service, and provides a clear summary of what it can offer each of them, such as: radio and television commercials for the advertising industry; voice-overs for retail kiosks, point-of-sale and in-store advertising; and voice-overs for video games.

Assignment

1 Place yourself as a brand journalist working in a particular industry and research that industry's overall presence on LinkedIn. Are the key companies and individuals there? Review relevant company pages and assess them.
2 Build up a picture of how the area you are researching is presented on the platform. Which brands are strong? What gaps are there? What inadequacies? If you were working for a particular brand within that industry, what strategy would you develop to engage on the platform?

How to use Pinterest for brand journalism

Pinterest is a photographic platform whose focus is on personal lifestyle; in addition, unlike many social media platforms, it has a predominantly female community base.

Research by Hubspot[28] reported by MemeBurn[29] found:

- Eighty-three per cent of Pinterest users are females, aged 18 to 34.
- Most pins are about design, fashion and home décor.

Hubspot, in a White Paper on using Pinterest for business, says: "A lot of big brands are taking notice of the power of online visual content for marketing and the emotions images elicit in readers."[30] It's particularly good for lifestyle brands. Alex Wheeler, vice president of global digital marketing at Starbucks, told CNN Money: "The beauty of that platform is its elegance and simplicity. [It allows Starbucks and its fans to show] shared values and product experiences that are very personal around life moments."[31]

So Pinterest is an effective way of connecting your brand to the wider lifestyle of your community. To make Pinterest work as part of your brand journalism strategy, you should present your brand, service or the cause you espouse as part of the lifestyle – and lifestyle aspirations – of your target audience. Pinterest is not just relevant to the materialistic in lifestyles: issues, causes and a desire to make a difference in the world can also work well on the platform.

Case studies: Brands that are doing a good job on Pinterest

Amnesty International

Amnesty (pinterest.com/amnestyusa/ and pinterest.com/amnestyusa/pins/) makes a presence on Pinterest suit its brand purpose by appealing to the wider interests of its community. It uses powerful imagery on its boards, and positions itself thus: "We're the world's largest grassroots human rights organization. We post on fair trade, book and movie recommendations, inspiring quotes and other good stuff that help make the world a better place."

In choosing the topics of its boards, Amnesty is looking – as well as at itself – at the other things those who choose to connect with it on Pinterest are interested in. Its boards are about the Amnesty worldview, and their general aspiration to "make the world a better place". So it has boards about its core concerns – such as Act, about getting involved in the current issues that Amnesty champions: "We've been fighting the bad guys since 1961. You can join us!" It also has Activists in Action: pinterest.com/amnestyusa/amnesty-activists-in-action/ and Human Rights Reading: pinterest.com/

amnestyusa/human-rights-reading-list/, which is about reading around the subject, but focuses on mainstream novels.

Some boards mix issues with commerce, such as one on Fair Trade: pinterest.com/amnestyusa/fair-trade/. They say: "We love #fairtrade and ethically made products! We'll share favourites from our store (shop.amnestyusa.org) as well as repins or other finds." Because Pinterest is a visual medium, Amnesty has a posters board, but also lighter stuff such as inspiring quotes and one called Fun: pinterest.com/amnestyusa/fun/.

ThinkProgress

Noah Chestnut, director of digital media at HPSInsight, wrote on *Quora* about politicians and political causes as brands on Pinterest.[32] Among those he includes is ThinkProgress: "This is a progressive blog run by The Center for American Progress."[33]

One of their boards targets the issue that Mitt Romney, who ran unsuccessfully against Barack Obama for the presidency in 2012, stayed at a succession of incredibly luxurious hotels as he campaigned. Chestnut says:

> The genius behind this board is that ThinkProgress does not write any copy for the hotels. The text taken from the hotels' own promotional material serves ThinkProgress' goals. A blog post stating that "Romney spends a lot of money on hotels" would not get much traction. A Pinterest board that reads like a brochure of a luxury tour of the United States is more memorable and drives conversations.[34]

Lands' End

The clothing manufacturer Lands' End (pinterest.com/landsendus/) does have boards on its clothing and footwear ranges, but also goes beyond product shots to create boards on themes around style, body image and dressing with confidence. They include Swimsuit Confidence: "Real women of all shapes and sizes showing their confidence during Lands' End's National Swimsuit Confidence Week"; and Dress Diaries: "Dress Diaries: Write the story of your life in a Lands' End Dress."

Assignment

Take a look at two brands in a given sector and compare their presence on Pinterest. Look for opportunities exploited and missed. Select a brand without a Pinterest presence and create a strategy for using the platform.

How to use Instagram for brand journalism

Instagram lets users take photos on their mobile phone, add filters and effects to them, and share them instantly, both on the Instagram app and also to other social networks, including Facebook, Flickr, Twitter and Foursquare. What sets it apart from most other photo-sharing platforms is the emphasis on high-quality photography, and sophisticated photo enhancement and editing.

It's good for mobile social sharing, which some analysts say explains why Facebook, on which users share 250 million images daily, but which has not been strong on mobile photo sharing, paid $1 billion for it in 2012. We'll look at other location-based applications in Chapter 9.

Jim Tierney, of Real Time Media, said on *Quora*: "Instagram works because it helps people connect on an emotional level that goes beyond simple photo sharing."[35] Instagrammers often like a photograph based on the technical proficiency or creativity of the photographer, so it has a strong aesthetic appeal. Jim goes on: "It also opens the user up to discovery outside of the typical 'walled garden' that sometimes comes with Facebook. Brands that are successfully implementing Instagram into their campaigns recognise this."

It won't work for all brands. Hubspot, in a post called "The Marketer's Scoop on Instagram and How to Use It" says: "While the application for service providers is not as easy to see, there does seem to be potential for product-oriented businesses to utilise Instagram."[36] They suggest using the platform as a sort of sounding board, taking photos of products that are in beta and getting feedback on them, for giving an insight into your brand by taking photos of the production process, and for highlighting creative ways to use a product. It also suggests running competitions, such as uploading an image of your latest creation and asking Instagrammers to name it.

What is missing in this approach is a recognition that Instagram is about high-quality photography. I believe missing out on that is to fail to exploit a key quality of the platform. To produce poor quality photographs is to invite the scorn of the Instagram community. It's also about location. Since photos can be geo-tagged, Instagram can work for brands with premises or where location is in some way important.

Competitions are a common way for brands to use the platform, and they are often run across Instagram and another platform – usually either Facebook or Twitter.

Case studies: Brands that are doing a good job on Instagram

Ford Fiesta

Tom Gibby, creative strategist at Blue Hive, said on *Quora*:

> Ford have just partnered with Instagram to launch a new photography competition [2012] called Fiestagram. The contest challenges Instagram

photography enthusiasts across Europe to upload photos in several categories inspired by the technologies and features of the Ford Fiesta. In each of the next six weeks, a new category (#Starting, #Hidden, #Listening, #Entry, #Music and #Shapes) will provide contestants with an opportunity to win a range of prizes, with the overall winner receiving a new Fiesta. Participants can interpret the categories in any way they wish and use any of the filters and effects available on Instagram to enhance the mood and feel of their images.[37]

The Fiesta competition was also featured on Ford's Fiesta Facebook page (Facebook.com/FordFiesta), and contestants entered by uploading photos with the hashtag #Fiestagram to Instagram. All submitted images appeared on galleries at the Facebook page, and the best were selected for use on live billboards and in real-life photography galleries across Europe. Ford says 16,000 pictures were submitted.

Of course, such competitions could be run purely on Facebook, so why use Instagram too? The answer is because Instagram can offer access to a different demographic. Like Pinterest, it is niche: more boutique store than high-street chain. So it will work for brands that are a bit different and want to maintain that difference. What it contributes to your brand journalism strategy is a presence on a fashionable platform where the community of generally highly skilled photographers appreciates good creative photography. To use the platform effectively, your photography has to be of a high standard.

Annie's Homegrown, a restaurant chain

We've seen above how brands twin Instagram with Facebook; here's one twinning it with Twitter. In a Hubspot post called "Best 10 Branded Companies on Instagram", Allyson Galle explained:

> Annie's Homegrown has done an excellent job of asserting its brand identity as an all-natural, organic, and healthy provider of foods Americans love, from macaroni and cheese to frozen pizza to fruit-flavoured gummy snacks. The brand understands how important these qualities have become to its target demographic, so its Twitter strategy is based upon sharing product news, tasty-sounding recipes, and Instagram photos.[38]

This is an interesting point. We can see Twitter as being largely "white label". It doesn't have a strong brand identity other than its openness to people to connect with a community they choose to be a part of. And because Twitter is easily used as a conduit to other platforms – blogs, websites and other social sites – it is an ideal place to promote brand journalism that resides on niche channels such as Instagram and Pinterest.

Assignment

Identify a sector that you believe Instagram could work for. Look for two brands in the sector, one that is using the platform, one that is not. Critique the first brand's use of the platform and put together an Instagram strategy for the second.

How to use Flickr for brand journalism

Flickr gets nothing like the publicity of some of the photo-sharing platforms we have looked at above, but it's still a contender. As Clive Andrews pointed out on the Nixon McInnes blog:

> In the world of social media, Flickr rules the roost when it comes to photos. Though Facebook hosts more images (over 60 billion compared to Flickr's mere 5 billion), Flickr has few rivals in terms of the way it allows photos to be grouped, arranged, discussed and used as starting points for conversations, debates, campaigns, projects and games.[39]

One key value of Flickr is its highly effective keyword tagging feature that enables you to make your material visible to search engine optimization (SEO), as well as internal searches from Flickr users. Clive goes on: "Several alternatives to Flickr do exist, some of which are highly sophisticated, but none have emulated Flickr's ability to accommodate communities gathered around photos."

So Flickr is good for grouping photographs around topics and engaging with communities that are attracted to those topics. In this it is closer to Pinterest than Instagram, which is a Twitter-like flow of posted images.

Brands that are doing a good job on Flickr

GM

GM uses its Flickr photostream (www.flickr.com/photos/gmblogs/) to show its wide range of products – past, present and future – and combines its own material with user-generated stuff.

LG

LG has used Flickr to crowd source content and host competitions. One, Viewtyfulworld (www.flickr.com/groups/viewtyfulworld/) had a great prize for the winning photographer – the chance to be published in *National Geographic* magazine. They kept the barrier to entry low, just asking for your best picture.

Nikon's Digital Learning Centre

The learning centre (www.flickr.com/groups/nikondigitallearningcenter/) is the Flickr arm of the Nikon School and Nikon Digital Learning Centre websites. It offers support and a resource for customers through tutorials, practical photography tips and advice.

Assignment

1 Find a brand that is using Flickr and one that is not. Critique the first brand's use of the platform and put together a Flickr strategy for the second.
2 Look at social photography sites as a whole. Identify a number of brands for which photography is important. Find out which platforms they use for photography. Do they simply post all pictures to several platforms or are there variations in how they use each of them? Assess their level of engagement on each of the photo platforms they use. Consider the differing appeals of each social photography platform for different types of brands.

How to use audio, particularly Audioboo, for brand journalism

Audio is used much less than video, which is probably an oversight for many brands. If any segment of your target audiences listens to podcasts, for example, you could be missing out on an opportunity to connect with them in a fairly meaningful way. Business-to-business (B2B) brands could be producing educational, informative or newsy audio packages designed for consumption on MP3 players.

So let's look at where audio fits into your brand journalism strategy. We'll concentrate on AudioBoo because it is a good example of a platform that emphasizes the social aspect of audio; but others are available. Audio-Boo allows users to easily upload audio to its website from the web or mobile. It's a sort of YouTube for sound. It's simple to use and integrates with other social media. You can share content; listeners can add their own audio comments to your soundtracks and submit their own audio to your channels. Brands and individuals can be followed and it integrates easily with iTunes, where you can create a branded podcast channel. There are smartphone apps as well as the desktop version, making it easy to record on the move: at a conference, meeting or other live event.

Mark Rock, AudioBoo founder and chief executive, told the *Financial Times* that his ambition was to be the Facebook of the spoken word. "Music has been done, text has been done, but no one has yet captured the uniqueness of the spoken word on the internet."[40] It hasn't, however, grabbed the popular imagination like YouTube has. It's a minnow in comparison, although it's as easy to record audio as it is video, and as easy to upload to AudioBoo as to YouTube. The free version limits you to 3 minutes of recording time, but use the pro version (audioboo.fm/about/upgrade) and you can record for 30 minutes for a small annual fee. They say: "We'll host your audio, take care of streaming bandwidth, integrate your podcast feed with iTunes, enable simple sharing with social networks and offer you a range of different embeddable players so you can easily include audio in your website or blog."

AudioBoo has few brand presences on it, but a ground-breaking link-up with the BBC in 2012 could see that change.

Case studies: Brands that are doing a good job on AudioBoo

BBC

The BBC chose AudioBoo (audioboo.fm/channels/bbc) as an official partner for publishing web clips of its programming content. This created a range of BBC-branded channels on the platform, and formalized unofficial use of AudioBoo by BBC producers, which had seen, for example, the *Today* programme on BBC Radio 4 get about 20,000 listens to the 24 "boos" it posted each week. The BBC's goal in the tie-up is to broaden its audience reach worldwide.

Boost for the troops

British Forces Broadcasting (BFBS) and *The Sun* teamed up (audioboo.fm/channel/boost-for-the-troops) with Audioboo:

> ... to help you support the men and women of the British Armed Forces. They do a difficult – and often dangerous – job, so let's get behind them and tell them how much we value their work. How? By sending an audio message (or "boo" for short). Tell a joke, sing a song or just say a simple thank you – it's up to you. And if the message is for someone in particular, make sure you include his or her details in the upload form. Boost for the troops is free and simple to use. So go on, boost our troops' morale today.

Christian Aid

Christian Aid (audioboo.fm/christianaid) has a couple of channels. Here's what they say about one of them, which is audio live from the field and has the ugly name ca_sitrep: (audioboo.fm/channel/ca_sitrep):

> On this channel our staff and partners report live from the field about work that is improving the lives of poor people in more than 60

countries. You can hear our humanitarian staff give the latest information on emergencies, such as floods, earthquakes and famines, and how we are delivering emergency relief to the people affected. And you can get the most up-to-date reports on our longer-term work to end poverty, delivered from within the communities themselves.

Users can add their audio to the channel.

Assignment

1 Find two brands in a particular sector, one that is using audio, one that is not. Critique the strategy of the one using audio and develop an audio strategy for the one that is not.
2 Alternatively, just pick a brand that is not using audio and develop a strategy for it. Be as creative as you can, drawing from the examples above and any others you can find.

Assignments relating to Chapter 8 in full

1 Pick a brand with a wide-ranging social presence, detail the platforms it uses and analyse how effective it is on each of them. Write a dissertation on that brand's social media strategy.
2 Draw up a social media strategy for a brand that does not have a substantial social presence – ideally one you are very familiar with or which you can gain good access to. Identify which of the platforms discussed above will be used and what your strategy will be on each of them.
3 Consider the ethical use of social media. Draw up guidance for social media engagement at a brand based on issues such as transparency discussed in Chapter 6.

Notes

1 *Mashable Business* report on Pagemodo research: mashable.com/2012/05/23/social-marketing-infographic/.
2 *Go Travel* report – *Facebook, Twitter Fail to Promote Brands; Offline Works Better*: technorati.com/lifestyle/travel/article/facebook-twitter-fail-to-promote-brands/.
3 eMarketer report: *Most Consumers Still Don't Talk about Brands on Social Sites*: www.emarketer.com/Article.aspx?id=1008773&R=1008773.
4 Marketing Pilgrim on how marketers use social media: www.marketingpilgrim.com/2012/07/90-of-marketers-using-social-media.html.
5 Ultimate Twitter Study researches how brands use twitter: ultimatetwitterstudy.com/.
6 Sprout Social, "5 National Brands Using Twitter Well": sproutsocial.com/insights/2011/11/national-brands-using-twitter/.
7 Kyle Lacey, in a case study of JetBlue's use of the platform: kylelacy.com/25-case-studies-using-twitter-to-increase-business-and-sales/.

8 Kissmetrics, from a case study of JetBlue: blog.kissmetrics.com/thrive-on-twitter/.

9 BrandGym blog: wheresthesausage.typepad.com/my_weblog/facebook.

10 Causes: www.causes.com/about?utm_campaign=home.

11 BrandGlue: www.brandglue.com.

12 Staffhacker on what a Facebook "like" can lead to: www.staffhacker.com/311/how-to-optimize-your-use-of-the-facebook-news-feed.

13 Success.com on Duck Tape as a case study for building your brand on Facebook: www.success.com/articles/1425-how-to-build-your-brand-with-facebook.

14 Steve Goldner writing about *American Idol* as a Facebook brand: socialsteve.wordpress.com/2012/03/19/making-facebook-work-for-your-brand/.

15 Catherine-Gail Reinhard in a *Mashable* post: mashable.com/2009/06/01/youtube-brands/.

16 Russell Working on Ragan.com: www.ragan.com/Main/Articles/Brands_use_YouTube_to_create_a_storytelling_presen_43130.aspx.

17 ComScore analysis of Google+ use: www.comscore.com/.

18 Search Engine Watch, "6 Successful Brands on Google+": searchenginewatch.com/article/2152861/Social-Media-Insight-from-6-Successful-Brands-on-Google.

19 Business 2 Community on successful brands on Google+: www.business2community.com/google-plus/6-brands-businesses-effectively-using-google-0174937.

20 Search Engine Watch, "6 Successful Brands on Google+": searchenginewatch.com/article/2152861/Social-Media-Insight-from-6-Successful-Brands-on-Google.

21 Business 2 Community on successful brands on Google+: www.business2community.com/google-plus/6-brands-businesses-effectively-using-google-0174937.

22 Pamela Vaughan writing on *Hubspot*: blog.hubspot.com/blog/tabid/6307/bid/31889/13-Brands-Using-LinkedIn-Company-Page-Features-the-Right-Way.aspx.

23 Inc.com, on LinkedIn company pages: www.inc.com/how-to-launch-a-linkedin-company-page.html.

24 LinkedIn's own marketing blurb for company pages: marketing.linkedin.com/.

25 Hubspot: www.hubspot.com/.

26 Hubspot on PR 20/20's LinkedIn company page: www.linkedin.com/company/pr-20-20.

27 Hubspot on use of the product/services tab: www.linkedin.com/company/voices-com/products.

28 Hubspot research: blog.hubspot.com/Portals/249/docs/ebooks/google_plus_vs_pinterest_where_should_you_market_your_business.pdf.

29 Hubspot research reported by MemeBurn: memeburn.com/2012/04/google-vs-pinterest-how-to-choose-the-right-platform-for-your-brand/.

30 Hubspot in a White Paper on using Pinterest for business: www.hubspot.com/.

31 Alex Wheeler, vice president of global digital marketing at Starbucks, quoted by CNN Money: tech.fortune.cnn.com/2012/05/30/brands-are-learning-to-say-cheese/.

32 Noah Chestnut writing on *Quora* about politicians and political causes as brands on Pinterest: www.quora.com/Noah-Chestnut.

33 Center for American Progress on Pinterest: pinterest.com/thinkprogress/.

34 ThinkProgress Pinterest board on Mitt Romney: pinterest.com/thinkprogress/luxury-hotels-of-the-romney-campaign/.

35 Jim Tierney of Real Time Media on *Quora*: www.quora.com/Jim-Tierney.

36 Hubspot in a post called "The Marketer's Scoop on Instagram and How to Use It": blog.hubspot.com/blog/tabid/6307/bid/29987/The-Marketer-s-Scoop-on-Instagram-and-How-to-Use-It.aspx#ixzz1vti854Ie.

37 Tom Gibby, creative strategist at Blue Hive, writing on *Quora*: www.quora.com/Tom-Gibby.

38 Allyson Galle writing on Hubspot: blog.hubspot.com/blog/tabid/6307/bid/32909/The-10-Best-Branded-Companies-on-Instagram.aspx.

39 Clive Andrews writing on the Nixon McInnes blog: www.nixonmcinnes.co.uk/
2011/02/15/flickr-new-rules-for-brands/.

40 Mark Rock, AudioBoo founder and chief executive, quoted by the
Financial Times: www.ft.com/cms/s/0/1a813116-8960-11e1-bed0–00144feab49a.
html#ix zz1xCxCfef5.

9 Brand Journalism for a Mobile Audience

Mobile Social Media Platforms, Apps, Augmented Reality and QR Codes

Goals of this module

- Assess the value of apps for mobile phones and tablets.
- Examine the use of third-party mobile social media platforms such as Foursquare.
- Explore the usefulness of augmented reality and quick response (QR) codes.

On the website

Find links to primers in the use of the platforms and applications discussed in this chapter, essential updates on the subjects covered, videos and links to all the sources quoted here.

The theme of this chapter is location, location, location. It's about making your brand journalism, and the brand or other organization you work for, accessible when your community members are away from their static devices, print products, TVs or radios. Of course, we want all our content available wherever our community wants it, but it is location-specific content that we are looking at in this chapter.

Comscore found that, each month, 3 billion search terms contain local terms.[1] Clearly, when location matters, it's vital to score well for local search terms. For some brands, location is obviously highly important. Any organization that has premises will benefit from interacting with its customers and potential customers around its locations: by using mobile social media platforms to enable those locations to be found, to encourage visits to them, and to reward those visits in some way. Those connections can be made in a number of ways.

One is through third-party mobile social media platforms such as Foursquare, and on location-enabled platforms that are part of a broader social platform, such as Google Local and Facebook for mobile. Other ways of connecting are through the creation of mobile phone and tablet apps by using augmented reality and QR codes.

We'll look at a number of platforms that can carry our brand journalism to a mobile audience; but, as ever, it's not the platforms *per se* that are important – it's the general principle of what can be done. And we'll discuss examples from brands of how each platform can be used as part of a coherent brand journalism strategy.

The challenge for brands, and for brand journalists, is to create content that is strongly location relevant so that it assists in the search for information, advice, recommendations and other material that can be accessed where it is most appropriate. This means understanding what members of your community need and want to know when they are in a particular location. At its simplest, this can mean identifying places your brand's products or services can be accessed close to where a person happens to be when they need them. But there is much more that can be done. Taking a brand journalism approach to location involves providing a range of rich, valuable information, news and entertainment that is closely focused on what people need or want to know right there, right then.

Mobile apps

There are mobile-friendly websites and there are mobile apps. The former are essential, the latter may or may not work for your brand. Here are the differences. A mobile website:

- is accessed through search or browsing
- has a static navigational user interface
- requires an Internet connection
- can't make use of phone features such as cameras and global positioning systems (GPS).

A mobile app:

- must be installed on a mobile device by the user
- has an interactive user interface
- can be accessed even when there is no Internet connection
- makes use of the phone's camera and GPS.

A search on a mobile device will return the mobile version of your brand's website, so it is findable by everyone. Mobile apps are faster, but their development cost is higher. They can be made available in app stores – and hence are easily findable – but there may be an approval process before they can be listed there. Because an app must be downloaded onto a mobile device, an individual must be convinced that the benefit they will get from the app is worth the effort of downloading it.

If location is integral to what your brand does, then a mobile app will be highly valuable. An app is like an automatic search engine that can deliver sifted information from a very large general database, showing only what is relevant to the person using the app in their current location.

There are two categories of app: native apps, designed to work on one of the main platforms – iPhone, Android and others – and web apps that work on any platform. You'll find links to information on commissioning and creating apps on the *Brand Journalism* website.

How brands are using mobile apps

So what categories of brand do mobile apps work best for? Here are some examples. Real-estate agencies have picked up on the benefits of apps for house hunters. Load one on your phone, set the parameters for what you are seeking, stroll around the area that interests you and the app will alert you when you are close to a suitable property that's on the market. Restaurants and other prepared food retailers employ them to enable users to find a restaurant location, book a table, order a takeaway and make a payment. Retailers are also embracing apps, but often use them simply as an enhanced product-browsing facility with in-built purchasing options. A search of the iTunes store reveals many negative comments from customers disappointed with such apps.

The challenge for a brand journalist is to combine trusted, authoritative content that helps an app user to reach a purchasing decision, with the added convenience brought into play with the phone's features. How can location be used? What about the phone's camera? Few brands bring brand journalism into their apps, but here's one that does – perhaps because it is a traditional journalism brand.

Vogue

Vogue Stylist, an app from *Vogue* magazine, pitches itself like this:

> You look forward to *Vogue*'s point of view every season – now, get that same unique perspective on fashion and style on your phone. Each month, Vogue Stylist gives you the back story on the top trends. Get inspiration from new looks curated by *Vogue*, and select and shop your favourite items from *Vogue*'s sponsors.

So that's one key element – bringing *Vogue*'s recommendations to the app and enabling purchases to be made. But as the *Wall Street Journal* reported, personalization is also brought to the app:

> The app can be used to upload items from one's own wardrobe and sort them by designer brand, colour or trend, as identified in the current *Vogue* issue. Users can search trends and find suggestions – populated by computer algorithms – based on the clothes they own and the ones

shown in that month's *Vogue*. The uploading and categorizing might be time consuming, but it is the thing *Vogue* executives are most excited about. The function is intended to draw in younger readers, whom the magazine isn't necessarily reaching yet. There are goodies salted through the application – discounts, exclusive products – which can be "unlocked" by snapping a photo of an ad – just a little extra inducement to buy the magazine.[2]

Any brand in the fashion business, any fashion retailer, buying guide or fashion media brand could do what *Vogue* has done.

Starbucks

Sprout Social, in a post called "Five Brands with Great Mobile Marketing Apps", singled out Starbucks as a good example of app development. Its app includes a store locator, and uses the smartphone as a loyalty card and to pay for purchases. Sprout Social says:

> One of the highlights of this app is the ability to create personalized drinks. It adds a game-like element that encourages shoppers to be creative and explore the full line of Starbucks products. For the health-minded, the app also includes nutritional information about its food and beverages. It's a good example of how you can make details about your merchandise accessible in a fun, new way.[3]

We'll look in more detail at what Starbucks makes available in-store via its data network in Chapter 19.

Waitrose

The UK supermarket chain Waitrose's app has a store locator, and offers a shopping list-building facility, recipes and "interactive cook's tools from weights and measures calculators to food and wine matching". Much of the recipe content is drawn from the company's customer magazine and static website, and includes how-to videos.

Waitrose's app goes some way towards drawing together content that reflects the lifestyle of the community with whom they are seeking to engage, with its recipes, guides and videos; but (at the time of writing) it could go further. For example, Waitrose's static website has a guide to picnic spots. A picnic spot locator in the app could use the phone's GPS. Also on the static site is a guide to a charity called the Woodland Trust, which preserves woodlands and opens them up to the public. Adding locations and other information about woodlands to the app would also be useful.

Not every brand that creates an app has a relationship with location. Many brands simply want to be findable on apps because that is where at least a segment of their community would like to connect with them.

Amnesty International

Amnesty International is such a brand. It uses apps in support of campaigns. At the time of writing, it had one in support of its campaign to bring democracy to Burma. This was a very simple app that invited you to take a picture of yourself, which would appear in the app behind superimposed bars to a campaign with the copy line: "While Burma's not free. I'm not free." It also has one called AiCandle which carries breaking news on human rights and allows downloaders to support Amnesty's latest campaigns – from prisoners of conscience to ending poverty.[4] Log in and the splash screen is an unlit candle. On-screen text asks you to use your voice to light the candle. The flame moves as you tilt your phone and gutters if you blow on it.

This is from Amnesty's description of the app:

> "The AiCandle is part of our suite of digital tools that empower people to take immediate action for human rights," said Owen Pringle, director of digital communications at Amnesty International. "The solidarity of our 3 million supporters across the world continues to make a positive difference to the lives of so many individuals. The AiCandle offers another way in which people can express that solidarity." Supporters are able to share news and actions with others via Facebook and email through the AiCandle.

Third-party mobile apps such as Foursquare

Foursquare is a third-party mobile check-in service and recommendation engine for venues and brands. There are others, including Google Local, but we'll stick with Foursquare here to demonstrate what such apps can do for you. While plenty of brands without physical locations have taken to the platform, simply because a segment of their community is on the app, we're going to concentrate here on how brands with premises use it.

Users check in to locations they visit to make themselves visible to friends in order to gain rewards and potentially become the mayor of a location. If your brand has physical locations, they can be registered on Foursquare. You can register your business and "claim" your locations, add tips and photos to your locations, and offer rewards or "specials" for check-ins and mayorships. So a coffee shop might offer a free pastry with your drink on a first visit or a free coffee after a tenth visit. There is an "explore" button that gives users suggestions on where to go based on information such as the time of day, the popularity of nearby places and past check-ins. You can create and customize a page for your business on the platform.

Lists can be created on Foursquare and others can follow your lists, so you can encourage Foursquare users to visit a range of locations. That list might be a guide to a town or to locations on a particular theme. When those who are following a list are near one of the locations on it, they'll get an alert suggesting they check in there. Typically, users connect their Foursquare account to their Twitter or Facebook ones, and their check-ins get posted there. This facility is not just of use to commercial brands. A public health authority or other organization promoting fitness, for example, could incentivize those whom it was trying to help by creating a list that includes gyms, healthy-eating places and other health-related locations, and reward check-ins with, say, reduced gym membership or special offers on healthy food options to encourage participation in a better-health scheme. The opportunity to collate such information can help you to create brand journalism that is more closely attuned to the audience you identify.

You'll find a basic guide to creating a Foursquare brand page on the *Brand Journalism* website.

How brands are using Foursquare

Mashable highlighted a number of big brands and how they use Foursquare.[5] Among them are the following.

Zagat

Zagat restaurant reviews says on its page (foursquare.com/zagat):

> We're excited to bring the enthusiastic Foursquare community together with ZAGAT's dining expertise. Now Foursquare users can benefit from official ZAGAT tips, show they love food by unlocking the new Foodie badge which will earn a 50% discount on a Zagat.com premium membership.

New York *magazine*

New York magazine uses Foursquare to encourage exploration of the city. It says on its page (foursquare.com/nymag):

> We've teamed up with Foursquare to bring you the latest tips from our expert food, fashion, and nightlife editors. Explore the best of New York with our picks for cheap eats, new stores, and awesome happy hour deals, plus insider info from all five boroughs.

Gucci

The Gucci fashion brand has its store locations on Foursquare and takes a wider brand journalism approach to its use of the platform by offering an exclusive take on luxury lifestyles. It says on its page (foursquare.com/gucci):

"Get insider tips from Frida Giannini, Gucci's creative director, who shares her favourite global hotspots in an exclusive series of city guides."

The Doors

The surviving members of The Doors use their Foursquare page to identify places with significance for the group (foursquare.com/thedoors), including where memorabilia can be found, locations that inspired songs and where the band has played. They say on their page: "Follow The Doors on Foursquare to discover elements of Doors history in your area, when you're travelling, and get access to content and clips when you're out."

Goodwill marketing

Brands also use Foursquare for goodwill marketing, making charitable donations for each Foursquare check-in at their premises.[6]

Google Local and Facebook for mobile

As with Foursquare, you can claim your business's location on Google Local. You'll find a primer in using Google Local on the *Brand Journalism* website. There is a user-generated content (UGC) aspect too; visitors can add content, and rate and review your business.

Using Facebook on a mobile device brings up a check-in tab, among others. Both these big players are likely to ramp up their investment in location-based applications, and one might easily buy Foursquare. We'll update on this issue on the *Brand Journalism* website as necessary.

Augmented reality and QR codes

First, what are they? This from Wikipedia's definition of augmented reality:

> Augmented reality (AR) is a live, direct or indirect, view of a physical, real-world environment whose elements are *augmented* by computer-generated sensory input such as sound, video, graphics or GPS data ... With the help of advanced AR technology (e.g. adding computer vision and object recognition) the information about the surrounding real world of the user becomes interactive and digitally manipulable. Artificial information about the environment and its objects can be overlaid on the real world.[7]

So, point your smartphone's camera at an object – it might be a building or other location, a product or an element in a print product, a poster or static advertisement – and a layer of digital information, which is invisible to the naked eye but can be read by that camera, can be read.

Inc.com said: "With augmented reality, marketers can take the physical world and combine it with the digital world, giving both users and brands the ability to connect even further with a product before, during and after making a purchase."[8] Some platforms, such as Aurasma (www. aurasma. com/), describe themselves simply as visual browsers, and it's likely this term will become the common descriptor.

A QR – or quick response – code is a type of barcode that can be read by the camera in a mobile device. Point the camera of a phone that has a QR code reader installed at such a code and the content the code links to opens up: it could be a web page, a video or any other content accessible on a mobile device. So, a QR code is a way of accessing augmented reality. The benefit is that codes remove the need for people to tap in a URL, or download an app, to get to your augmented material. One of the best known augmented reality platforms is Layar (www.layar.com/).

Layar

Here's Layar's take on augmented reality:

> Layar specializes in mobile augmented reality – the most popular medium through which the average person interacts with AR content. The mobile AR world consists largely of two different types of experiences: geolocation- and vision-based augmented reality.
>
> Geolocation-based AR uses GPS, compass and other sensors in a user's mobile phone to provide a "heads-up" display of various geo-located points-of-interest. Vision-based AR uses many of these same sensors to virtually display digital content in context with real-world objects – like magazines, postcards or product packaging – by tracking the visual features of these objects.[9]

So one branch of AR – geo-located points of interest – concerns linking rich content to a building or landmark. This is great for travel guides, for example, or for a brand to deliver information or entertainment relevant to a person's current location. The other branch of AR involves adding a layer of content relevant to that displayed in a static item. So a poster might have a QR code that takes you to that brand's Facebook page or to a video. A magazine can have both editorial content and advertising linked to an additional layer of information relevant to that content.

Among the categories on Layar are accommodation, architecture and buildings, art, beauty, health, city tours, education, employment, and charity and community.

Blippar

Blippar (blippar.com/) is another well-known AR platform, and is much more closely aligned to brands than Layar, which has many non-commercial users.

Indeed, Blippar's slogan is that it "brings brands to life"[10] and it is aimed specifically at brand-consumer engagement. Typically, open the Blippar app on your phone and point the camera at a product from a brand that is using the platform, and you'll get competitions, recipes or other content designed to enhance a user's experience of the brand.

How brands use augmented reality

Many brands concentrate on showing customers where they can consume its products locally.

Stella Artois

Stella Artois, for example, has an augmented reality iPhone app called Le Bar (demo video here: youtu.be/sTERI1s-UyA) that lets you find a local bar serving the beer. Open the app and the camera automatically engages. Superimposed on what the camera sees are tags with bar locations. Tap a tag and you get directions to that location. Another area of functionality lets you find a taxi home after your drink.

A lot more could be done to build on such an app. It could develop the bar experience with brand journalism such as pub quiz questions, sports news and games commentary.

Cadbury

Cadbury created an augmented reality game with Blippar called Qwak Smak. Users load the app, point the camera at one of a number of Cadbury products and cartoon ducks appear around that image as rendered on the phone's screen. Then they can whack the ducks and submit their score for the chance of winning a prize.

Transport for London

Transport for London's Oyster card uses Blippar to inform passengers about the journey they are undertaking. Point the app at your Oyster card – a pre-pay ticket for funding multiple journeys for regular travellers – and you get updates on any delays or other problems.

The Invisible Artist

Among the less commercial uses of augmented reality on Layar is The Invisible Artist (www.layar.com/layers/tmonkeybk/). It's a tour of London's principle contemporary art galleries conducted "in the company of a real insider. Our guide will tell you about the architecture of the building, the kind of work shown there, and some of the varied artists the gallery has exhibited."

Galleries including London's Royal Academy create apps for particular exhibitions, building a multimedia location-specific guide to the art that a user is viewing. They'll include video interviews with the artists alongside text about aspects of the work or of the exhibition.

Assignment

1 Take a look at one or more brands for which location is important and identify which of the above platforms they use. Look at their mobile apps, their engagement on third-party apps such as Foursquare, and their use of visual browsers or augmented reality platforms and QR codes.

2 How good is their use of each platform? Can you gauge how popular they are with users?

3 Do their mobile apps take the brand journalism approach? If not, what brand journalism could usefully be added to them?

Notes

1 Comscore research into search terms that contain local terms: www.comscore.com/Press_Events/Press_Releases/2011/9/comScore_Releases_August_2011_U.S._Search_Engine_Rankings.

2 *Wall Street Journal* reporting on *Vogue*'s app: online.wsj.com/article/SB10001424052748704240004575085673152523904.html.

3 Sprout Social, "Five Brands with Great Mobile Marketing Apps", sproutsocial.com/insights/2012/05/top-mobile-apps-brands/.

4 Amnesty International's AiCandle app: www.amnesty.org/en/news-and-updates/amnesty-international-launches-iphone-app-human-rights-2011-04-13.

5 *Mashable* on big brands on Foursqare: mashable.com/2010/08/24/big-brands-foursquare/.

6 Clickz.com on goodwill marketing on Foursquare: www.clickz.com/clickz/news/2122595/brands-foursquare-goodwill-marketing.

7 Wikipedia on augmented reality: en.wikipedia.org/wiki/Augmented_reality.

8 Inc.com on using augmented reality: www.inc.com/guides/201104/how-to-use-augmented-reality-in-advertising.html.

9 Layar's explanation of augmented reality: www.layar.com/what-is-layar/.

10 The Next Web on Blippar: thenextweb.com/apps/2011/08/17/blippar-the-augmented-reality-app-for-brands-launches-with-cadbury-chocolate-bar-game/.

10 Brand Journalism Content Creation and Curation

Examining Blogs, Live Blogging, Curation, Data, White Papers, e-Books, RSS and Email Newsletters

Goals of this module

- Survey a wide range of content creation platforms.
- Demonstrate the value of curation as a brand journalism tool.
- Show the value of blogs to brands that have expertise in a given subject.
- Explain when a brand can use White Papers and e-books effectively.
- Look at additional distribution strategies for the content that brands create.

On the website

On the website you'll find primers in the use of each of the platforms we discuss below, as well as links to all the references given here.

In this chapter we look at areas in which a brand and a brand journalist can demonstrate their expertise. We will look at creating brand journalism content and some of the ways in which content can be distributed – at brand as publisher, and brand as curator. So we look at blogs, White Papers and e-books as methods by which the brand, and its in-house experts, can demonstrate deep knowledge in its area of expertise. We explore live blogging as a way to cover an event or a fast-developing story.

We add curation to that as a service to a community – doing the leg work of bringing disparate nuggets of information that they'll find useful together in one easily accessible place. Content creation and curation offer an opportunity for your brand to become what is often called a thought leader – to make a really substantial contribution to the knowledge pool in your industry and to pass on valuable knowledge and information to your community. We examined this business goal in Chapter 3.

We look at data journalism as a method through which a brand that produces research findings can make those findings easily absorbable by an audience, and make that raw data available to others to turn into visualizations. We add in really simple syndication (RSS) as a method of research and a bundling and distribution tool, and email newsletters as one further important method of distributing that information.

Each of these areas is hugely valuable to business-to-business (B2B) brands, but their usefulness is not exclusive to them. Any brand that has expertise can demonstrate it through these methods. Any brand community that needs or wants information can be served.

There can be several goals for such content creation and curation: lead generation, search engine page rank improvements, thought leadership, audience engagement and brand awareness. Such engagement can be measured and offerings refined in the light of those outcomes. Knowing what the goals are in any content creation and curation programme is a vital first step.

Content creation and curation

Blogs

Blogs are an absolutely central part of brand journalism, as they are of traditional journalism. This is where a brand becomes a publisher. It's the blog that gives you content to link to on social platforms such as Twitter and Facebook. I like the approach, espoused by Robert Peston, the BBC's business editor, of creating what is known as a beat blog. A beat is an area of expertise. And just as a traditional journalist has an area of expertise, so do many of those working for a brand, business, charity or any other type of organization. Robert Peston's blog (www.bbc.co.uk/blogs/thereporters/robertpeston/) offers a great model for brands and brand journalists.

A beat blog created by a brand can be used to demonstrate expertise, to educate and to establish trust. Blogging lets you contribute to current discussion, to comment on industry issues and developments. It can also be used to break news about your brand and to increase community engagement. Comments left on successful blogs will help a brand to understand what really matters to the community whom they seek to serve.

An expert at a brand, someone who is doing detailed research, analysing business options and reaching conclusions about how to conduct that business, could – if they can write – turn that process into an engrossing blog. So a wine buyer, product developer, research chemist, programmer, sales rep, retailer, charity worker, or just about any other category of individual could use a blog to explore the work they do and to communicate an insider's guide to that work with a community. If they can't write, they'll need the editing skills of a brand journalist to turn what they produce into an effective piece of brand journalism.

How brands use blogs

Here are some brands that demonstrate a range of things you can do with a blog.

Whole Foods Market

The organic retailer's blog is a cookery guide, with regular recipes, such as a seasonal guide to using cherries (blog.wholefoodsmarket.com/2012/07/cherryriffic-recipes/). It talks about current offers (blog.wholefood smarket.com/2012/07/summer-giveaway-way-better-snacks/). It gets relevant staff to write about issues they deal with, such as a post from the receptionist at the Whole Foods Market's global support offices on the frequently asked questions she gets from customers, investors and potential employees (blog.wholefoodsmarket.com/2012/07/faqs-from-our-global-office-3/).

Zillow

Zillow (www.zillow.com/blog/) is a real-estate brand that blogs on everything to do with buying and selling homes and moving house. That includes making the house look as good as it can, with tips on repairs and improvements; advice on mortgages and insurance; and how to avoid unscrupulous removals companies.

It takes a wider brand journalism approach with a section of the blog on celebrities who are moving home – an area that will attract those who have no immediate interest in moving, but who will begin to build a relationship with the brand. It covers market trends, establishing itself as a trusted commentator and adviser on important financial matters. It also blogs news and advice on general finance, with posts on wider topics, such as "Financial Questions to Ask before You Get Married" (www.zillow.com/blog/2012-02-14/financial-questions-to-ask-before-you-get-married/).

The Zillow blog is full of effective brand journalism that acts as a multi-sectioned resource for householders.

Eloqua

Eloqua (blog.eloqua.com/) is a specialist company in marketing automation whose blog explores the role that innovation plays in revenue generation. I want to use it as an example of how commenting on a breaking news story via a blog can work for a brand.

As David Meerman Scott reported, when Oracle, another brand in Eloqua's sector, announced the acquisition of a third brand, Market2Lead, the official announcement was very brief and factual. With journalists and others searching for information on this breaking story, Eloqua's CEO posted on what the acquisition meant for the sector. He wrote, in part:

> I expect Oracle's entry to make a major difference in the attention paid to this sector. It's going to open marketers' eyes, and, as a result, expand the market. This is exactly the type of movement this industry needs. You see, the potential market for lead management systems is less than 10 per cent penetrated.[1]

That post got Eloqua into the story as reported by a wide range of journalists and commentators.

Who should blog?

IBM says everyone should blog.[2] As *Mashable* reported:

> When IBM decided they wanted to start using blogs, they didn't just create one blog, they created an entire network. IBM created a way and allowed their employees to write about their experiences, what they're working on, or any other topic of choice.[3]

In its introduction to the many hundreds of blogs it hosts, IBM says:

> As they'll tell you themselves, the opinions and interests expressed on IBMers' blogs are their own and don't necessarily represent this company's positions, strategies or views. But that doesn't mean we don't want you to read them! Because they do represent lots of business and technology expertise you can't get from anyone else.

Mashable comments:

> IBM capitalizes on the intelligence of their employees to give consumers insight into what happens behind the scenes. By giving the industry experts they've hired a voice, IBM is able to highlight the people behind their products. Users get to see how IBM operates, and are given a direct connection with IBM employees.

Guest blogging

As well as posting on your own branded blog, your experts can guest blog on other blogs read by your industry. As *Social Media Examiner* reported, guest blogging enables your experts to build a profile in the industry and to increase your credibility and reach on social and online media. It gives an example from Intel.[4]

Intel

Ekaterina Walter is a social media strategist at Intel. She posts authoritatively on her own Building Social Bridges blog (www.ekaterinawalter.com/), where she is identified as a key Intel staff member, and on other sites, including *Mashable* (mashable.com/author/ekaterina-walter/).

Social Media Examiner explains:

> The company lets Ekaterina build her own personal brand. She always links to her personal blog while making it obvious that she loves working at Intel. Ekaterina has become a social media celebrity and Intel handles that perfectly. It brings the company credibility, which is an invaluable advantage.[5]

Live blogging

Live blogging is the real-time reporting of an event. Live bloggers will sift a wide range of potentially curatable content from on-the-spot reporters, official sources, media outlets and those using social media – Twitter, Facebook and the rest – to add their coverage and comment on a story. The basis for live reporting is usually text, but the addition of still pictures, live-streamed video clips and on-the-spot audio using AudioBoo or other platforms can add greatly to the effectiveness of a live blog.

The format is familiar from ball-by-ball football commentary on websites, and can be practised very effectively on platforms such as Cover It Live (www.coveritlive.com) and Storify (storify.com/). You'll find links to primers on live blogging on the *Brand Journalism* website.

How brands can use live blogging

Dell, General Electric, Virgin America and Adobe have all used Storify; but their efforts are generally disappointing when compared with traditional news brands' live blogging. To make a comparison, contrast the brand examples below with what is produced at:

- *The Guardian*'s News blogs (www.guardian.co.uk/news/blog
- *New York Times*'s the Lede (thelede.blogs.nytimes.com/); and
- BBC's Live Stream format – one example here: www.bbc.co.uk/news/uk-18234049.

Dell

Dell's social stories on Storify are indexed at this page: storify.com/Dell. They've storified think tanks, forums and conferences. One, a collaborative exploration of how the office is changing (storify.com/Dell/the-evolving-workforce; you'll find it on the *Brand Journalism* website) hits the brand journalistic goal of providing a community with information on a topic that is much broader than their purchase of office equipment from Dell.

The live blog kicks off with this:

> For efficiency's sake, it used to be the norm to fill up office buildings with employees and lock them into a schedule that had everyone on the

premises at the same time. These days, that approach makes less and less sense for more and more companies. What's your ideal working environment?

It goes on to ask for workplace stories and post contributions from third parties as well as Slideshares and videos from Dell employees.

General Electric (GE)

GE storified (storify.com/generalelectric) a major conference called GE Works, with themes including Future American Workforce (storify.com/generalelectric/ge-works-day-4). It isn't a particularly full use of Storify as a multimedia live blogging platform. It's actually just a record of tweets about "salient comments on what we'll need to do in order to re-skill the American workforce for next-generation jobs". This is OK as far as it goes, but they could have used video of panel discussions and key speakers to bring depth and allow greater involvement from the wider community not at the conference.

General Electric and Virgin America combined on a story called "Leap Forward" (storify.com/generalelectric/virgin-america-ge-leap-forward-towards-the-future-). They said of it:

> On June 15th, Virgin America took a leap forward with the announcement that its new planes would be powered by GE's 15 per cent more fuel-efficient LEAP engines. Virgin America & GE wanted to celebrate with fans – from carbon offsetting to innovations about the future of flight and free tickets, check out how the day unfolded.

Again, it's mainly a list of corporate tweets from the two parties and gained virtually no involvement from the wider GE/Virgin community.

Curation

Curation is all about spotting and passing on material that your community will be interested in. So as well as putting your own content in front of people, you can say, in effect, "Take a look at this which x produced; I think you'll find it interesting." That can be done as simply as re-tweeting a good tweet, liking a Facebook post or commenting on it, up to building a topic that you curate on a platform such as Pinterest, (www.pinterest.com) Tumblr (www.tumblr.com) or Scoop.it (www.scoop.it). Such curation adds to the richness of the content surrounding your brand's online presence.

This comprehensive approach to curation can establish your brand as a trusted content source. You can curate an industry, an issue, a hobby or pastime – whatever your brand's area of expertise or involvement is. Do curation well and you also become a highly useful knowledge resource. To achieve that you must draw together all sorts of information that your community members would have to work hard to find on their own. As you pull in material from a wide range of sources, you present your brand as open to independent content and views. If your curation is well defined and targeted, it can make your curation platform an essential destination for your community.

To do that you'll need a high level of knowledge of your community and what they want or need to know. You may well find there are several separate areas you should be curating. If you'd like a primer in curation, you'll find one on the *Brand Journalism* website. Among the curation platforms available is Scoop.it, which I use for curating the *Brand Journalism* topic (www.scoop.it/t/brandjournalism).

It seems likely that as brands find more options to tell their own story, they'll look beyond the brand as publisher model and to the brand as curator – a facilitator of conversations around a topic or industry. Josh Sternberg, in a post at Digiday, comments on this development and shows why brands might prefer curation to publishing:

> Digital media has emboldened many brands to consider themselves publishers ... The problem is publishing is a lot harder than it looks, or rather it's a lot harder to do it with the consistency, day after day, that's needed to build a long-term audience. That's leading some brands to hook onto the idea that their role lies more in the curation of content.
>
> Curation is the vogue digital term for the ability to not only aggregate and distribute carefully selected information, but also to provide a unique voice on top of the original pieces of information. In the age of Twitter and Facebook, it seems like all the world is curators now. Brands want in on the action.[6]

But there can be dangers in curation for brands. As Stephanie Schwab said on *Social Media Explorer*:

> For many brands, curating outside content can be very scary – it means using content that others have developed to build your brand, and that loss of 'control' doesn't always sit well with upper management. But a savvy reader who's got their finger on the pulse of your industry could do an excellent job as "editor", bringing the best of the web in your niche or vertical directly to your followers and fans.[7]

I'd say use a brand journalist for that; but even then, curation still requires far fewer resources than content creation, so it can offer good returns on time invested in it.

So how should you approach curation as a brand journalist? In a post called "How to Curate Content for your Brand", Stephanie Schwab recommended:

Determine how to attract not only current customers but potential new customers to your content by thinking a bit outside the lines of your actual brand premise. If you sell a travel product, perhaps your content could include links to destination reviews by travel bloggers, news about airlines and fares, and links to images of great destinations.

People who are thinking about travelling or travel frequently will appreciate the content, and, when they're in the market for your travel product, they may think of you. If you hew too narrowly to your own product or topic, you may miss a chance to attract new audiences or to get engaged with an influencer just outside your sphere.[8]

How brands are using content curation

Josh Sternberg at Digiday gives the following examples.[9]

IBM's A Smarter Planet

A Smarter Planet (smarterplanet.tumblr.com/) is a stream of curated content about innovation, one of IBM's core competencies. A second curation site, Social Business (ibmsocialbiz.tumblr.com/), curates the innovative use of social networking in business, and a third, Smarter Cities (smartercities.tumblr.com/), has this approach: "What will make our cities smarter? You! Contribute an idea, link or picture: tell a story or share an insight in words, video or [audio] ... Let's build a planet of smarter cities. Together."

American Express's Amex Open Forum

Open Forum (amexopenforum.tumblr.com/) is described by Amex as "an online community for business owners, connecting them with insights, advice, and tools to help them manage and grow their companies". It combines material produced by the brand, plus "our editors' picks from around the web".

Intel's IQ

Bradley Silver, in a post at curation platform developer Atomic Reach's blog, looks at Intel's digital magazine *IQ* (iq.intel.com/):

The company is using a combination of original content written by staff, news from the web, and curated content selected by Intel employees ... [It] is using the platform to connect the Intel brand to 'younger demographics'. What we find most interesting about the strategy is [that] the editorial focus of the site is not Intel or its products, but rather, technology-related stories that are interesting, informative, educational and engaging to the audience Intel is hoping to reach.[10]

Data journalism

Data journalism is a major new area of story finding, exploring and telling. It involves taking large sets of figures and finding stories within them, and – often – creating visualizations out of them. Visualizations can be maps, graphs or tables that help to express the story that was hidden within the data.

Data journalism is also about presenting data or visualizations that others can delve into and then make their own connections, spot their own stories and reach their own clearer understanding of the issues the data covers. If you'd like a primer on data journalism, you'll find resources on the *Brand Journalism* website.

Data journalism has developed as a discipline because of a combination of the huge amount of easily obtainable, digitally formatted data now available and the development of powerful tools for scouring data to reveal stories within it. Brian Reid, on the WCG World blog, related that to brand journalism, saying: "We must ... become increasingly aware of the data our companies and our clients push out into the world, even seemingly worthless information, and ask ourselves if that data can be examined – or mashed up with other data sets – to tell a story."[11]

Fiona Cullinan uses data as part of her work for brands such as Grant Thornton, an audit, tax and advisory service for business.[12] Cullinan makes raw data sets from the company's survey data available on visualization sites such as Many Eyes "for financial, business and data journalists to use in their own stories and infographics". For example, one data set she published showed the percentage of women in senior management roles worldwide over time.[13] That information can form the peg for a story in a wide range of media outlets.

White Papers

Commercial White Papers are in-depth analyses of issues that matter to a given audience. They are used particularly in B2B enterprises to argue the benefits of a particular technology; launch new products or highlight existing ones; offer solutions to specific problems; present research findings; recommend an approach to a business issue; or highlight a particular product or service.

Typically, White Papers are produced in PDF form, with high design and presentation values. They are usually at least ten pages long, with illustrations, charts and references. To work, they need to offer something of real value to a given community. In a Hubspot post entitled "How to Write a

White Paper that will Capture Leads" (which is just one of the goals of White Papers) is a check list for approaching White Papers that I adapt here:[14]

- Find a topic that feeds a need. You must know your target market; what do they want to know and what's already out there?
- Put your heart into it. Analyse the data and add value by evaluating options and presenting them to your readers in an easy to understand way.
- Make it substantial. It's a good idea to make each section a "bite-sized" chunk, maybe one page with charts or graphics that covers a certain point.
- Make it authoritative. Your mission isn't to be the only expert in the field – it's to be the latest expert with the freshest insights.
- Create a great landing page. Include a summary. Tell them why it's important to them.

You'll find links to primers in creating a White Paper on the *Brand Journalism* website.

How brands are using White Papers

Hubspot

Hubspot, a marketing software company, creates many White Papers for Internet marketers.[15] Typically, they offer a free basic-level paper followed by more advanced levels that require payment. Many other companies of all kinds and sizes leverage their expertise.

Bournes

A removals company, for example, has expertise in how people should pack for a house move. Bournes put together a guide to packing for moving house, and tweeted links to it.[16]

Fast Signs

A company that designs and manufacturers signs has expertise on how signage can be used in a wide range of contexts, including at a press conference. So Fast Signs created a White Paper called *How to Improve Your Press Conference with Visual Communications*.[17]

e-Books

An e-book – which is a book-length publication in electronic form – is clearly a major undertaking for a brand. For an e-book to work, it has to address a major topic that is important to the community with whom your brand is seeking to engage. The boost to thought leadership, brand aware-ness and profile in presenting a guide that solves a real problem faced by members of your community can be immense.

So one theme often followed in e-books is problem-solving. But e-books can also feature a learning programme about a major new development in an industry, or a newcomer's guide to that industry. If your brand sells a pro-duct or service that requires training to use it effectively, an e-book training manual could be highly valued.

IBM

IBM, for example, publishes e-books on using its software products.[18] e-books can also be used as a tool for causes and against big brands. There are e-books that claim to reveal the secret recipes for McDonald's and KFC's products.

Human Rights Watch

Human Rights Watch offers free e-books on topics such as cruelty and neglect in Russian orphanages[19] and academic freedom in Indonesia.[20] Many e-books are free, but not all.

Whole Foods Market

Whole Foods Market publishes a free cookery e-book.[21]

Amnesty International

Amnesty International charges for e-books on the state of world human rights and also embraces physical publishing, tying up with a traditional publishing house.[22]

You'll find links to primers in creating e-books on the *Brand Journalism* website.

Content research and distribution

I'll just touch upon these tools since learning to use them is covered in almost any journalism course. You'll find more about them on the *Brand Journalism* website.

RSS

RSS, or really simple syndication, is, according to Wikipedia: "a family of web feed formats used to publish frequently updated works – such as blog

entries, news headlines, audio, and video – in a standardized format".[23]
Brand journalists can use RSS feeds in two ways:

- to gather information
- to distribute it.

Feeds bring us breaking news, press releases and other material instantly from all the sources we need to monitor. Feeds save us from having to remember to go to dozens of individual web addresses to check what's new.

We can further distribute our own published news and information by making it available as an RSS feed or feeds. Using RSS to gather information involves identifying all the sources that are valuable to you in your work as a brand journalist. Distributing via RSS involves, first, making your content, such as blog posts, available as RSS feeds. If your website is created on Wordpress, Blogger or another common blogging platform, it will have an RSS feed built into it as standard. If you have content on your website such as breaking news, job opportunities or other defined areas, each can be made into an RSS feed.

RSS can also be used for curation. Google Reader, for example, lets you build bundles made up of numerous individual RSS feeds. Mash them together into a bundle and Google generates one new RSS feed that you can distribute. You can do the same on Yahoo Pipes.

So you might draw together all the important sources of information in a particular area and use it personally as an easy way to monitor many sources of material, but also make it available to your community by allowing them to follow that feed. Such bundles can be embedded in your website or blog.

For a primer on this topic, go to the *Brand Journalism* website.

Email newsletters

Email newsletters are a convenient additional distribution channel for your blog posts and other material that you have produced. They are another way for your community to choose to interact with you. You can, of course, create original content for a newsletter; but if you have a full programme of brand journalism, it's much more likely that you'll use the email newsletter to promote what you are doing elsewhere. An effective email bulletin is designed as a series of tasters of content, with links through to that content in full. You'll find links to primers in creating email newsletters on the *Brand Journalism* website.

Regular email bulletins are very useful, both for brands and for their communities. Brands and brand journalists like them because the reader doesn't have to remember to tap in our URL to get to our website. Instead, if they open the email bulletin, they find headlines and brief introductory paragraphs and can click from them straight into blogs, websites, White Papers or e-books – whatever content we are promoting. Once there they can move around or go back to select another story that they like the look of.

Assignment

Survey one or more brands' use of the content creation, curation and distribution platforms we have discussed in this chapter. How good is their brand journalism on each? How coherent is their brand journalism strategy?

Notes

1 David Meerman Scott writing about Eloqua: www.webinknow.com/2010/06/real-time-blog-post-gets-eloqua-ceo-tons-of-b2b-ink.html.
2 IBM on their blogging strategy: www.ibm.com/blogs/zz/en/.
3 *Mashable* on IBM's blogging strategy: mashable.com/2009/02/06/social-media-smartest-brands/.
4 *Social Media Examiner* on guest blogging as a strategy: www.socialmediaexaminer.com/8-brands-that-benefit-from-guest-blogging/.
5 Ibid.
6 Josh Sternberg writing at Digiday: www.digiday.com/publishing/brands-apply-for-content-curator-roles/.
7 Stephanie Schwab writing on *Social Media Explorer*: www.socialmediaexplorer.com/social-media-marketing/content-curation-its-whats-for-breakfast-these-days/.
8 Stephanie Schwab, "How to Curate Content for Your Brand": www.stephanieschwab.com/2011/02/15/curate-content-for-brands/.
9 Josh Sternberg writing at Digiday: www.digiday.com/publishing/brands-apply-for-content-curator-roles/.
10 Bradley Silver writing at Atomic Reach: blog.atomicreach.com/?p=895.
11 Brian Reid writing on the WCG World blog: blog.wcgworld.com/2011/01/why-data-journalism-is-the-future-of-media-and-pr.
12 Fiona Cullinan on her data use: fionacullinan.com/2012/06/in-defence-of-brand-journalism/.
13 Fiona Cullinan with an example of a data set: www-958.ibm.com/software/data/cognos/manyeyes/datasets/33db47e2c43e11e08730000255111976/versions/1.
14 Hubspot, "How to Write a White Paper that Will Capture Leads": blog.hubspot.com/blog/tabid/6307/bid/6496/How-to-Write-a-Whitepaper-That-Will-Capture-Leads.aspx.
15 Hubspot creates many White Papers for Internet marketers: www.hubspot.com/internet-marketing-whitepapers/.
16 White Paper from removals company Bournes: www.bournes-uts.co.uk/book/Guide%20to%20packing%20for%20moving%20house/#/1/.
17 White Paper from a sign manufacturer: www.fastsigns.com/Blog/qs/how_to_improve_your_press_conference_with_visual_communications.
18 IBM e-books: www.ibm.com/developerworks/wikis/display/db2oncampus/FREE+ebook+-+Getting+started+with+IBM+Data+Studio+for+DB2.
19 Human Rights Watch e-book on cruelty and neglect in Russian orphanages: www.hrw.org/legacy/reports/reports98/russia2/.
20 Human Rights Watch e-book on academic freedom in Indonesia: www.hrw.org/legacy/hrw/reports98/indonesia2/.

21 Whole Foods Market cookery e-book: www.kobobooks.com/ebook/The-Whole-Foods-Market-Cookbook/book-lviy7ayYMEKXep5Jytm-SQ/page1.html.
22 Amnesty International e-book on the state of world human rights: www.amazon.co.uk/Amnesty-International-Report-2012-ebook/dp/B008515ISA.
23 Wikipedia definition of RSS: en.wikipedia.org/wiki/RSS.

11 Specialist Online Communities and Webinars

Goals of this module

- Explore when specialist online communities and forums can work for a brand.
- Discuss the value of webinars.

On the website

On the website you will find links to primers in the areas covered, videos and further resources, as well as links to all the sources quoted here.

We've looked at some of the big social platforms; but what if your community isn't on them? What if it is on specialist forums? In this chapter we'll consider the value of specialist forums and how to interact with them.

We'll also look at webinars, which are interactive workshops, seminars or lectures transmitted over the web and which can add great value to your content on a specialist forum.

Specialist online community forums

You'll find specialist online forums being used for a range of specialist consumer, professional groups and business-to-business (B2B) communities. Sometimes those forums are an integral part of a specialist consumer website – for example, Mumsnet (www.mumsnet.com/) for mothers. Examples of professional groups' forums include TES Connect (www.tes.co.uk/) for teachers and the General Medical Council (GMC) (www.gmc-uk.org/) for doctors.

Some brands set up or "sponsor" forum-based sites for professional groups. Examples include The CMO (www.thecmosite.com) site for senior marketing staff, which is sponsored by IBM, and Open Forum (www.open-forum.com/) for small businesses sponsored by America Express. There are also many independent forums set up by specific interest groups, both on major social platforms such as Facebook and LinkedIn, and also on a wide range of other smaller ones. Brands and brand journalists may wish to interact on those, acting as brand advocates.

We'll look at the necessary protocols for using them successfully.

Specialist consumer communities and forums

These can be very lively places. On Mumsnet, for example, discussions can take place that have an impact upon the political agenda. But can brand journalists use them? Mumsnet has over 1 million unique users every month and 25,000 daily posts on its discussion boards.

The 2010 UK general election was dubbed the Mumsnet election because politicians – who queued up to do web chats on the platform – believed that whoever could win this community over would triumph. Mumsnet director Justine Roberts, interviewed in *Director* magazine, said that the idea was ludicrous: "There are over a million mums on Mumsnet, but the idea that they are going to vote in a cohesive way is just mad. This is a group of individuals with strong opinions and they are politically diverse ... there wasn't one collective Mumsnet vote."[1]

But you can understand why politicians and brands would like to tap into that community. In the same *Director* article, Rebecca Harrison, qualitative insight director for brand experts Added Value, said: "I have been surprised about the relationship women have with sites like Mumsnet, they seem to rely on them a lot." Mumsnet is a source of information, advice and product recommendations. Many campaigns begin there, although Roberts says it's not a top-down thing. Often, members set up a group on Facebook and are joined by others.

One campaign that affected brands was called Let Girls Be Girls against the sexualization of young girls. It saw major retailers agreeing not to stock clothing that prematurely sexualizes. Following it, brands including Tesco and Asda have adopted a policy of seeking guidance from Mumsnet on what is seen as appropriate and what isn't.

There is also a "social shopping" recommendations area called Mumsnet Swears By where Mumsnetters can pass on their recommendations for products and services.[2] One further benefit of a forum is that it generates content. Forums are often a mix of editorial content – sometimes aggregated from third parties – and user-generated material. So, is Mumsnet a place for brand journalism?

What is clear is that, as a brand journalist, you need to be locked in to any forum that affects the community whom you seek to serve. The experience of Tesco and Asda shows that a forum such as Mumsnet can be a hugely valuable way of understanding how your community thinks about key issues and for learning what it considers appropriate and inappropriate. Listening in on relevant discussion threads is an important part of your job.

Starting a discussion strand in order to conduct research is clearly perfectly possible; but should you do it? Transparency is key here. If you want to engage on Mumsnet, or on any other community site, do it openly. Tell the community who you are and who you work for. If they think you shouldn't be there they'll tell you.

What you certainly shouldn't do is go into Mumsnet Swears By posing as an ordinary member and promote your own brand. If you are tempted, *Marketing Week* reported: "The forums are already very sensitive to any media using the site without declaring themselves as such and are quick to report such suspicions to the moderators."[3] You can also ask to engage with Mumsnet direct. Mumsnet works with some brands, but it rejects others. Roberts told *Director*:

> We have a core policy, which is that we are here to make parents' lives easier so there are some brands and products that don't fit very well with that. But it is an open dialogue with Mumsnetters and we'd always go with the consensus on the site. McDonald's is on our 'no' list but they came to us not long ago and asked to do a web chat. We put this to our members and there was a 50/50 split, but the ones who didn't want to do it felt very strongly about it so we decided not to.

Mumsnet partners with some brands. Roberts told *Director*: "We do a lot of insight, product testing and R&D so we could be included right from the genesis of a product to the testing of it. Ford last year gave 12 of our members a Ford Galaxy which they then filmed themselves using. These films were brilliantly authentic and very realistic." They want to work with organizations that share Mumsnet's concerns and goals, so if your brand is a good fit, the platform could be an effective place for your brand journalism.

Building a close relationship with forums that complement your brand is clearly an important part of your brand journalism.

Specialist professional communities and forums

If your brand is relevant to a particular profession, then you need to be intimately aware of what members of that profession are saying – about you and, more generally, on any relevant forum. Additionally, professional forums are an important place for your in-house experts to be engaging. You may well be one of those experts. Those running such forums will want your brand's specialists taking part because it increases the value of the discussion to their community.

Again, transparency is vital, but the community will recognize that your acknowledged experts have important contributions to make to key debates, and as a brand journalist you should be encouraging them to do so. If you can achieve a positive engagement with those running the relevant forums, you may be able to suggest discussion threads and offer your experts and contributors to them. If your journalistic instinct is right, you'll be contributing positively to the spread of news-awareness, knowledge, information and expertise within your community.

Ethical questions concerning the use of community forums

There have been attempts to change opinions by getting a significant number of relevant individuals to post on specialist forums in favour of a particular brand. Furlong PR wrote about information technology (IT) products and services company Microsoft's attempt to influence discussions about it:

> New York based advertising agency JWT were tasked with engaging with IT 'decision makers' in the world of business technology – a close knit world which can be difficult to penetrate through traditional advertising strategies. The agency aimed to join in online conversations relevant to Microsoft products and contribute in real time, with content targeted at "fence sitters" across the web.
>
> The agency's news team listens to and monitors all online conversations on a daily basis, relevant to Microsoft Enterprise Software, identifying potential conversations to join. A team of 40+ specialist IT bloggers are then activated to join the identified conversations, and briefed with speaking on Microsoft's behalf. Additionally Twitter feeds such as ExecTweets IT, audio interviews, round tables and live chats with industry analysts were hosted, with the aim of publishing in places where the key decision-making conversations were happening.[4]

Furlong says it worked, that these contributions saw it "accepted as a valued resource in the 'tight knit' IT community within 7 months"; that they "established one of the most popular Microsoft blogs with over 1.4 million total page views"; that "top bloggers averaged over 19,000 page views per post"; and that the "IT audience engaged with Microsoft experts via live chats, roundtable discussions, white papers and audiocasts, generating 8.8 million user engagements so far."

Should you get involved in such practices? The only way you can do so ethically is to be entirely transparent about your allegiances. If you, or anyone working for you, is tasked with speaking in favour of a brand, they must make clear their status as a brand representative. For the ethical brand journalist, transparency is key. After all, as we saw in the Mumsnet example, communities are pretty quick to pick up on being marketed to, and they don't like it.

You'll find a video explaining the JWT approach to brand journalism on the *Brand Journalism* website. Ethical questions regarding this issue were covered in more detail in Chapter 6.

Establishing your own community forums

Brands sometimes aim to create or sponsor a professional forum that is so successful it more or less monopolizes discussion in an area where they have a keen commercial interest. They may, if they get carried away, talk about them "owning" the discussion.

This is a very bad attitude to adopt. As we all ought to know, no one can own anything on the web. The best we can do, in terms of forums, is to create or sponsor one that is a welcoming home to the community with whom we wish to engage. We can do that with good brand journalism. The Business to Community blog posted a list of the benefits of creating a forum:

> By combining editorial content, user-generated content and networking, online communities provide many benefits to brands:
>
> - They provide a venue to highlight thought leaders, which can help you extend your brand.
> - They provide a way to cut customer support costs if members are sharing ideas.
> - They enable you to collect audience insights and perform market research.
> - They give you an opportunity to make money with ad revenue or by providing special access to members.[5]

But many forums fail – you send out invitations to the party, but no one turns up. So how do you know whether an in-house forum will work for your brand? Let's take TES Connect as an example of how a brand got it right. iPublishing Consultants wrote about how and why TES, which was a traditional print brand, set up their forum and in the process became the world's largest social network for a single profession.[6] Gail Robinson, community producer at TSL Education, said: "I think it happened almost by accident. The BBC had quite a lot of education forums and had closed them down for some reason. The TES took up the slack and so inherited a community that we built from there."

So, one indicator of possible success is that an existing discussion place is lost to a community. Or, perhaps, no appropriate discussion forum exists for them. Question one, therefore, asks: is there a need? If you face a dominant rival such as TES Connect, you are better off building a relationship with them rather than striking out on your own.

Robinson is asked about TES Connect's attitude to other organizations that are interested in facilitating teacher engagement (unions, professional institutions) and says:

> Some of the unions do have their own forums and we have been speaking to them a little bit, they say that they find it very difficult to

generate enough activity on a forum and look on ours with admiration that we can do that. We've worked a little bit with the unions to bring them onto our forum areas.

Another key question is knowing whether you have a community who likes to talk. If individuals have plenty of opportunity to communicate with others in their profession through means other than a specialist forum, they may not be interested in yours. Robinson explained that teachers like to talk and can be isolated:

> If you're the only history teacher, for example, in a smallish second-ary school, you've got nobody else to talk to about your subject, so you can go on the forum and get together with other history teach-ers. Teaching a particular subject can be quite a lonely job, and this is where you can get support from people who are not part of your own school, where if, say, you admitted to any kind of weakness or uncertainty you might find it coming back at you. So we've got a great audience.

A further important tip is to let the community develop the discussions it wants to hear. Robinson said: "if you try to control the engagement between people too much, they resent it. The forums work because there's a real sense of ownership from the people on there, that they feel that this is their place to be."

That can mean there are clashes between your brand's policies and the views being expressed in the forums:

> What happens on the forums can conflict with the way that the paper [or brand] presents itself, and its views on certain issues, so you have to make it very clear that these two things are different and what is expressed on the forums are the views of the people participating.

For TES, the forums opened them up to a new market – in their case, "a younger market to the audience that the print product typically gets".

You'll find links to primers on setting up and running a forum on the *Brand Journalism* website.

Brand-sponsored forums

Just as an adjunct to the section above, here are a couple of forums spon-sored by brands but run semi-independently of them. These are customer hubs – places which facilitate members of a particular community gathering to learn, discuss and share information, and hence make great places for a brand to listen in to the community it aims to serve.

Open Forum, sponsored by American Express

We looked at Open Forum (www.openforum.com/) briefly in Chapter 10 as an example of brands curating content. Open Forum is a good example of a site that is both rich in created and curated content, and which also functions as a powerful forum for a community. American Express describes it as "an online community to exchange insights, get advice from experts, and build connections to help you power your small business success ... Open Forum accounts are linked to Open Card accounts on AmericanExpress. com through usernames and passwords."

So AmEx uses the forum as a brand journalism approach to a key group of customers: small business owners. It seeks to help them develop their enterprises by forging business connections and providing practical information from important third-party providers, including *Mashable* (www. mashable.com). The community can network on the forums, too.

The CMO Site, sponsored by IBM

The CMO Site (www.thecmosite.com) describes itself as "an executive social network that provides CMOs [chief marketing officers] and other marketing executives from the world's leading organizations with a real-time, online venue where they can convene to discuss how they're delivering on the most critical marketing priorities of the day."

Their offer is a clearly targeted one. They say:

> How can CMOs best navigate a course through this new, technologically driven marketing landscape? The answer is to turn to the wisdom of the marketing crowd and forge their strategies on the anvil of their peers' experiences. The CMO Site is designed to facilitate that exchange of information by providing a congenial forum for marketing education, discussion, and debate.

It's obviously a brand journalism exercise, run by editors with backgrounds in journalism, as well as in business and marketing. There is very little evidence of IBM's sponsorship, except for transparency disclosures when the forum's journalists write about IBM.

Webinars and webcasts

Webinars are interactive workshops, seminars or lectures transmitted over the web. It's the interactive element that differentiates a webinar from a webcast, in which communication is one way. Webinars are mostly used for B2B and specialist consumer audiences, and typically involve an expert, or panel of experts, plus a facilitator discussing a key topic.

Their advantage is that they are a seminar or other learning event which you can make open to all. Webinars should share experience or expertise, not simply demonstrate the benefits of a particular product or service (unless that is what you know the audience wants). They can be used as open question and answer sessions, where you offer up an expert for an hour. They can also be used for group coaching.

High-quality, focused training is expensive and time consuming if you have to travel to another city to get it, so webinars have great value. Some brands charge for them, others get as much data as they can from attendees. Others use them simply to build relationship with their community. Many companies working in fast-moving areas such as social media use webinars. Hubspot offers free webinars on subjects such as building your LinkedIn group and the science of lead generation.[7] The UK's Customs and Revenue service offers webinars explaining complex tax areas to businesses and the self-employed.[8] Webinar Vet uses the format to educate veterinary students.[9]

Assignments

1   Pick an industry and research the forums available to its members. Are there many forums or few? Is there one dominant player? Do the most successful forums tend to be run or sponsored by brands, or created by community members? How well is this community/industry served by existing forums? What improvements could be made? Is there room for a new forum? If you had to build relationships with this community, how would you go about that while using forums? Would you seek to form relationships with existing forums, create your own, join debates and influence them?

2   Consider further the ethical implications of taking part in community forums. Conduct a survey designed to identify how much covert use there is of forums by brand representatives. Draw up a code of practice for the use of forums.

Notes

1 Justine Roberts of Mumsnet, interviewed in *Director* magazine: www.director.co.uk/magazine/2011/4_April/justine-roberts-mumsnet_64_08.html.
2 *Marketing Week* on Mumsnetter social shopping: www.marketingweek.co.uk/opinion/blogs/ruth-mortimer/will-mumsnet-get-consumers-social-shopping/4002363.article.
3 Ibid.
4 Furlong PR on Microsoft's efforts to influence discussion about it: www.furlongpr.com/social-media-case-study-microsoft/.
5 The Business to Community blog on the benefits of creating a forum: www.business2community.com/online-communities/why-content-marketers-need-to-take-notice-of-online-communities-0202830.

6 iPublishing Consultants on why TES set up its forums: www.i-publishing consultants.com/tes-connect.

7 Hubspot webinars: www.hubspot.com/marketing-webinars/.

8 UK Customs and Revenue webinars: www.hmrc.gov.uk/webinars/index.htm.

9 Webinar Vet: thewebinarvet.com/.

12 Your Branded Websites as Information Hubs for Customers and Potential Customers

Goals of this module

- Demonstrate the importance of making your branded website a valuable information hub for your community.
- Outline the central position that branded websites have in your overall brand journalism strategy and content creation.

On the website

You'll find essential updates, further resources, links to primers in the areas covered, videos and links to all the sources quoted here.

Taking a brand journalism approach to your websites involves making them much more than a mere holding page on the World Wide Web – which is all that a lot of corporate websites amount to. Branded websites should be designed as information hubs for customers and potential customers. We've spoken before about how so much research and information gathering is done online. A brand's website ought to work as an important part of the research a visitor does before reaching a significant decision: from selecting goods or services to deciding which political party to back, from choosing to support a particular cause to donating to a certain charity.

In producing brand journalism – and also in designing a site and establishing its structure – the key questions are: who will come and what will *they* want to learn or do? Who do we want to come? What would *we* like them to learn? What would we like to interest them in? You'll get several categories of visitors and they'll be seeking a range of information or want to do a variety of things.

Some key goals of visitors can be satisfied very easily. If you are a charity and are running an appeal, many will come to make a donation – so a great big Donate button on the homepage sorts them out. If there is a big piece of company news just breaking, make that easy to find. Other visitor goals are not so easy to satisfy. To work out what they are, and how best to satisfy them, brand journalists need to think like their customers, and to put the customer and their needs and wants at the heart of what they do on the website.

Remember why we got involved in social media. It was to reach audiences who wouldn't otherwise have found our main branded websites. We interact with them on those social platforms and can often give them the information they need right there and then; but we'd like to deepen the relationship wherever and whenever we can. We'd like to persuade those who have more than a passing interest in us to engage with us on a more significant level.

We want to draw them in from social media sites such as Twitter, Facebook, YouTube, Pinterest, Google+ or wherever to our rich brand journalism content. So we try to get them to click on links that take them to it. And where does that rich content sit? On our branded websites and blogs.

In this chapter we'll examine two branded websites in some detail: one from a major corporation, Boeing, the other from a big charity, Oxfam. We'll look at the brand journalism they contain and at how they work in conjunction with a brand's social media and other presences. We'll also consider some other examples of branded websites that fulfil the goals of brand journalism.

We are concentrating on content in this chapter. What we won't look at is how those branded websites are structured and designed, and how the architecture and navigation functions. If you'd like tuition in these areas you'll find a primer on the *Brand Journalism* website.

Boeing

Plane-maker Boeing (www.boeing.com/) places brand journalism right at the heart of its site, with a picture carousel at the top of the homepage scrolling through half a dozen feature stories that are told through text, stills and video. Todd Blecher, communications director at Boeing, writing about the company's approach to brand journalism, actually provides a useful starting point to any brand journalism strategy.[1]

Blecher believes that an organization has to build its brand journalism capabilities in a manageable way. It's not something that can be done immediately. Blecher's approach fits how we approached things in Part I – in particular, to two principles we established: that you must have a solid brand journalism delivery structure within an organization; and that your brand journalism strategy must stem from business goals. If it doesn't, he says, brand journalism content "will communicate in a vacuum, with little benefit to the organization and of little interest to audiences".

Stories that have worked for Boeing and a couple that haven't

Blecher says that when brand journalists think of what's interesting to their audiences and create engaging content, they generate stories that prove really popular. He gives this example, headlined "Boeing 747–48 Performs

Ultimate Rejected Take-Off". You'll find the video element of the story on the *Brand Journalism* website.[2] Blecher says:

> This story is about testing the brakes on our new 747. The test involves speeding an airplane down a runway then hitting the brakes just before take-off. It ends with the brakes on fire, which is eye catching, to say the least. That story had it all for our audiences: iconic airplane, an interesting test activity, and great visuals. We've had more than 1.1 million views, and our key messages about safety and durability reached more people through our website, YouTube channel, and Facebook page, than we would've reached with a traditional news release.

A second example of a successful story is "Phantom Eye High Altitude Long Endurance Aircraft Unveiled".[3] Blecher says: "It has more than 400,000 views, a lot for a military story as those usually appeal to a niche audience. This one broke out by presenting a new and unique vehicle in a way that sparked imaginations and discussions." Again, you'll find the video element of that story on the *Brand Journalism* website.

Stories that didn't work

Blecher is honest enough to give two examples of stories that didn't work. One is about a retiring security dog.[4] The other is about designs for World War II era uniforms:[5] "Our audiences didn't know what to make of either of them."

What Boeing is getting right

Marketing strategist David Meerman Scott put the secret of Boeing's brand journalism success down to something that every journalism student learns in their first week: don't write about things, write about people.[6] Meerman Scott says:

> The Boeing Company recently launched a completely new approach to the web. The dramatic shift in direction brings what was a dull technology and product-focused site to one focused on brand journalism, with interesting stories about people. The new Boeing site does an excellent job at putting a human face on the company.

He quotes Todd Blecher as saying: "'Now on our site we show there are real people who work in the company.'" Meerman Scott goes on: "An interesting aspect of the brand journalism approach now used at Boeing is that each of the stories carries a byline of the person who wrote it. 'The bylines are another way that we humanize the stories,' Todd says." Meerman Scott singles out a story called "Freezin' in Florida". He says:

I particularly liked "Freezin' in Florida", about testing the 787 Dreamliner in the largest refrigerated hangar in the world. The hangar simulates temperatures as low as minus 65 degrees Fahrenheit or as high as 165 degrees Fahrenheit. There is a fascinating two-minute video of the very, very cold airplane featuring the people who are testing it.

"Rather than have a standard news release that describes testing, we take you inside the hanger to actually show what people have to do to freeze the airplane," Todd says. "No airplane comes together without the people who work on it. Now we're talking about our technology from the perspective of the people."[7]

You'll find the "Freezin' in Florida" video on the *Brand Journalism* website.

Boeing also creates sites around major events, such as the UK's Farnborough Air Show. Such sites act as multimedia news platforms. As with the main site, the emphasis is on videos that tell a story rather than sell a product.

Oxfam

Oxfam (www.oxfam.org.uk/ and www.oxfam.org/) is a charity, but one that employs a head of news, as well as head of public relations (PR), and a news and multimedia manager. So it's also a news organization – and a very strong brand, as we'll see in the next chapter.

While the site's homepage is focused on key areas (make a donation; how you can help; what we are doing right now; and where your money goes), it is underpinned with highly innovative journalism allied to campaigns. The goal of the brand journalism is to encourage donations. The technique used is the same one used by Boeing: they tell stories about people, but not in the way you might expect from a charity dealing with death, disaster, malnutrition and starvation.

Take the Oxfam See for Yourself campaign.[8] This involved taking an ordinary Oxfam supporter out to one of the areas in which the charity works, together with a film crew, so she could see for herself the difference a small donation can make. Here's the text that accompanies the video on the Oxfam website:

Watch Jodie's film: see why regular donations are so vital. Until you see it for yourself, it can be hard to understand how giving £3 a month to Oxfam can transform people's lives. So we've done something completely new. We're taking people like you out to see our work first-hand and meet the people they're helping (costs are covered by an anonymous donor). We believe it's the best way to show you what regular donations can really do. In February 2012, Oxfam supporter Jodie Sandford travelled with us to Zimbabwe. The trip was hard work and emotional. She visited Oxfam projects, met the people we're working with, and asked the questions you'd ask. Now Jodie's home, she's keen to show you what she saw. So watch Jodie's film – and find out why regular giving is so vital.

The films were shot by Duckrabbit, (www.duckrabbit.info), a digital production company that works with documentary audio, stills photography and video. Duckrabbit also made TV commercials from the film, an example of how brand journalism and traditional advertising and marketing can be made to mesh.

Duckrabbit says:

> The work produced from this trip represents a unique approach to fundraising advertising. None of the adverts or online materials have been scripted – they are produced from the authentic reactions of an Oxfam supporter to what she saw and heard in the field. We were inspired by the hard work and commitment we saw from the Oxfam team we worked with in Oxford and particularly their people in Zimbabwe who showed us exactly why Oxfam is an organisation worth supporting.

Oxfam's videos are linked to, and one is featured, on the *Brand Journalism* website.[9]

Other examples of brand journalism at work on branded websites

Monster

Monster (www.monster.com and www.monster.co.uk) is a recruitment company, and it uses brand journalism to make its customers – both those seeking work and those looking for employees – as informed and effective in their searches as possible. It has a huge amount of information on recruitment and hiring, and plenty of careers advice on education and training, job hunting, interviewing, salaries and career development. The section on writing a CV/résumé alone has dozens of screens of information. There are also advice forums. Anyone seeking work, or looking for new hires, will find this hugely rich information hub a great place to improve their chances.

All the information is straightforward and unbiased – why would it be anything else? You could use it to access Monster's services or apply it to a job/employee hunt elsewhere. So, it works for the customer and it works for Monster because every article will pop up on search results for those looking for specific information, and will pull them in to the branded Monster site as potential customers.

Some brands create websites that are not under their main corporate URL and don't carry their usual branding. Such sites are specifically designed as content hubs for key elements within their overall client base – key communities with whom they want to engage with. HSBC is an example.

HSBC and Business without Borders

David Meerman Scott writes about Business without Borders (www.businesswithoutborders.com/) as being: "a terrific example of brand journalism at work. It is a site specifically designed for an important HSBC buyer persona – people responsible for expanding U.S. businesses into international markets."[10]

The site is designed to provide information that will help such people succeed in their businesses. It is designed to look very much like a financial news site, has its own editorial staff, as well as using material from the Economist Intelligence Unit, the *Wall Street Journal* and Bloomberg Master Class. Much material is free, but there is a members' area with additional resources. Meerman Scott says: "HSBC is educating and informing their market."

Here's another spin-off brand website dedicated to brand journalism.

Cisco's The Network

Technology company Cisco has its main brand website (www.cisco.com/), but it has also created something called The Network: Cisco's technology news site (newsroom.cisco.com/). John Earhardt, director of social media communications at Cisco, leads the social media team within corporate communications. He's responsible for Cisco's use of Facebook, Twitter, Ustream, LinkedIn, its corporate blog and the corporate newsroom.

John outlined the motivation in creating The Network:

> The Network is our effort to tell stories and share information on the topics that are the most important to Cisco, namely: Video, Collaboration, Core Networks, Data Center, Cisco Culture ... and, more parochially to my team, Social Media ... We will create, share and curate content on these topics as a part of our overall Cisco voice. We have engaged world-class reporters who have worked at *Fortune*, *Forbes*, *Wall Street Journal*, AP [Associated Press] and more to create content on the technology news topics that we want our audience to care about and, ultimately, share with their social footprint. The purpose of these stories isn't to showcase Cisco or our technology, but to create compelling content in the topical areas that we care about. This is content that you might read on any other technology or business news site. We are supporting the generation of this content in the hopes that our audience shares it and becomes more educated on the topics that are important to Cisco and to our customers. Some are calling this "branded journalism", but I just call it content creation around the topics that we care about.[11]

He also addresses the question of content that promotes Cisco in this supposedly open environment and says that the mechanisms they have introduced mean there is a level playing field:

> Sure, we're also going to use The Network to tell our own stories on innovation or highlight our smart employees and the good work they are doing. We hope our audience finds this information compelling and "share worthy" as well, but because we will embed the number of views a piece of content gets, its tweets, its Facebook likes, etc. into the actual piece and allow our readers to sort content by most viewed and most shared by week, month and year, they can easily see what others are reading and sharing.

Assignment

Identify two brands in the same sector: one that demonstrates a strong use of brand journalism on their website, one that does not. Critique the former brand's site and develop a brand journalism content strategy for the latter.

Notes

1 Todd Blecher writing about the company's approach to brand journalism: www. briansolis.com/2011/11/the-force-behind-successful-brand-journalism/.
2 Boeing story example – "Boeing 747–48 Performs Ultimate Rejected Take-Off": www.boeing.com/Features/2011/05/bca_747–48_RTO_05_04_11.html.
3 Boeing story example – "Phantom Eye High Altitude Long Endurance Aircraft Unveiled": www.boeing.com/Features/2010/07/bds_feat_phantom_eye_07_12_10. html.
4 Boeing story example about a retiring security dog: www.boeing.com/Features/ 2010/05/feat_rocky_retires_05_10_10.html.
5 Unsuccessful Boeing story example about designs for World War II era uniforms: www.boeing.com/Features/2010/09/corp_rosie_09_20_10.html.
6 David Meerman Scott on Boeing's brand journalism: www.webinknow.com/2010/ 05/the-plane-truth-brand-journalism-and-the-new-boeing-site.html.
7 David Meerman Scott on Boeing's story "Freezin' in Florida": www.boeing.com/ Features/2010/04/bca_cold_soak_04_22_10.html.
8 Oxfam's See for Yourself campaign: www.oxfam.org.uk/what-we-do/seeforyour self?intcmp=hp_37_hych4_sfy_2012-06-25.
9 Oxfam videos by Duckrabbit: duckrabbit.info/2012/05/oxfam-see-for-yourself/.
10 David Meerman Scott on Business without Borders: www.webinknow.com/2011/ 09/hsbc-new-business-without-borders-site-is-brand-journalism-done-right.html.
11 John Earhardt on the motivation in creating The Network: www.briansolis.com/ 2011/06/ciscos-forary-into-brand-journalism/.

13 How Traditional Media, Including Customer Magazines, Fit into a Brand Journalism Strategy

Goals of this module

- Outline the importance of traditional media as part of many brand journalism strategies.
- Demonstrate the value of customer magazines.
- Explore the concept of creating unconventional relationships with traditional publishers.

On the website

You'll find essential updates, further resources, plus links to all the sources quoted here.

Brand journalism isn't just about social media, nor is it only about creating content online. A brand will also often want to maintain a presence on traditional media. That can include creating customer magazines; developing innovative, mutually beneficial relationships with traditional media companies; and the old practice of buying space for advertorials or sponsored features. It can also include creating advertising with an editorial style and content – in essence, putting brand journalism in bought space. It frequently also means integrating brand journalism with an advertising campaign so that the two dovetail together.

Not all of that content will be created in most cases by brand journalists. But brand journalists will need to be intimately involved in the development of a brand's overall media strategy so that they can fulfil their role in it. We looked, in Chapter 7, at Red Bull as an example of how all the elements we are surveying individually in the rest of Part II fit together to make up a coherent brand journalism strategy. Here, we'll consider in detail how traditional journalistic platforms fit into that whole.

Customer magazines

Customer magazines – often produced by third-party specialist publishers, but also created in-house by some brands – are a very well-established part of a brand journalism strategy, in many cases predating a brand's work on other platforms. This is a hugely successful area.

Readership for the most successful customer magazines outstrip even those for major traditional media titles. Tesco magazine overtook *The Sun*, the UK's most popular daily newspaper, in terms of readership, with 7.2 million to *The Sun*'s 7.1 million in 2012,[1] although this is disputed by some commentators.[2] In the UK, of the top ten consumer magazines, half are produced by or on behalf of brands. *Marketing Week* reported that:

> Branded customer magazines are continuing to challenge consumer titles with new launches and improved circulation figures ... as brands seek to bolster marketing messages with branded editorial content. ...
>
> Half of the Top 10 titles and 25 of the Top 100 by average circulation are magazines produced by brands as part of their marketing communications and more than 60% of customer titles in the Top 100 are new entries or increased their circulation, according to the Association of Publishing Agencies (APA).
>
> The supermarkets dominate the cooking and kitchen category, while *Saga Magazine*, published by the organisation that targets over 50s, is the fifth most actively purchased title with an average circulation of 616,097 for the first six months of this year.[3]

Because of the success and established nature of branded customer magazines, they often form a key part of a brand journalism strategy.

Why have a customer magazine?

Why do brands want magazines? Because they offer relationships with consumers and control over the environment that third-party consumer media doesn't. The Content Marketers' Association blog listed seven reasons why they work.[4] In summary, these are as follows.

Tangibility

Many customers like reading material that they can hold in their hand, pick up and put down at will, and return to often. They value the quality of the product.

Ability to engage

Customer magazines offer a platform through which brands can truly engage with consumers. Because the magazines are valued and represent a non-invasive "soft sell", they help to build a long-term affinity between consumer and brand and boost trust and customer loyalty. One challenge for journalists on such magazines is to create content that readers will value and return to frequently. Food retailers find that recipes achieve this.

The Association of Publishing Agencies' (APA) *Advantage* study investigated how long the average consumer reads a magazine.[5] Readers spend an average of 25 minutes with a customer title, the equivalent of 50 30-second TV ads. Magazines have proven to be hugely effective in building a rapport with customers and encouraging them to integrate the brand within their lifestyle. While the customer recognizes that the offering is a brand communication, they don't necessarily feel they are being sold to. Rather, they see the magazine as the result of the brand putting time and effort into creating something that will entertain and benefit them.

Some magazines are sufficiently highly valued for brands to be able to charge for them.

Targeted nature

Magazine content can be designed to appeal to a specific customer base, making customer publications highly targeted according to interests, lifestyle and stage of life.

Measurability

To quote the APA directly: "As one of the most targeted forms of communication, the medium offers the chance to see exactly who the magazine has gone to and therefore which consumers have engaged and responded positively to the content that they have been targeted with."

Provision of information

In terms of delivering on a range of marketing objectives, encouraging loyalty comes top, with providing information to customers a close second, according to Mintel research commissioned by the Advertising Standards Authority (ASA).

Also, says the ASA: "Royal Mail research found that recipients of both physical print combined with online brand communications can spend up to 25 per cent more with a brand due to its ability to open up dialogue with potential and current customers."[6]

Entertainment value

Customer magazines are often produced to the same high quality as newsstand titles and, hence, deliver product and other brand information alongside first-rate features, interviews, fashion, travel, or whatever content is relevant to both brand and customer lifestyle.

Communication of complex brand messages

The APA says that customer publications allow brands to communicate a range of underlying, often complex messages.

We can add to that list an eighth virtue: cheapness.

Cheapness

In an article in the *New York Times* looking at the growth in customer publishing from fashion brands comes this quote from Alice Litscher, a professor in fashion communication at the Institut Français de la Mode in Paris: "Why spend €40,000 a page to advertise in *Vogue* when, for the same amount of money, you can publish an entire magazine?"[7]

The growth of customer magazines is also part of a recognition that conventional advertising is less effective. The same article states:

> "The consumer is much more likely to engage with independent editorial content than with conventional, purely product-focused advertising," said Max Vallot, marketing director of BLK DNM, which introduced the jeans brand and a magazine at the same time last May. "It's much harder to differentiate a brand through product than through advertising today, which is why we're investing in new ways of 'advertising'."

While many customer magazines work by presenting a brand's products within a lifestyle, and by building content around that lifestyle rather than just the product, others are more ambitious. The fashion chain Benetton's *Colors* magazine (www.colorsmagazine.com/), for example, embodies the values of the brand, but has no connection with the products that the company sells. It was conceived in 1991 as a standalone product, and while it has undergone some radical changes in strategy and content, it still holds to this core function. Benetton's advertising director, Paolo Landi, says:

> We set up *Colors* as a way of communicating the intelligence of the Benetton brand to an extremely sophisticated consumer. That consumer doesn't respond so well to traditional advertising. *Colors* is a real magazine about the rest of the world, but it's also a way of marketing the ideological commitment of the Benetton company. While the magazine still costs us money, we are taking more and more advertising in it, often from our rivals, so we are roughly reaching break-even – although it's still not profitable.[8]

Colors is published in eight bilingual editions and is sold in 120 countries. It is edited by two South African photographers – Adam Broomberg and Oliver Chanarin. It has this editorial policy, according to Charnin, quoted in the same article:

"If you look at issue 50 it's almost like journalism from the 50s when *Life* magazine was really kicking. It was about going into a place and staying there for a long time, investing time and money and no one's really doing that anymore."

The magazine now covers what the editors call closed communities – mental hospitals, old people's homes, refugee camps or, in issue 50, prisons. Staff spend three weeks in every community they cover, like a refugee camp in Tanzania. "We went to the camp in 2001 and there hadn't been a journalist there since 1997," says Broomberg. "We took Stefan Ruiz, who does high-end fashion ads for Caterpillar and Camper. The idea was to take a fashion photographer into a zone where reportage photographers usually go."

Benetton has also made the magazine a key part of a wider, ambitious marketing project.

Marketing magazine reported that Benetton has made *Colors* a part of a multimedia, participatory marketing exercise, bringing together the themes of an exhibition about it at the London Design Museum and content from the magazines, and projecting videos and animations on those themes onto the videowalls of its flagship European stores:[9]

The retailer aims to create a "new customer experience where the individual's approach becomes a participatory experience". Visitors will also be offered copies of the *Colors* magazine alongside other in-store initiatives inspired by different cultures, young people's creativity and the future of new media.

Creating unconventional relationships with traditional publishers

A brand's approach to the use of old media can also involve developing a relationship with a traditional publisher. We looked at Oxfam's innovative approach to brand journalism in Chapter 12. The charity is also a model for the way in which it integrates that brand journalism with a presence on traditional media.

Here's how Oxfam used brand journalism to raise awareness and public concern over the issue of climate change in the run-up to a major climate change conference. The problem was a traditional journalistic one: how to tell the story of climate change through specifics – people and a place. First they selected Gabura, an island off the coast of Bangladesh, which had been ravaged by a cyclone. Rising sea levels caused by global warming were to blame.

How they told the story of the people in that place was innovative: Oxfam twinned with *The Guardian* to produce an interactive online documentary, published on their website and on *The Guardian*'s.[10] The viewer selects how they want to explore the subject, choosing between a range of different individual stories. The screen is split, with the left-hand area linking to stories about before the disaster, the right-hand side linking to stories of the aftermath. Readers can select which of these stories they want to explore.

Barbara Stocking, president of Oxfam, explained the approach in a *Guardian* article:[11]

> It is the people in poorer communities whose voices are all too often drowned out in the drumbeat of reports, debates and summits. To avoid this, Oxfam has produced a short interactive online documentary that captures the moments leading up to the storm. Through extraordinary footage, the documentary chronicles the life of rural Bangladeshi farmers and the plight of the storm on their livelihoods – their farms flooded, their harvest ruined, their homes drenched and destroyed. It's an effort to indirectly democratize the discussion on climate change ... [The interactive documentary] allows you both to bear witness to the impact of climate change and to choose your own journey through the story.

So Oxfam, a non-governmental organization (NGO), has teamed up with a traditional journalistic organization to produce an innovative new style of interactive documentary in order to raise public awareness of an issue and to influence policy-makers.

Alongside the video on their website, Oxfam set up an email so that viewers could write to the policy-makers and urge them to watch the film. In another campaign, Oxfam twinned with *Q*, the music magazine, for a fund-raising initative called OxJam.[12] OxJam was a month-long series of many local volunteer-organized music events, promoted both by the charity and within *Q*. The partnership with *Q* involved a special online edition of the magazine "all written by and about the people who've organised, played or partied at OxJam events across the UK".

Oxfam said:

> *Q* are going to be on the look-out for reports and photos from organisers, performers and punters. It's going to be a great opportunity for aspiring journalists and photographers, and also for acts and promoters who want to get their name out there ... you now have the added bonus of knowing you might then see a review of your event in *Q* magazine.

Assignments

Specifically on this chapter

Research two brands within the same sector, one with a customer magazine, one without. Find out how successful the magazine is. Make a journalistic analysis of its strengths and weaknesses. Then consider the brand without a magazine. Research their customer base and develop an editorial strategy for such a magazine.

Relating to the whole of Part II

1   Take a brand that does brand journalism across a wide range of platforms and analyse its effectiveness.
2   Take a brand that has a weak or non-existent brand journalism offering and create a coherent strategy for it, using all appropriate platforms.

Notes

1   The *Financial Times* on *The Sun*/Tesco magazine readership: www.ft.com/cms/s/0/fa5455e2–324e-11e2-b891–00144feabdc0.html#axzz2DViyGTZ5.
2   PaidContent on Tesco magazine and *The Sun* readership, *Marketing Week*: paidcontent.org/2012/11/19/does-a-supermarket-magazine-really-have-more-readers-than-the-sun/.
3   *Marketing Week* on brand magazines challenging consumer magazines: www.marketingweek.co.uk/new-brand-magazines-challenge-consumer-titles/3029401.article.
4   The Content Marketers' Association on reasons for having a customer magazine: www.apa.co.uk/about-us/seven-reasons.
5   The Association of Publishing Agencies' (APA's) *Advantage* study: www.google.co.uk/url?sa=t&rct=j&q=&esrc=s&source=web&cd=1&ved=0CCIQFjAA&url=http%3A%2F%2Fswedishcontent.se%2Fdownload%2F406-CFEEE673A745783F9C33E517F954A5D2%2FAdvantage_exsum.pdf&ei=TF6FUJe4MKb80QXOuYGgBA&usg=AFQjCNGXmHrivw3c53_gUNLTy0VRKVoPVQ&sig2=Ez2G58YD8rwydA9QoM7tgA.
6   Ibid.
7   *New York Times* article on the growth in customer publishing from fashion brands: www.nytimes.com/2012/02/22/fashion/22iht-rbrand22.html.
8   Benetton's advertising director, Paolo Landi, quoted in *The Guardian*: www.guardian.co.uk/media/2002/may/27/mondaymediasection4.
9   *Marketing* magazine on *Colors*: www.marketingmagazine.co.uk/news/1123963/.
10 Oxfam/*The Guardian* interactive online documentary: www.guardian.co.uk/environment/interactive/2009/nov/06/oxfam-bangladesh-cyclone-aila.
11 Barbara Stocking, president of Oxfam, writing in *The Guardian*: www.guardian.co.uk/environment/interactive/2009/nov/06/oxfam-bangladesh-cyclone-aila.
12 Oxfam/Q partnership OxJam: www.oxfam.org.uk/Oxjam/LatestNews/OxjamFestival/QPartnership.

Part III

Brand Journalism Storytelling Paths

In Part I we looked at how to develop a brand journalism strategy. Part II surveyed the media and platforms on which we can create brand journalism. In Part III we will look at what I'm calling brand journalism storytelling paths. By storytelling paths I mean the methods by which a business goal can be supported with a particular brand journalism strategy, using a range of media and journalistic techniques.

Through a series of case studies, taking archetypical story types, we show how the brand journalism created has been designed to deliver a particular goal for a brand. So we examine, in each case, how the brand did these things:

- establish the audience to be targeted
- identify the business goals
- create the brand journalism strategy
- use a range of publishing platforms
- measure the outcomes of the strategy.

In the chapters that follow we will examine these story paths:

- launching a product
- promoting and covering an event
- publicizing a travel destination
- building an information resource
- fundraising
- building a geo-located information and entertainment resource
- launching a customer magazine
- creating a media toolkit
- developing a company news resource
- managing a crisis
- establishing a personal brand.

14 Launching a Product
How Ford Uses Social Media to Launch New Cars

Goal of this module

Map the process of creating a brand journalism strategy to support the business goal of successfully launching a product using Ford as an example.

On the website

See examples of the brand journalism created for Ford, videos, and find links to all sources quoted here.

Ford's Fiesta Movement

Ford has developed an approach to marketing new vehicles that involves having consumers who are in the target market for the product, and who are influential on social media, engage in a series of challenges that create citizen-generated brand journalism content about the car.

The approach was first used with the North American launch of the 2011 Fiesta and called the Fiesta Movement. It has been updated and developed for subsequent launches, including the Focus. Focus Rally: America was a reality show-style contest in which Ford Focus drivers raced across the US, completing challenges with help from their social media followers. Other launches on a similar theme have included Random Acts of Fusion for the 2013 Ford Fusion. We'll focus here on the Fiesta Movement.

The audience

Ford went for the sector known as Millennials: 18- to 32-year-old, city-dwelling, import-loving professionals. Eddie Reeves of Reeves Strategy Group said:

> One of the most important strategic successes of the campaign was its discipline in market targeting. There had to be substantial internal pressure to broaden the effort beyond the sometimes-fickle Millennials, but

because Ford held firm, it has established a crucial beachhead with a market segment whose importance will only grow over time.[1]

The business goals

Ford's business goal was to succeed in a sector of the automobile industry in which it had no great reputation. It wanted to establish itself as the maker of good small cars. That required changing perceptions of the company, which was known in the US as a manufacturer of trucks and sports utility vehicles (SUVs). They estimated that would take a year.

The American Association of Advertising Agencies said that Ford in the US lacked credibility with the young city-dwelling target audience for compact cars.[2] In launching the Fiesta, a brand that was successful in Europe, they needed a strategy that would prove they "got it": that they knew people wanted small, efficient cars that weren't an embarrassment to own. But to succeed, Ford also had to change the perception in the US of what a small car could be.

Ford's analysis was that, in the North American market, small car meant "econo-box that will rattle you from Point A to Point B", but that rising fuel prices meant small cars were becoming increasingly popular.[3] Here's Ford on the challenge it faced:

> The very people Fiesta had been designed for, young city dwellers, weren't willing to listen to Ford talk for 30 seconds, let alone for 12 months. Their current perception was that Ford was "a truck company" that "also makes Mustangs". How do we sincerely engage them for the 12 months leading up to the official launch of the vehicle?[4]

Ford's strategy was this: "We wanted Fiesta to stay true to the Ford brand tone of voice of authenticity by using real people (who, coincidentally, would likely carry more weight with our target – young city dwellers who had their doubts about Ford being relevant to their lives)." They decided to give 100 "well-connected, engaging, and, most importantly, real people" a Fiesta for a year, pay for their insurance and fuel costs, and get them to carry out a series of challenges in their cars that they would blog about and post about on social media.

Scott Monty, Ford's global head of social media, said: "We put the brand in the hands of the people who would own it, and let them tell the product story for a solid 12 months, staying true to the Ford brand strategy of authenticity while introducing Fiesta to a whole new Ford customer."[5] How they chose those influencers is illuminating.

Ford knew it needed a disciplined distribution strategy and created:

> ... the Influencer Algorithm and chose our 100 best shots at success. We came up with a specific set of criteria to determine if someone had

the online social currency required to get one of the precious 100 Fiestas. We developed a specific algorithm ... that determined a person's "social vibrancy". This algorithm accounted for each individual's current status in the online world – we wanted, and frankly needed, people who were already being followed and watched and clicked on by our target customers – we specifically vetted from the over 4,000 applicants those who could best command an audience and spread the word. The 100 most socially vibrant applicants became official Fiesta Agents.[6]

You can see one application video on the *Brand Journalism* website.
   Harvard Business Review said of the strategy:

There is an awful lot of aimless experiment in the digital space these days. A lot of people who appear not to have a clue are selling digital marketing advice. I think the Fiesta Movement gives us new clarity. It's a three-step process:

1   Engage culturally creative consumers to create content.
2   Encourage them to distribute this content on social networks and digital markets in the form of a digital currency.
3   Craft this is a way that it rebounds to the credit of the brand, turning digital currency (and narrative meaning) into a value for the brand.[7]

The brand journalism strategy, and the platforms used

Harvard Business Review interviewed Bud Caddell of Undercurrent, the digital strategy firm responsible for the campaign and quoted Caddell explaining:

The idea was: let's go find twenty-something YouTube storytellers who've learned how to earn a fan community of their own. [People] who can craft a true narrative inside video, and let's go talk to them. And let's put them inside situations that they don't get to normally experience/document. Let's add value back to their life. They're ... always hungry, they're always looking for more content to create. I think this gets things exactly right. Undercurrent grasped the underlying motive (and the real economy) at work in the digital space. People are not just telling stories for the sake of telling stories, though certainly, these stories have their own rewards. They were making narratives that would create economic value.[8]

Ford had a hand in what they did, requiring these Fiesta agents to complete missions or challenges – a series of ad agency-created activities that might or might not actually involve their Fiesta. One involved seeing who could get the highest number of people in a car. Those selected were given plenty of choice in what they did on their missions. They chose to do many things:

delivering meals on wheels; giving treats to deprived children; adventures including wrestling alligators. One even used the car to elope.

Each agent documented what they did on Facebook, Twitter, YouTube, Flickr and elsewhere. The campaign was organized into chapters, earlier ones focusing more on the people driving the cars, later ones on the cars themselves. Ford ran branded social media accounts including:

- Twitter (twitter.com/fordfiesta)
- Facebook (www.facebook.com/fordfiesta); and
- YouTube (www.youtube.com/user/FiestaMovement/feed).

It built other content marketing alongside this, including an Ask Ford Fiesta Twitter account (twitter.com/FordFiestaAsk) where it asked: "Have questions about the Fiesta? Get real answers from real people. Just use the hashtag #FordFiestaAsk." Ford also aggregated all the content at its Ford Social website (social.ford.com/).

At the end of the experience, Scott Monty blogged:

> We brought together more than 90% of the Fiesta Agents in person, their friends, and fans of the Fiesta Movement to celebrate the conclusion ... It was a remarkable event ... featuring the band Parachute, a short awards ceremony ... and the first reveal of the 2011 Ford Fiesta.[9]

They also achieved the world's largest Tweet-up, and got into the *Guinness Book of World Records*.

The result

Ford says:

> The target [audience] kept doing what they did best – they paid attention and passed it on. And then they started hand-raising ... spec'ing Fiestas online ... seeking out test drives ... and then they started pre-ordering online ... and we hadn't even shipped the first one.
>
> Our target watched and paid attention to what the agents got up to, leaving comments, replying to videos, and linking to agent content on their own sites. The agents were online celebrities worth regularly checking in on and pushing out to their friends. The target was choosing to engage with the Fiesta ... Our agents created:

- 31,000 pieces of original Fiesta content
- 17 million consumer engagements
- 58% brand awareness of Fiesta prior to launch
- over 100,000 hand-raisers

- 52,000 test drives
- over 10,000 online vehicle reservations.[10]

However, two years after the launch, *Forbes* was reporting that sales of the car had slumped.[11] Did that mean the citizen-generated brand journalism strategy had failed? The *Forbes* report points out that, in the interim, cars better suited to this target market – including the Focus from Ford – had become available. But Scott Monty told *Forbes* it wasn't just about sales: "Whether or not sales resulted from any particular effort [Ford gets the attention of] a whole set of consumers who otherwise wouldn't have paid attention and [this] gives us credibility in terms of being a brand that 'gets it'."[12]

Forbes continued:

> Monty said essentially that social media is meant only to start the job of marketing a new car, not to finish it. "The sales cycle of our vehicles is a complex process with multiple data points that inform each buyer's decision," he said. "Social media typically fits at the higher end of the funnel as it contributes to awareness and consideration. When you consider that consumers gather facts from about 18 different sources on average before they make a decision on buying a car, it's important to remember that social media is only one of those."

Assignments

1 Research your own product launch story path, covering the full process from establishing the target audience, identifying the business goals, and developing the brand journalism strategy to deliver on those goals, the platforms to use and the results achieved.
2 Consider the ethical implications of the Fiesta Movement approach. Were the "agents" to whom Ford gave the cars acting independently of the company? Was the content created objective? Draw up ethical guidance for such a campaign that ensures transparency.

Notes

1 Eddie Reeves on Ford's social media strategy: www.smmmagazine.com/magazine/issue03/smm-strategies.html.
2 The American Association of Advertising Agencies on Ford's strategy: www.jaychiatawards.com/gallery2010/gallery_bronze_fiesta.html.
3 Ford on its Fiesta Movement strategy: www.jaychiatawards.com/documents/gallery2010/FiestaMovement.pdf.
4 Ford on the challenge it faced: www.jaychiatawards.com/documents/gallery2010/FiestaMovement.pdf.
5 Scott Monty, Ford's global head of social media, on the Fiesta Movement: www.scottmonty.com/2009/12/fords-got-reason-to-fiesta.html.

6 Ford's influencer algorithm: www.jaychiatawards.com/documents/gallery2010/
   FiestaMovement.pdf.
7 *Harvard Business Review* on Ford's strategy: blogs.hbr.org/cs/2010/01/ford_recently_
   wrapped_the_firs.html.
8 *Harvard Business Review* interview with Bud Caddell of Undercurrent: blogs.hbr.
   org/cs/2010/01/ford_recently_wrapped_the_firs.html.
9 Scott Monty of Ford on the success of the Ford Fiesta Movement strategy: www.
   scottmonty.com/2009/12/fords-got-reason-to-fiesta.html.
10 Ford on what the strategy achieved: www.jaychiatawards.com/documents/
   gallery2010/FiestaMovement.pdf.
11 *Forbes* reports that sales of the car had slumped: www.forbes.com/sites/dalebuss/
   2012/05/02/fiesta-sales-slump-suggests-the-end-of-the-movement/2/.
12 Scott Monty quoted in *Forbes*: www.forbes.com/sites/dalebuss/2012/05/02/fiesta-
   sales-slump-suggests-the-end-of-the-movement/2/.

15 Promoting and Covering an Event

How Blogging and Social Media Can Be Used Before and During a Conference, Convention, Exhibition or Sports Game

Goal of this module

Demonstrate, via three contrasting case studies, how brand journalism can be created both before and during a major event to build interest throughout the build-up period, and to produce live coverage during the event.

On the website

Find further examples and links to all the resources quoted here.

FC Barcelona

With this first case study we'll concentrate on a brand journalism strategy designed to connect with an audience through live reporting and fan engagement during football games both at the ground and around the world.

The audience

Barcelona Football Club estimates that it has 349 million fans or followers internationally, including 145 million in the fast-growing Asian market and 77 million in the US.[1] Although its Nou Camp stadium has the biggest capacity in Europe at 99,354, this still means that only a small proportion of the worldwide fan base can actually buy match tickets and get to games. So the club uses new media not only to inform those other millions, stretching from South-East Asia to North America, but to attract overseas supporters to become FC Barcelona customers too.

The business goals

FC Barcelona (Barca) uses social media extensively to build its brand and to engage with fans. The club says that involvement during games is the pinnacle of that engagement, and involves a mix of live reporting and live interaction between fans and the club, and with each other. The importance of fan engagement, and enhancing the live experience on various platforms, is key to Barca's social media strategy and central to its overall business strategy.

Digital-Football.com reported that the club was converting its stadium into a mobile-friendly zone and was using social media for initiatives including live reporting on games and live broadcasts of training on YouTube:[2]

> With smartphone adoption rapidly increasing, it makes sense that clubs begin to look at the role of mobile in the game, whether that is mobile marketing, geolocation, mobile sharing and even mobile tickets. ... if you want to have a social presence that maximizes huge attendances, then you have to ensure that your environment is conducive for data sharing. There's little point spending thousands on a social media campaign if you can't even effectively market to your own fans in your own house!

Pasi Lankinen, FC Barcelona's business intelligence manager, told the BBC (as above) that the goal with live reporting via social media was: "To use the emotion of fans to create clients and consumers. We have been looking at ways of expanding, and generating revenue. We have expanded fan numbers in our country and in Europe. Now we are looking at gaining a global, profitable, fan base." This means using live content on social media as a way of generating revenue.

Lankinen said that the situation with a club such as his was different than most brands that use social media, and which were seeking to gain fans. Barca has the fans. So, compared with general brands: "we are trying to do the reverse, we are trying to use the emotion of fans to create clients and consumers – and not just viewers – around the world".

As part of that commercial drive, the club has "lowered the threshold of consumption" – or financial level at which fans make a purchase. Whereas before the club aimed to get fans to buy a replica shirt as their first purchase, now the first point of commercial contact could be for a Barca mobile app costing as little as 75 cents. "That then gives the chance to take fans to the next commercial consumption level", says Lankinen. He explains that the road to profitability is in driving their huge social media following towards Barcelona's own website and apps (or to the websites of their sponsors), and then making a sale there.

But it isn't just about sales. It's also about building relationships internationally and spreading the club's values and identity:

> FC Barcelona uses social media as a service channel. Twitter, Facebook and YouTube are the best way to connect to a lot of people around the world. We are proud of our values and our identity and this is a good

way of spreading them. So, the return of investment is not only in economic terms.

The brand journalism strategy and the platforms used

The strategy is to use social media platforms including Facebook, Twitter and YouTube to enable fans, both at games and remotely, to interact with the club, players and other fans. Main Twitter accounts are one in English (twitter.com/FCBarcelona), the other in Spanish (twitter.com/FCBarcelona_es). Barcelona's corporate website, with six language options (www.fcbarcelona.com/), has a social media hub (www.fcbarcelona.com/club/barca-2-0/social-media). Among the streams there are the hashtags #fcblive – active during games – and #fcbarcelona for general news about the club.

On Facebook, Barcelona has an app called FCB Alert which tailors content specifically for different groups or individuals based on their respective interests, demographics and geography using the data that exists within Facebook. The app includes exclusive content, news, interactive features and the ability to buy merchandise within Facebook. Econsultancy reported: "Fans can interact with games, polls and a range of other multimedia content which can also then be shared with other Facebook users."[3]

On YouTube (www.youtube.com/fcbarcelona), Barca has 291,000 subscribers and total views of 97 million. The channel, which features live streaming of training, includes a link to the club ticket sales and also to its online shop. The club is on other channels, including Google+ (plus.google.com/116151548242653888082/posts), where 2 million followers have it in their circles, and the Chinese social media platform QQ (t.qq.com/FCBarcelona), on which it has 1.5 million.

The club has seven mobile phone apps (fcbapps.fcbarcelona.com/); six – including the Barcelona Live app – are free. Some are traffic generators and loyalty builders; others are more focused on monetizing. There is also a Barca TV channel (barcatv.fcbarcelona.com/).

While some clubs seek to ban or restrict the use of social media by players and staff, Barcelona encourages it. But it is conscious of the potential dangers and has an education strategy in place to ensure that they think about what they post and avoid bad practices: "We don't like to restrict the use of social media. We just try to give all the information, tools and support to all FC Barcelona employees, football players included, in order to be aware of."[4]

The result

FC Barcelona has the most liked Facebook page (www.facebook.com/fcbarcelona) in global sports, at 31 million, and it ranks in the top 50 of all

Facebook pages.[5] On Twitter, the English language account has 6.5 million followers, the Spanish language one 3 million.

According to Reputation Metrics, Barca is:

> ... the top football team in the world in terms of media value. FC Barcelona has 103 points of media value [points are awarded for media mentions of players and the club]. This is four consecutive seasons as world leader. Second most valuable team is Real Madrid, with 79.5 points ... Media exposure is the core factor in football and other professional sports influencing brand value. The business of sport entities is selling spectacle to fans. Media coverage is an excellent proxy for the size of the spectacle a sport brand is creating. In our previous studies, we have found a direct relationship between media value and revenues.
>
> Total revenues have increased from 290 million euros in June 2007 to 461 million in June 2012, a 58 per cent rise. In the same period, Manchester United increased revenues to just 18 per cent.[6]

RSA Conference

The RSA Conference is a major annual event for companies involved in the information technology (IT) security business.[7] Promotion of the conference is in the hands of Shift Communications.[8] During recent years the agency has moved beyond relying on traditional media to promote and cover the event, to working with bloggers and developing a social media strategy. CEO Todd Defren has blogged about what they did, the lessons learned and success achieved.[9]

The audience

The RSA Conference is designed to attract IT security industry organizations and individuals and was set up in 1991 as "a forum for cryptographers to gather and share the latest knowledge and advancements in the area of Internet security."[10] It now creates "opportunities for conference attendees to learn about IT security's most important issues through first-hand interactions with peers, luminaries and emerging and established companies" and "plays an integral role in keeping security professionals across the globe connected and educated".

The business goals

- Build interest in the conferences, increase attendance and engage more closely with the industry.

The brand journalism strategy and the platforms used

The strategy has developed over recent years. One area has been that of blogging and the crucial question for an industry event that wanted to ensure coverage was of a high standard: "What makes a blogger a blogger? How should we think about their credentials versus the *bona fides* of a *Wall Street Journal* reporter?"[11] Agency and organizers worked together to set strict guidelines for assigning bloggers' credentials. "The focus and longevity of the blog, frequency of updates, Technorati rankings and number of page views were all taken into consideration. Bloggers who made the cut were given full journalist privileges." Accredited bloggers were given an official online seal to display on their blogs.

Social media was also developed.[12] Twitter was used to keep the security community informed before, during and after conferences:

> We spent a lot of time promoting the #RSAC hashtag to a number of influencers and other security-minded folks. We wanted to be sure to differentiate between RSA Conference's "official" tweets (primarily focused on announcements, troubleshooting, etc.) with conversations about the show. In fact, a handful of security acolytes used the hashtag to arrange some unsponsored tweet-ups, tangential to the show venue.

The result

Twitter follows increased by 1500 per cent over the previous year, and promoting the hashtag led to 7500 tweets using it during the subsequent show:

> This allowed our RSAC client contacts to answer a range of logistical questions from users and to take a pulse on the crowd's reaction to everything from showfloor amenities to speakers' performances. If we noted rave reviews (or pans) of individual speakers, it was also duly noted for [next year's] planning. At each step, across the last few shows, RSAC's embrace of users' content and feedback has been rewarded with greater knowledge about its audience and a closer relationship with attendees: an object lesson for conference organizers across industries. It also seemed to help on the "traditional" PR side: coverage in mainstream journals such as the *Wall Street Journal* increased 83 per cent over [the previous year].

The Senior PGA Championship

The Senior Professional Golfers' Association (PGA) Championship is an annual golfing tournament.[13] For a recent event, in Cleveland, the PR 20/20 agency was hired to handle local media relations.[14]

The audience

Golf fans who might attend the championship.

The business goals

They needed to build awareness and interest prior to the event, and distribute information and content of interest to fans both before and during the event. Keith Mohering of PR 20/20 wrote: "To support our event marketing plan, we recommended launching a social media campaign to help generate awareness and build excitement by giving fans a behind-the-scenes look at a major golf championship. We got approval in mid January and launched the campaign on February 2, three months and 16 days before the event."[15]

The brand journalism strategy and the platforms used

The agency began by taking a natural and organic approach to building followers for the event. They had three months, but recommend starting as early as you can. Because time was short, it took two approaches to build a Twitter following for the event: monitoring on-topic golfing tweets and joining in conversations; and using online tools to identify Twitter followers who mentioned an interest in golf in their profiles. The agency used both TwitterGrader[16] and Twitter's search facility to do this. They set a goal to reach 500 followers by the start of the championship week; but conscious that users are more inclined to follow you if there is no great discrepancy between your following/follower stats, they built their follows steadily, in line with their growing band of followers, keeping the two figures within 200 of each other.

Here are the criteria they used for following people:

- Clevelanders who listed golf in their profiles (this proved to be the least successful strategy)
- Ohians who listed golf in their profiles
- golf twitterers with the best Twitter grades
- all professional golf tournaments
- all twitterers discussing golf, PGA and senior PGA, and various player names (this proved to be the most successful strategy)
- followers of other professional golf tournaments.

Platforms used were a twitter account @SeniorPGA2009, a Flickr account (www.flickr.com/photos/seniorpga2009), a blog (www.SeniorPGA2009.Wordpress.com), as well as a championship branded website (www.pga.com/seniorpga/2009/). They were unable to host the blog on the website for technical reasons.

To identify what content would work best, the agency asked Twitter followers:

> The overwhelming answer was pictures – images they can't see on TV or in the newspapers. This was consistent with the answers another Champions Tour event (@RegionsCharity) got when they asked their followers the same question.
>
> Leading up to the event, we posted pictures of clubhouse and course construction, media day, practice rounds and player arrivals. During the event, we showed pictures of players, the course, media interviews, putting green, driving range and fans getting autographs. Each picture we posted to Twitter would get between 20 to 30 views, with player photos generating the most traffic.
>
> On Flickr, the most popular photo album was from media day, which involved a press conference, golf, a chipping contest on Progressive Field and the returning champion throwing out the first pitch.

Blog, website and social media were integrated. Blog articles served as source material for tweets, and Twitter was the second highest driver of traffic to the blog, behind the event website. The blog was pitched like this:

> [It] was created to give fans behind-the-scenes access to Cleveland's first major golf championship in more than 10 years. Readers will be some of the first to view breaking news about the championship, including player commitments, clubhouse and course preparation updates, special opportunities to get involved, and Championship scores and highlights.[17]

The blog covered champions' tour updates, past Senior PGA championships, pre-championship events and Canterbury's (the host course) history with the PGA of America. During the week of the championship they posted live updates and news about player arrivals, tee times, pairings, practice rounds and championship scores, with updates and recaps. There was also information for those attending the championship, including parking arrangements, weather forecasts, the best course locations to see the action and places to see the players up close. On Twitter they posted live updates, and also answered questions.

Before the event, the workload was light, but close to and during it, the team was very busy. They recommend assigning closely defined roles to each team member, such as obtaining interview quotes (which were very popular), event recaps and posting interesting facts and figures.

The result

During the three-month campaign, there were 908 Twitter followers, 400 more than the 500 target.

Assignment

Plan a brand journalism strategy for an event. If you can do this for real, all the better. Set a business goal, develop a brand journalism strategy with its own goals designed to help deliver the business goal, decide what platforms to use and the content to create, and measure your success.

Notes

1 BBC report on FC Barcelona following: www.bbc.co.uk/news/business-18065300.
2 Digital-Football.com on FC Barcelona's mobile strategy: digital-football.com/recommendation/fc-barcelona-see-the-real-value-in-social-media-interview/.
3 Econsultancy on FC Barcelona's FCB app for Facebook: econsultancy.com/uk/blog/9397-fc-barcelona-launches-fcb-alert-app-for-facebook.
4 Digital-Football.com on FC Barcelona's social media strategy: digital-football.com/recommendation/fc-barcelona-see-the-real-value-in-social-media-interview/.
5 Digital-Football: digital-football.com/recommendation/fc-barcelona-see-the-real-value-in-social-media-interview/.
6 Reputation Metrics on FC Barcelona's media value: reputation-metrics.org/2012/06/06/football-media-value-report-2012/.
7 RSA Conference: www.pr-squared.com/index.php/2009/07/social-media-case-study-twitter-alights-at-rsa-conference.
8 Shift Communications: www.shiftcomm.com/.
9 CEO Todd Defren on the strategy: www.pr-squared.com/index.php/2009/07/social-media-case-study-twitter-alights-at-rsa-conference.
10 RSA Conference: www.rsaconference.com/about/.
11 RSA Conference brand journalism strategy: www.pr-squared.com/index.php/2008/04/social_media_conference_planni.
12 RSA use of social media: www.pr-squared.com/index.php/2009/07/social-media-case-study-twitter-alights-at-rsa-conference.
13 Senior PGA Championship: www.pga.com/seniorpga/2012/.
14 PR 20/20 agency: www.pr2020.com/page/7-tips-to-event-marketing-using-social-media.
15 Keith Mohering writing on the PR 20/20 blog: www.pr2020.com/page/7-tips-to-event-marketing-using-social-media.
16 TwitterGrader: www.hubspot.com/blog/?Tag=Twitter%20Grader.
17 Senior PGA Championship blog: seniorpga2009.wordpress.com/about/.

16 Publicizing a Travel Destination
How a Ski Resort Uses Brand Journalism on Social Media to Increase Visitor Numbers

Goal of this module

Chart the processes involved in promoting a travel destination using social media backed with traditional media to strengthen relationships with visitors, publicize events and help visitors along the purchase journey.

On the website

Find further information and links to all the resources referenced here.

Whistler Blackcomb

Whistler Blackcomb is a Canadian ski resort.[1] Amber Turnau,[2] social media project manager at 6S Marketing, gave an account in a Hootsuite[3] seminar[4] in which she explained how her company worked with the resort to use brand journalism content distributed via social media to promote the resort.

The audience

Guests – current, past and future.

The business goal

The goal was to increase business at the resort. The traditional route to gaining business online had been to offer a click-to-buy facility on the branded website. The brand journalism strategy was, said Amber Turnau, designed "to ease consumers into the purchase journey using social media".[5]

To do that they created events – and produced brand journalism content around them – that would increase awareness. So the marketing funnel was extended from a short click-to-buy one into a process in which potential visitors could "see pieces of inspirational content on social media ... then go through a process of consideration and validation, asking people on Twitter what they think, looking at reviews on Trip Advisor". The marketing team monitors this process and tries to assist people along the way, answering questions, and offering advice and recommendations.

The aim, alongside triggering purchase decisions, is "to get a loyalty loop with people becoming ambassadors for the brand [who] use social media to pass on to friends, colleagues, peers and encourage them to try Whistler".

The brand journalism strategy and the platforms used

One content strategy the resort uses is to establish events through which journalism showcases the appeals of the resort. But it must be of high quality to get maximum re-sharing. Amber says they "use a lot of photography and video content on social media because it best reflects the experience visitors will have when they get here". She gives the example of a Deep Winter pro ski and snowboarder photography competition, run in conjunction with the clothing company ARC'TERYX. As with other Whistler campaigns, they factored the social into every aspect in order to get the story to travel as widely and swiftly as possible.

Whistler invited professional photographers – who are often also skiers, snowboarders or mountain bikers – to take three days to shoot the resort in midwinter, edit what they produced into slide shows and play them before an audience of 1000 at a judging evening. So they needed to engage athletes, photographers and audience pre-event, and drive ticket sales.

They used the #deepwinter hashtag to curate the live content streaming out as the professional photographers went about their work. Some were live tweeting from their shoots all day, and there were videos posted, quotes and photos documenting behind the scenes during the shoots. Social platforms used included the "pillar channels" of Twitter, Facebook and Foursquare, as well as Flickr, YouTube and Vimeo. Trip Advisor is also key.

Whistler Blackcomb has a social aggregator site called the Movement where it curates social media engagement in platform-specific streams, so it is effectively a portal into the Whistler experience.[6] They often support such initiatives with print campaigns designed to push readers to the Movement, and use social content as the text within those ads.

There was also a Deep Winter website, with a mobile version and a live app with information about current conditions on the mountain: "lift status, trail conditions, weather, maps, webcams and more",[7] as well as global positioning systems (GPS) to enable users to track their day on the slopes and to buy passes. The team uses Hootsuite and other tools to schedule tweets and other social postings, to track mentions and conversations about the resort, and to enable it to step in where it feels appropriate.

Amber Turnau says: "You'll find people looking at the general topic but who haven't engaged with you and you can initiate conversations with them, tell them about yourself." They also pull metrics from Hootsuite, Google Analytics, Sitecatalyst and Facebook Insights to measure engagement with their targets. For future campaigns, they plan to work more with key influencers.

The result

The midwinter campaign achieved this:

- 4.7 per cent Twitter follower increase
- 168 re-tweets of #deepwinter
- 664 mentions of #deepwinter
- 5474 click-throughs to Deep Winter URL
- 5.2 per cent Facebook fan increase
- 770,041 Facebook page impressions in the campaign
- 4030 Facebook likes of Deep Winter content.

Using social media led to:

- 23 per cent decrease in total cost per campaign impression
- 82 per cent decrease in total cost per engagement; and
- 86 per cent decrease in total cost per website visit.

Turnau says: "The figures persuaded senior marketing and other management to adopt this strategy with every campaign they do."

Assignment

Plan a brand journalism strategy for a resort or other travel destination. Set a business goal, develop a brand journalism strategy with its own goals designed to help deliver the business goal, decide what platforms to use and the content to create, and measure your success.

Notes

1 Whistler Blackcomb: www.whistlerblackcomb.com/.
2 Amber Turnau: www.linkedin.com/in/amberturnau.
3 Hootsuite seminars: blog.hootsuite.com/.
4 Hootsuite's Crafting the Perfect Social Media Campaign seminar: blog.hootsuite.com/perfect-social-campaign/.
5 Amber Turnau: blog.hootsuite.com/perfect-social-campaign/.
6 The Movement: movement.whistlerblackcomb.com/.
7 The Movement live app: www.whistlerblackcomb.com/app/index.aspx.

17 Building an Information Resource
How a Government Department Created a New Web and Social Presence

Goal of this module

Chart the process involved in creating a major information resource that uses branded websites, social media, blogging and location-specific applications to deliver information where and when users need it.

On the website

Find further resources, including a video presentation on the strategy outlined here, as well as links to all the resources quoted.

US Department of Energy

The US Department of Energy's job is to communicate energy-saving advice to consumers.

The audience

There were two audiences: the general public, who needed to be connected with regarding energy-saving issues; and energy specialists, technicians and individuals involved in energy policy on Capitol Hill.

The business goals

The US Department of Energy's (DOE's) public communications strategy was seriously flawed and needed a complete overhaul. The initiative was led by Cammie Croft, who moved from the position of deputy new media director for President Barack Obama to become senior adviser and director of new media and citizen engagement at the DOE.

Croft told *Federal Computer Week* that there were three main business goals, or "imperatives". First imperative: "Use energy.gov to deliver local services and information to consumers and businesses."[1] Second imperative: "Serve specialized audiences through sub-domains and affiliate sites." Third imperative: "Connect with users where they are already engaged." They did that through social media, blogs and third-party sites where issues such as discussion of energy use and saving on bills were relevant.

Croft said on Blip TV that the site she inherited didn't tell the story. It should have played a vital role in "building the clean energy economy, protecting national nuclear security and expanding our knowledge on the frontiers of science and technology. These are very important and critical things that the department of energy does but in no way did this site tell that story".[2]

There were two additional goals:

- Eliminate wasteful spending.
- Improve digital communications.

When Croft began, the DOE had 87 individual websites, with an additional 399 sub-sites. Eliminating presences that were outmoded or which duplicated other presences helped to achieve the two additional goals:

> All those sites had a wide array of user experiences that make things very confusing for the audience to figure out how to find the information and services that they provide. So pulling all the information into one place makes it easy and a more pleasurable experience in finding what you're looking for.

This departmental business goal fitted the wider government goal of website reform, reducing the 24,000 .gov domains and the 125,000 sub-domains. Another part of the business strategy was to develop better relationships with two key groups: the leadership: the many scientists and other specialists within the department; and the grassroots: the many people across the department doing communications work.

With the leadership, Croft said, her team needed "to recognize that they were bringing an expertise to the table and should not be micromanaged". They also needed to get these experts to trust the communications team. With the grassroots communications staff: "They need to know what impact the new strategy would have on their day-to-day work. So we created a web council to bring together all the people who work on digital strategy and communications and get their guidance on next steps."

The brand journalism strategy and the platforms used

In order to implement the business strategy, Croft put a new framework in place. She developed an office of digital strategy that was empowered to own the department's digital presence – which meant it could, for example, act to reduce the 21 logos from interested bodies that appeared on the homepage of the previous version of the site. The digital strategy office included (she said on Blip TV):

> ... an editorial team, a team of digital communications specialists curating content from across the department and elevating that on top level pages, a multimedia team working on video photography, data visualisations, infographics, plus a user experience team.[3]

Croft explains that the main content strategy was "achieving national goals by supporting individual decisions". To do so, they established a user-focused content strategy in which they organized content to accord with what users were searching for. The content strategy followed the three imperatives of the business strategy outlined above, ensuring that the brand journalism strategy could deliver on the business strategy.

The first imperative, "Use energy.gov to deliver local services and information to consumers and businesses", is delivered through the orientation of the top-level pages of the branded website. These pages are designed to create a ladder of engagement, with four stages: inform, inspire, act, feed back. They have a range of information that informs, including statistics, information on energy policy, and the penalties for high energy use and incentives to cut consumption. They have content designed to inspire browsers through success stories and local projects. Consumers are encouraged to act through energy incentives, contests and challenges, and to share via social media. They are also given feedback through visuals that explain the impact of the actions they have taken.

The second imperative, "Serve specialized audiences through sub-domains and affiliate sites", is delivered by having, within the topic-orientated structure of the site, links to more specialized information suitable for researchers, advocates, academics, policy-makers, staff and contractors, press and media. The specialized content is made visible in the same arena as the general consumer and business information by having the content team curate information from sub-domains and affiliates and having "it bubble up to the top levels of the site". So, for example, click on a page about vehicles and you get general information about vehicles, but you also get links to make specialists aware of information appropriate to their specialism on sub-sites. In this way energy.gov is a portal: an umbrella site spanning all the many sites that used to exist individually.

The third imperative, "Connect with users where they are already engaged", is delivered through partnering with third-party sites. It reflects the fact that people are finding energy information in other places. So, for example, when it's tax return time and people are filling out their returns on turbotax.com, the energy.org team can provide their tax-saving information on that site. They also use social media to spread the word.

To make the abstract issue of energy consumption and saving relevant to the individual, the site uses personas to demonstrate what individuals can do. One persona is a contractor called Pete who wants to buy a new truck. Pete cares about his money, his job, his family and his environment. He doesn't know about how to save energy, the sources of his power, and what the cost of energy will be next year. Energy.org has that information, and if it can get it to Pete in the places he will find it, and in a form that makes sense to him, the brand journalism can do two things. It can help Pete to save money by buying an energy-efficient truck. When Pete does that, it helps the Department of Energy to deliver on the national priorities that it has been set.

Croft's first step, before revamping the website, was to create a social media strategy. She told *Federal Computer Week*:

> When I came to Energy, there was no central office thinking holistically about an online presence. One of the first things we took on was our limited capability to disseminate information in a dynamic way: no Facebook or Twitter account, and no blog. So we set those up.

The DOE has these social media accounts:

- Facebook: www.facebook.com/energygov
- Twitter: twitter.com/energy
- YouTube: www.youtube.com/user/USdepartmentofenergy
- Flickr: www.flickr.com/photos/departmentofenergy.

News and Blogs (energy.gov/news-blog) is a second-level area on the main branded website.

To create the new branded website, the DOE turned to an agency called Huge (www.hugeinc.com/). In order to deliver on the core requirement of empowering individuals to act, they say:

> We isolated local content from national content. There were a number of content types that could be served to individuals based on their zip code: rebates, tax incentives, news and specific maps and data info-graphics. By chunking out this content when a user enters their zip code, we were able to serve them the most relevant content for them to immediately get context of how the Department of Energy is working for them and also encourage them to act quickly.[4]

Other content initiatives on the main site include a live chat series with experts, called Energy Matters, and first-person profiles that use multimedia to show the impact of government energy policies upon individuals. There are also data visualizations, including an interactive map of every alternative fuel filling station in the US, covering biodiesel, electric, hydrogen and others, and giving its location, the fuels it stocks and its opening hours.

Another visualization, on the energy economy, shows state-by-state energy production, consumption and expenditure. All the source data can be downloaded and reused.

The next goals as of early 2013 were to add more tools to the site and to work with developer partners on energy apps for mobiles.

Croft gives these key points on what it takes to build an enterprise platform for government:

- Have a clear vision the team understands.
- When seeking the talent you need, think outside the box when looking for the team you need to succeed.
- You need empowered decision-makers – people who are prepared to make a decision, own it and not be afraid.
- A user-focused content strategy: organize your content based on the topics that people are searching for, rather than on your organization's structure.
- Have friends through the food chain – from the very top of the administration "all the way down to the folks who are posting press release for your smallest programme".
- Keep innovating – once you launch, you are never done.

The result

In a video interview, Croft stated that in getting on Facebook and YouTube: "Instantly we saw a 30 per cent increase in our traffic and the people we were reaching through our online communications."[5] On Blip TV she said that the re-launched energy.org site saw an increase in unique visitors of 328 per cent during the first six months and a very significant shift in the type of visitor: "Before, 42–48 per cent of visits were coming from within in the department of energy. Within 6 months of launch just 9–12 per cent from within in the building. We were reaching external audience never reached before."[6]

Assignment

Analyse how a major government department or public body has used brand journalism to inform its audience.

Notes

1 Cammie Croft quoted in *Federal Computer Week*: fcw.com/Articles/2011/04/11/QA-Cammie-Croft-DOE-social-media.aspx?Page=2.
2 Cammie Croft talking on Blip TV: blip.tv/drupalcondenver/the-story-of-energy-gov-the-ins-and-outs-of-turning-energy-dot-blah-into-energy-dot-awesome-603 6600.
3 Ibid.

4 Huge on the DOE contract: www.dopedata.com/2011/08/04/energy-gov-a-content-strategy-case-study/.
5 Cammie Croft interviewed by Alexander Howard: youtu.be/4F8UHNF6oSA.
6 Cammie Croft interviewed on Blip TV: blip.tv/drupalcondenver/the-story-of-energy-gov-the-ins-and-outs-of-turning-energy-dot-blah-into-energy-dot-awesome-6036600.

18 Charity Fundraising

How charity:water Uses Social Media
and Powerful Storytelling to Raise Funds
for Its Cause

Goal of this module

Analyse how charity:water uses brand journalism to realize its mission to provide access to clean, safe drinking water in impoverished nations.

On the website

Find video and other resources relating to this case study, as well as links to all the sources referenced here.

charity:water

The audience

Generation X donors (born any time from the 1960s to 1980s) who are just starting to develop their giving habits. Seventy per cent of fundraising is done online, so a social-network engaged audience is key. As well as the general public, charity:water targets non-profits, non-governmental organizations (NGOs), foundations, social enterprises, cause organizations, businesses and their corporate social responsibility divisions, video producers, educators and journalists.[1]

The business goals

charity:water aims to approach raising money for good causes in a new way. Founder Scott Harrison set out to build a brand that could deliver on the goal of providing clean water for everyone:

> To solve a problem this big, we needed to create an epic brand, an aspirational and transparent brand. So many charities seem to market guilt. We tell a story of opportunity. We needed to present the problems, the solutions and the joy that results when those solutions are implemented, in beautiful ways.[2]

Paull Young, its director of digital, said on ResponsSys:

> At the core of our marketing we're trying to build a really strong brand that people can connect with and look up to like they do with Nike or Apple, for example. The non-profit sector doesn't typically put a lot of stock in branding, while for us, it's really at the core of who we are.[3]

The charity aims to provide a different experience for donors. It recognized that the user experience of charities was poor – you make a donation and their next communication is to ask you for more money. The founders were also conscious of a concern among potential donors that their money would not reach the people whom it was intended for. So they have used digital media to build total transparency, what they call the power of proof, where a donor can see exactly how their money has been spent, right down to seeing the specific project they have contributed to on a Google map. Donors are kept updated on the progress of the project during the 18 months it takes to complete.

The charity does not dig the wells itself – local partners do that – leaving it free to focus on the marketing message rather than dealing with buying drilling rigs and the logistics of getting them where they are needed.[4] It is able to guarantee that 100 per cent of any donation is used on an actual project because it raises money to cover its operating costs from a different source.[5]

There are three elements to their business strategy, according to Paull Young:[6]

1 Inspire through storytelling

The goal is to inspire potential donors to fundraise by "telling them a story they can connect with. Our founder is a natural storyteller, he's really our storyteller in chief; I work with some of the best creatives".[7]

2 Provide a platform to let people make our story their story

Any individual can make their own page on the charity:water website and tell their own story in their own way.[8] Young gives examples of individual fundraising efforts, such as a woman who said she would swim from Alcatraz to San Francisco without a swimsuit if 1000 people pledged a donation. Another couple postponed their wedding until they had raised $5000 to build a well.

3 Customer experience

As well as giving total transparency, charity:water aims to make the process of giving fun, with initiatives such as asking those who would give you birthday presents to donate to the charity instead. Young says: "They have a great time, their friends love donating and the campaign looks like a hero ... those are the fundamental drivers of our digital growth."

The charity also differs in two others ways: it always tells positive stories and it rarely asks for money. Young explains:

> Traditional fundraising, especially direct marketing fundraising, frequently plays with guilt, or frequently makes people feel bad. I often see commercials that make me upset and instantly want me to give $20. We prefer to tell positive stories, stories that inspire people, stories that people will want to share. Who would share a sad dog video on their Facebook page? You'd have to be a sociopath. Positive stories are important in this new sharing web economy.
>
> We don't ask for money much at all ... we want people to commit, to fundraise, to inspire their friends to give, we don't just want their wallet. So at the end of the year the email you'll get from charity:water will hopefully inspire you, it will excite you as opposed to an email with a huge donate button that wants 20 bucks from you now.

David Connell, digital media communications director for Ocean Conservancy, explains the appeal of the business strategy like this:

> charity:water doesn't think like a non-profit, they think like a consumer-focused tech start-up. They want to make their product (yes, all non-profits are selling a product) a must-have among the coolest, trendiest people in their target demographic. They then let these cool, trendy people tell their friends who are also cool and trendy (but perhaps less so) about the product and it takes off from there through an ever-widening pyramid of influence.[9]

charity:water's strategies focus on activating individuals and asking them to engage their network because they know that the whole of a person's network is greater than the sum of its parts.[10]

The brand journalism strategy and the platforms used

Paull Young says that charity:water was one of the first charities to successfully use social media, coupled with powerful imagery and a compelling story, to garner millions of supporters. For example, it uses two branded websites with distinct strategies behind them.[11] On MyCharityWater.org, donors create a profile, start and manage a fundraising campaign and activate their personal network to get behind their efforts through Facebook, Twitter and email.

On a second site, WaterForward.org, individuals activate their social networks through a process that charity:water calls "paying it forward". You give a sum to the charity in the name of someone in your social circle, and they are invited to make a donation of their own, again paying it forward to someone in their circle. The site takes the form of an online book, featuring pictures of all those who have donated.

The MyCharityWater site has a Water Projects section with powerful brand journalism. There is a section on Videos from the Field and another on Stories from the Field.[12] charity:water's storytelling is highly professional. It plays to viewers' emotions like the first-class popular journalism or documentary-making that it is. For example, "Rachel's Gift, One Year Late" is a text, stills and video feature about a nine-year-old girl who pledged to raise $300.[13] She didn't quite make it, but told her mother she would try harder next year. She was killed in a car accident one month later. Those touched by her death pledged $1.2 million. On the anniversary of her death, the charity took her mother and grandparents to Ethiopia to show them some of the people whom Rachel had helped.

A Photo of the Day feature, each a powerful image accompanied by short updates, is promoted through Twitter posts and Facebook updates. The challenge, as any storyteller would find, is to make the impact of poor water upon health, food supply and the general economy of a region into powerful brand journalism. charity:water manages it by using the journalistic technique of telling such stories through the experiences of individuals whom the viewer/reader can relate to on an emotional as well as an intellectual level.

There's also a Campaigns to Watch area that demonstrates just how inventive donors are in creating ideas that make great copy.[14] Some are simple – a bearded man asks you to donate to one of two funds: one for him to keep the beard, the other for him to shave it off. Whatever the outcome, all funds pledged go to the charity. Others feature companies that will give a donation for each purchase made with them, such as a donation for each use of a store's loyalty card. Another key engagement/storytelling tool is email bulletins. charity:water uses email updates extensively, says Paull Young, to "drastically increase the number of touch points we have with our donors during the 18 months it takes to build the water project they've funded".[15] The hope is that the emails "help us to create deeply personal communications with each donor, creating long term donor relationships". charity:water is on Twitter (twitter.com/charitywater) and Facebook (www.facebook.com/charitywater).

Social media engagement is vital, but it only works because of the content that charity:water can push through it. Young says: "Using social media is about what content you've given them, and key [are] the 10,000 people who love us the most",[16] and emphasizes that content creators must ask themselves: "What can I give them that they want to share?"

The result

charity:water had 1.5 million Twitter followers and 250,000 Facebook page likes in early 2013. The organization has helped 2.5 million people in 19 countries via more than 250,000 donations in the past five years, according to founder and CEO Scott Harrison.[17] In the latest available annual report (www.charitywater.org/annual-report/11/our-work/), charity:water reported: "In 2011, we more than doubled the amount of funds we granted to the field. At the end of 2011, our total investment in water projects was $37 million, and with that, we'd served over two million people."[18]

Assignment

Develop a brand journalism strategy for a charity. Cover the full process from establishing a target audience and identifying the business goals, to developing the brand journalism strategy to deliver those goals, the platforms to use and the results achieved.

Notes

1 charity:water's target audience, as reported by SocialBrite: www.socialbrite.org/2012/01/17/how-charity-water-changes-lives-through-multimedia/.
2 Scott Harrison interviewed on *Venture Beat*: venturebeat.com/2011/11/16/how-charitywater-became-techs-favorite-non-profit/.
3 Paull Young quoted in ResponsSys: www.responsys.com/blogs/nsm/2012/04/charity-water-inspiring-a-grassroots-movement-through-digital-marketing.html.
4 Vimeo video on the charity's strategy: vimeo.com/12985172.
5 Social Edge on how the charity covers its administration costs: www.socialedge.org/features/job-listings/charity-water.
6 Paull Young in a YouTube video: youtu.be/fSMZt52ic1Q.
7 Paull Young on his own website: www.paullyoung.com/.
8 charity:water website: www.charitywater.org/?gclid=CLOWuvuOqbMCFQzKtAod0XEAmQ.
9 David Connell on the charity's business strategy: www.davidconnell.net/2011/05/05/so-you-want-to-be-like-charitywater-10-brand-challenges-between-you-and-cool/.
10 YouTube video on charity:water's strategies: www.youtube.com/watch?v=u7HL61J54jI.
11 charity:water's distinct strategies on its two branded websites: www.youtube.com/watch?v=u7HL61J54jI.
12 Videos from the Field and Stories from the Field: www.charitywater.org/projects/fromthefield/index.php.
13 "Rachel's Gift, One Year Late": www.charitywater.org/blog/rachels-gift/.
14 Campaigns to Watch: www.charitywater.org/blog/category/updates/campaigns-to-watch/.
15 Paull Young quoted on ResponsSys: www.responsys.com/blogs/nsm/2012/04/charity-water-inspiring-a-grassroots-movement-through-digital-marketing.html.
16 Paull Young in a Vimeo video: vimeo.com/12985172.
17 Scott Harrison on the charity's website: www.charitywater.org/about/scotts_story.php.
18 charity:water annual report: www.charitywater.org/annual-report/11/our-work/.

19 Building a Geo-Located Information and Entertainment Resource

How Starbucks Uses the Full Range of Geo-Location Tools to Tell Its Story in Each of Its Stores

Goal of this module

Explore how brand journalism can be used by a brand with many locations.

On the website

Find supporting material and links to all the sources quoted here.

Starbucks

The audience

Starbucks holds around 33 per cent of the market share for coffee in the US. The bulk of its outlets are in city centres and up-market suburbs. According to *Small Business*: "Starbucks' primary target market is [high-income, urbanite] men and women aged 25 to 40. They account for almost half (49 per cent) of its total business. Young adults [often college students], aged 18 to 24, total 40 per cent of Starbucks' sales."[1]

The business goals

Starbucks has always styled itself as the third place between home and work – a haven in which customers can relax, work if they want to, communicate both in person and digitally, and generally feel comfortable. Now it has created what it calls its fourth place, a digital content network accessible from its stores. Much effort has gone into location-based marketing built on relevant content, plus incentives and loyalty rewards.

It offers free in-store Wi-Fi which gives access to a wide range of digital content that can be tailored to each of its store locations; a mobile-phone payments system; a powerful presence on each of the main location-specific social networks; and the use of augmented reality and quick response (QR) codes.

Adam Brotman, chief digital officer, spoke to Interbrand about the role of digital technologies in telling the Starbucks story:

> Digital is hugely important, video in particular but also imagery, [because of] the two-way and real-time interaction that digital allows, all those are important in telling whatever story we have to tell ... Where digital comes in ... is we for years have relied and still do on the green-aproned store partners to listen to our customers, tell our story, occasionally promote something, but mostly just have a relationship with our customers, know the customers ... digital gives us an opportunity to not put all of that weight – to tell our story, to build our brand – all on the shoulders of our store partners.[2]

Digital enables Starbucks to replicate something of the one-to-one relationships it hopes its staff have with customers in its stores in the world of mobile electronic communications.

Mobile Marketing and Technology reported:

> Starbucks sharpened its focus by moving away from mass marketing to a one-to-one focus, putting the customer at the centre of its marketing efforts. Starbucks has developed a mobile marketing program that successfully blends loyalty, incentives, and commerce. The important part of the effort, from a mobile wallet and mobile payments perspective, is that Starbucks has sharply focused on incentives and loyalty to drive business results, not just the addition of a new mobile payment option.
>
> What immediately comes to mind for many is the Starbucks store finder app. That makes it easier for consumers to find a Starbucks location. Starbucks also has developed mobile programs that allow consumers to shop, search, and purchase through contactless payments. But Starbucks also has integrated web, app, text messaging, out-of-home, display, location-based services, in-store, and direct mail programs.[3]

We'll look at those initiatives in detail below.

Another strong community focus stems from Starbucks's commitment to helping the local communities around each of its stores. Geo-location is not the whole of the Starbucks brand story, nor is it the whole of their content strategy, but it is a very significant part of that story simply because having a largely bricks and mortar consumer business dictates that it be so.

The brand journalism strategy and the platforms used

Starbucks is using content to build its relationship with its customers, effectively turning each of its stores into a digital information and entertainment hub – what the brand calls its fourth space, after the third space of the physical store and its physical offerings of coffee and food. That content is a mix of universally relevant news, information and entertainment, plus a wide range of location-relevant and specific content, depending on where the store you are in is located.

Content is also closely bound up with the array of incentives, rewards and loyalty initiatives that Starbucks also uses to forge a closer relationship with its customers. The strategy of aiding communities around each of its stores is partly met through geo-located schemes to encourage customers and staff to take part in local initiatives.

While we are concentrating here on location-based storytelling, it's worth mentioning that Starbucks uses content in other ways, too, notably with its My Starbucks Idea initiative, where customers can make their suggestions, see them discussed and voted upon by others, have them considered by Starbucks and, in hundreds of cases, implemented.[4]

Let's look at the main platforms that Starbucks uses.

Starbucks Digital Network

Log on to Starbucks Wi-Fi and you also get access to a collection of free and premium digital content, delivered through a partnership with Yahoo. *The Drum* reported: "The network will offer benefits that elevate the value of free wi-fi and invite to a one-of-a-kind destination featuring free access to various paid sites and services, exclusive content and previews, free download, career tools and local community news."[5] *The Drum* itemized the content on offer, which includes online channels featuring news, entertainment, health, business, careers and local neighbourhood information. Journalism content comes from, amongst others, the *New York Times, Patch, USA Today*, the *Wall Street Journal*, Yahoo! and *Zagat*.

Geo-located information, reports *The Drum*, includes:

> ... the Run, Ride and Walk finder online application for local community relevance. The app will provide access to geo-targeted maps of more than 300,000 routes that highlight Starbucks stores along the way, and customers can upload their own trails that begin or end at their local Starbucks ... As part of the My Neighborhood channel, DonorsChoose. org, will help match customers with local K-12 public school classrooms in need of support. DonorsChoose.org is a nonprofit website where public and charter school teachers describe specific educational projects for their students, and donors can choose the projects they want to support. Contributors can give as little as $1 to help bring a classroom project to life. After project completion, the donor receives photographs and thank-you letters from the students they helped.

Starbucks Melody, an unofficial fan site, asked Brotman about hyper-local and user-generated content on the network, and reported:

[He] said that the idea behind this digital content is that much of it is intended to be hyper-local. By clicking on the tab which has the name of the Starbucks you're at, you connect with the possibility of a Four-square login, and there is all kinds of local information such as the temperature outside, and even what's playing inside the store.[6]

Mobile apps and mobile payments

Starbucks's mobile app combines a store finder and information resourced on the firm's products with a loyalty and rewards card, plus mobile pay-ments.[7] Users can pay for their coffee, check their balance, reload their card and view transactions. The app is strongly focused, in terms of the functions it covers, on being a useful utility around the act of getting a coffee, from finding the café to paying for the drink.

SMS

Mobile Marketer reported that Starbucks has used SMS to build its My Starbucks Rewards programme, through which customers earn rewards such as free drinks and refills when paying with a Starbucks Card.[8] It invited customers to opt in by texting the keyword GOLD to the short code 697289. SMS is used to promote special events, such as a Frappuccino Happy Hour.

Augmented reality

Starbucks has used augmented reality to enable interaction with special coffee cups produced for occasions such as Christmas and Valentine's Day.[9] Pointing your phone's camera at the cups brings characters or design ele-ments such as Valentine hearts featured there into animation. You can interact with them by tapping the screen – for instance, a skiing boy on the Christmas cup does a somersault when you tap him. The app also includes social sharing capabilities: you can send e-cards and holiday offers from Starbucks.

QR codes and games

Starbucks strategically placed QR codes (or mobile barcodes) on fliers, pro-moting new coffee roasts such as blonde, medium and dark.[10] Customers could scan a code to vote for their favourite roast. They could also watch a video about the company's coffee. *Mashable* reported that it has also used them as part of traditional media promotions – for example:

> ... in ads in popular magazines like *People* and in daily newspapers as well as on billboard ads. The ads promote Starbucks' mobile payment

app and give additional information, often in video form, about coffee sold at the stores.

Mike Wehrs, CEO and president of Scanbuy [which produced the campaign for Starbucks], says one QR code might, for example provide a sample of music that people listen to in the region where the coffee was picked or a description by some coffee experts about what makes that coffee unique. "This is bringing to the Starbucks consumer the ability to interact," says Wehrs. "We can show a very evolved shopping experience through some advanced technology."[11]

Starbucks also produced a QR code scavenger hunt in partnership with Lady Gaga. When customers scanned QR codes on in-store banners, chalk-boards and posters, they saw clues in the seven-round hunt. Players had to visit certain blogs and Starbucks digital properties, decode cryptic messages and use logic, plus their knowledge of maths, literature and pop culture, to solve the clues. The clues, arranged into rounds, were calibrated to encourage group play and prizes were awarded.

The game tied in with the release of a Lady Gaga album and, on release day, a special edition of the music was streamed on the Starbucks Digital Network. There were also free downloads and exclusive videos. The game had two goals for Starbucks: to build deeper relationships with its most engaged customers and, *Mashable* reported, "as a way to connect the store – what Starbucks refers to as the 'third place' – to Starbucks Digital Network, its content network and 'fourth place'".[12]

Starbucks Community Service

Enter a zip or post code on the community service website and you get a list of all the community initiatives at that location.[13] And there is an invitation to get the local store to help you: "If you would like the store local to you to support your charity or group, there are lots of options", including displaying your poster in the café, holding your meetings there and gaining support for the charity from the store. The stories of the individual initiatives are told on the site.

What was not available at the time of writing was an app that automatically identified local projects – something that could be incorporated within the main Starbucks app described above.

Let's look now at the social platforms that Starbucks uses. We're focusing here on social platform use as it relates to location.

Foursquare (foursquare.com/starbucks)

Starbucks has a custom barista badge to reward regular customers, and it has developed a number of initiatives on the platform. It has donated cash to an AIDS prevention charity for each check-in over a given period. It provided a national offer for mayors of any store to get a discount at any Starbucks across the US.

Facebook (www.facebook.com/Starbucks)

Media Funnel points to Starbucks's use of localized content on its brand pages, as well as of geo-targeting.[14] Facebook enables the geo-targeting of content based on the language and location of the recipient, and promotion of exclusive products developed to appeal to regional tastes in, for example, China or Indonesia.

Instagram (instagram.heroku.com/users/starbucks)

GeekWire says:

> The way that Starbucks makes its Instagram account pay off is through the interplay with other social media sites like Twitter and Facebook. Among other things, Starbucks posts photos of coffee-taste testing at headquarters and in-store experiences from different locations around the world. They then share these photos on Facebook, which allows fans to comment. In essence, their Instagram strategy works because they are sharing photos that interest their followers. In addition, they've created a slide show on their site to promote fans' photos. Starbucks has made it really simple by using the #starbucks hash tag.[15]

Pinterest (pinterest.com/source/starbucks.com/)

Buzzbrothers Social Media blog says that Starbucks follows the essentials for success on the platform:

> Share what users like and want, make them your cherished brand ambassadors, engage in meaningful ways to foster conversations around your brand. In one short sentence: get into your fans' heads. Our favourite board that illustrates very well this motto is the Coffee Moments Board, where they pin images of recipes of various drinks based on coffee and most importantly of people enjoying their Starbucks coffee.[16]

The result

Starbucks was rated number one in a study of the most socially engaged companies by the research organization Phase One:[17]

The researchers found that social media users are drawn to brands that convey a social benefit. When the user affiliates with the brand, the user is sending a message to those in his or her social network about how he or she wants to be perceived. In this way, the brand reflects the user's idealized self – the "Me Statement".

We looked at this phenomenon in Chapter 7 in relation to Red Bull.

The report goes on: "This very public aspect of social media can be quite different from the private self: those aspects of one's self that, while true, are not for public broadcast. Marketing messages that tap into the private self may drive sales, but they won't drive social media engagement."

With Starbucks:

> The study found that a focus on a me statement (the idealized self embodied by a brand) was the key factor in driving social media engagement among the most engaged brands. For example, Starbucks ... uniquely delivers its story with consistent messaging and strategy across all of its touch points, appealing to the idealized self.
>
> To achieve this successful social media engagement, Starbucks focused its web page, Facebook page and television advertisements on the individual and his or her individualized experience with the brand. For example, Starbuck's Facebook page engages the visitor by speaking to his or her coffee preferences and personal stories.

We can see this strategy applied on the geo-located contact points discussed above: from apps that provide utility and let you select your favourite stores, coffees and food; to a digital content network that lets you select the news, information or entertainment that suits your mood when you are in a store.

The report continues: "Starbucks taps into visitors' desires for individualized experiences that appeal to their unique preferences" and the location in which they are having those experiences. Starbucks's community engagement programme also lets customers demonstrate their idealized self by taking part in activities to help that community.

Assignment

Develop a brand journalism strategy for a consumer brand with physical premises in a number of locations. Cover the full process, from establishing a target audience and identifying the business goals, to developing the brand journalism strategy to deliver those goals and the platforms used.

Notes

1 *Small Business* on Starbucks's target audience: smallbusiness.chron.com/starbucks-target-audience-10553.html.

2 Adam Brotman quoted by Interbrand: vimeo.com/42624362.
3 *Mobile Marketing and Technology* on Starbucks's marketing strategy: mobilemarketingandtechnology.com/2011/11/28/starbucks-among-top-10-mobile-marketers-of-2011/.
4 My Starbucks Idea initiative: mystarbucksidea.force.com/.
5 *The Drum* reporting on Starbucks's digital network: www.thedrum.co.uk/news/2011/01/12/starbucks-bring-free-digital-network-uk#yuf3mIj3OkQL9GVF.99.
6 Starbucks Melody fan site on hyper-local and user-generated content on the company's network: www.starbucksmelody.com/2010/10/28/having-a-french-press-with-the-new-starbucks-digital-network-and-adam-brotman-sr-vp-digital-ventures/.
7 *Mobile Marketer* on Starbucks's mobile apps and mobile payments strategy: www.mobilemarketer.com/cms/news/content/12852.html.
8 *Mobile Marketer* on Starbucks's SMS strategy: www.mobilemarketer.com/cms/news/content/12852.html.
9 *Mobile Marketer* on Starbucks's augmented reality strategy: www.mobilemarketer.com/cms/news/content/12852.html.
10 *Mobile Marketer* on Starbucks's QR codes and games strategy: www.mobilemarketer.com/cms/news/content/12852.html.
11 *Mashable* on Starbucks's use of QR codes: mashable.com/2011/10/26/starbucks-qr-codes/.
12 *Mashable* on Starbucks's games strategy: mashable.com/2011/05/19/srch/.
13 Starbucks's community service strategy: community.starbucks.com/index.jspa.
14 Media Funnel on Starbucks's Facebook strategy: mediafunnel.com/facebook/what-you-can-learn-from-starbucks-facebook-strategy/.
15 GeekWire on Starbucks's Instagram strategy: www.geekwire.com/2012/advanced-guide-instagram-build-brand/.
16 Buzzbrothers Social Media blog on Starbucks's Pinterest strategy: live.buzzbrothers.ch/post/27904741871/pinterest-how-5-top-brands-are-doing-it-right.
17 Phase One research into Starbucks's performance as a socially engaged company: www.phaseone.net/news/starbucks-rates-number-1-in-study-of-most-socially-engaged-companies-by-research-firm-phaseone/.

20 Launching or Re-Launching a Customer Magazine

How Waitrose Repositioned Its Customer Magazine and Extended Its Brand Journalism Strategy

Goal of this module

Explore the place of a customer magazine in the brand journalism strategy of a brand using Waitrose as an example. (We used Waitrose in Chapter 2 as a demonstration of how to create a customer persona. If you haven't yet read that chapter, it may help to do so now.)

On the website

Find further information, background material and links to all the sources quoted here.

Waitrose

The audience

Waitrose, the supermarket group owned by John Lewis, has only a 3.9 per cent market share among UK supermarkets, according to research collated by *In Publishing*, but a clearly defined up-market appeal.[1] It has a market share of 6.6 per cent in the highest earning managerial and professional demographic, the highest proportion of shoppers from the professional A and B classes, at 47 per cent, the next highest being Sainsbury's at 34 per cent and Marks & Spencer at 22 per cent.

The business goals

The magazine revamp and repositioning, in which *Waitrose Food Illustrated* was replaced by *Waitrose Kitchen*, tied in with a move to convince consumers that they could do their everyday shop at Waitrose. A budget Essentials range was introduced, supported with an advertising campaign, and in-store recipe cards featuring two very different chefs – Delia Smith, who represents tradition (and for many years was closely associated with rival supermarket Sainsbury's) and restaurateur Heston Blumenthal, a high-profile

Michelin-starred chef who represents a more *avant-garde* image of the enjoyment of good food.

The Marketing Practice saw the way in which the repositioning of the supermarket was handled as showing the way forward for content marketing, reporting that the brand took over entire commercial breaks for a video featuring the two chefs cooking together. It commented: "everything seems to be geared up to meet Waitrose's goals – the recipes are about showing that you can do your 'everyday' shop at Waitrose".[2] The advert is on the *Brand Journalism* website.

The Essentials marketing strategy which *Waitrose Kitchen* tied in with had great success, winning an award from *Marketing Week*, which reported:

> The launch of Essentials allowed the retailer to give shoppers a range of good quality everyday food products at entry level prices, appealing to customers feeling the pinch of the recession but not alienating its well-heeled shoppers or straying from its core brand.
>
> Rupert Thomas, the chain's marketing director, says: "Waitrose was thought to be pricey and the brand image wasn't consistent across categories in the store so whatever strategy we took needed to address that."
>
> He adds that it was important not to pitch its new own brand label as a discount brand and to communicate that all its products maintained the high quality standards that Waitrose is renowned for, such as always using free range eggs.
>
> Andy Nairn, executive planning director at MCBD, the agency that created the ad campaign for the launch, believes that Essential Waitrose engaged with consumers and the … judges because it was a real business transformation-strategy story.
>
> "It was the creation of a new brand – not just an advertising campaign. It could have gone wrong and alienated Waitrose shoppers, not brought people on board. Waitrose created a £600m brand in less than a year and it smashed all the projections of growth," he says.[3]

The brand journalism strategy and the platforms used

Waitrose's magazine is published by the John Brown customer publishing group. They say:

> Waitrose marketing challenged John Brown to evolve our multi-award-winning *Waitrose Food Illustrated* (WFI) magazine into a fresh, new magazine that would resonate with everyday family cooks and healthy eaters, as well as the upmarket foodies WFI had traditionally courted.
>
> Our solution was *Waitrose Kitchen*, a more accessible, more practical magazine that's firmly keyed into the Waitrose marketing strategy, while

still retaining the ethos that made WFI such a success. Like WFI, *Waitrose Kitchen* is sold in-store, as well as being delivered to cardholders.[4]

The first issue of the revamped magazine (April 2012) featured Heston and Delia on the cover, and a mid-market rather than up-market look. The magazine's repositioning brought a stronger emphasis on recipes and was supported with 4000 recipes online (www.waitrose.com/home/recipes.html).

Waitrose extended its brand journalism offering with *Weekend* newspaper. The 16-page 400,000 circulation publication was described by Waitrose as: "Free every Thursday – Your essential guide on what to do, watch, eat, cook, read, buy and visit this weekend."[5] The newspaper features food news, reviews, recipes and promotional offers. The Pelissier Communications blog lists the benefits of the newspaper:

- Physically touches customers every weekend.
- Provides something of value and relevance (and not only about food).
- Effortlessly plonks its brand across millions of kitchen tables.
- Cements brand loyalty.
- Saves customers money through the use of coupons.[6]

There was also a Waitrose smartphone app which, in addition to recipes, includes a shopping list-building function, offers, a branch finder and a cook's tools section.

Waitrose coordinated the print magazine and newspaper with a branded website featuring a recipe database (www.waitrose.com/home/recipes.html). It also has these social presences:

- Twitter (twitter.com/#!/waitrose)
- Facebook (www.facebook.com/Waitrose)
- YouTube (www.youtube.com/user/Waitrose).

The result

John Brown says: "The refresh has been a resounding success. Sales of *Waitrose Kitchen* outstrip those of WFI, proving we have gained readers (ABC: 339,109); and advertising, in very challenging times, is outperforming the market with a 4 per cent year-on-year increase in revenue.[7]

Assignment

Carry out your own analysis of a customer magazine and what it does for its brand. If possible, get access to the person who commissions the magazine, and the data the brand has, and present a full analysis of the business goals, brand journalism strategy and results achieved.

Notes

1 Research collaged by *In Publishing* on Waitrose: www.inpublishing.co.uk/kb/articles/waitrose.aspx.
2 *The Marketing Practice* on Waitrose: blog2.themarketingpractice.co.uk/marketing-mit/waitrose-showing-the-way-for-b2b-content-marketing.
3 *Marketing Week* on the Essentials range: www.marketingweek.co.uk/what-next-for-waitrose-essentials/3022412.article.
4 John Brown customer publishing group on Waitrose's magazine: www.johnbrownmedia.com/case-study-waitrose.html?lang=en-gb&displaymode=Approved
5 Waitrose on its *Weekend* newspaper: www.waitrose.com/home/inspiration/waitrose_weekend.html.
6 Pelissier Communications blog on the benefits of Waitrose's newspaper: www.joepelissier.co.uk/marketingtips/marketing-newsletter/.
7 John Brown on Waitrose's magazine: www.johnbrownmedia.com/case-study-waitrose.html?lang=en-gb&displaymode=Approved

21 Creating a Media Toolkit

How a Charity Uses a Media Toolkit to Communicate with a Number of Audience Sectors

Goal of this module

Demonstrate how a brand can inform any story told about it by other media, and also inform audience sectors, including staff and supporters.

On the website

Find further resources and links to the video and other sources quoted here.

Creating a media toolkit is a basic essential for any brand journalism strategy. Having a good one can make the difference between your brand being a key part in your own story as it is told by other media or being left out.

When a story breaks, particularly if it is an important and fast-developing one, media organizations scramble for information about the brand involved. If they can find what they need on the brand's websites and other presences, and the quality is right, they will use it, alongside other material. If they can't find that material from you, you risk being left out of your own story. We're not talking here about the instant comment and analysis you will want to post to get your voice heard, but about having the essential background about your brand already available to be grabbed by whoever needs it.

Media toolkits have both external and internal applications for an organization. External applications: a media toolkit is a multimedia resource for journalists in traditional media that contains a comprehensive package of information which will enable them to include you in a story. Internal applications: a toolkit can also set out guidance for those within an organization who need to get their message across to external media.

Company news is one stream in a media toolkit. Company news can also be released direct to the consumer via social media.

Porchlight

The audience

Porchlight is a charity dedicated to helping the homeless and is based in Kent, south-east England (www.porchlight.org.uk). Content is directed mainly at local media, with some website materials aimed at supporters, and social presences directed at the general public, potential fundraisers and volunteers in the area where the charity operates.

The business goals

Porchlight says: "We help anyone who is homeless or threatened with homelessness. We also work with any vulnerable people who need support and advice." In particular, Porchlight can intervene to help rough sleepers. It widely publishes its contact details and requests that anyone who sees a rough sleeper let them know.

The brand journalism strategy and the platforms used

Porchlight's website includes a media centre (www.porchlight.org.uk/media-centre/) with multimedia toolkits (www.porchlight.org.uk/media-centre/media-toolkits/) on particular stories and wider issues. There are also individual press releases (www.porchlight.org.uk/media-centre/press-releases/) and a real-life stories resource (www.porchlight.org.uk/media-centre/real-life-stories/). Only summaries of those stories are on the website. The media must contact them for the full text and images, which gives them control over the distribution of this valuable and sensitive material.

Video and audio resources (www.porchlight.org.uk/media-centre/video/) include first-person accounts of homelessness; documentaries featuring interviews with individuals whom the charity has helped; and details of a campaign asking members of the public to let the charity know the location of rough sleepers. There is also a fundraiser video about a new initiative, and another with guidance on fundraising featuring inspiring stories, such as the group that abseiled down the 100 foot side of a shopping centre. There is a report on a homeless football world cup, held in Milan and featuring a team made up of individuals whom the charity had helped, and a video report on a rough sleeping conference organized by the charity and attended by professionals from across the housing and homelessness sector.

Photography resources include photosets on stories involving the charity, as well as sets illustrating the charity's work and activities. A blogging area includes one from the chief executive (www.porchlight.org.uk/about/blogs/): "Find out what chief executive Mike Barrett thinks about the current social and political issues that impact on vulnerable and homeless people."

Publications include *The Porchlight Post*, an online magazine distributed to the charity's supporters. They also publish reports that they have commissioned, such as one by the University of Kent on provision for homeless singles in the county.

Porchlight's main social media channels are Facebook and Twitter. On Facebook (www.facebook.com/Porchlight1974) the main image contains details on how to report a rough sleeper to the charity for immediate intervention. Status updates are social – for example, raising the question of how a homeless person had been portrayed on the latest episode of *East-Enders*, and gaining comments on the opinions expressed. On Twitter (twitter.com/Porchlight1974) there are tweets on charity initiatives and ways in which readers can support them – such as schemes where you give a donation to a charity as you make a purchase – as well as appeals for volunteers required for particular tasks in the near future and re-tweets on issues around homelessness.

In addition, all of the charity's videos are hosted on YouTube (www.youtube.com/Porchlight1974) and its photographs are on Flickr (www.flickr.com/photos/porchlight/).

The result

No hard figures are available, but the organization sees its media toolkit as boosting its profile in both its policy and geographic areas of operation.

Assignment

1 If you work on a brand which has a media toolkit, assess the quality of the material in it and decide how useful it is. Make any necessary improvements.
2 If you work on a brand without a media toolkit, create one. Start with the audiences for the toolkit, see what business goals it might support, decide on the range of content you require and the platforms to publish it on. Set goals for the toolkit and assess how effective it is over time.
3 If you don't work on a brand, you may be able to get a small brand without a toolkit to allow you to create one for it.

22 Developing a Company News Resource

How Dow Chemical Reports on Itself and Its Activities as a Problem-Solver and Educator

Goal of this module

Demonstrate how a company can use news storytelling to present itself in a positive light.

On the website

Find further resources and links to all the sources quoted here.

Dow Chemical

Dow Chemical is in many respects a good example of a company using storytelling to its own advantage and of being involved in the news about itself in a positive way. So it makes a good case study of a company news story path.

But there is one big cloud over Dow. It's called Bhopal. The Bhopal Disaster didn't happen to Dow, but it is still feeling the consequences. And while its presentation of itself is positive in many ways, it isn't over Bhopal. So while we look in this chapter at good-example Dow, we will look at bad-example Dow in the next chapter as a case study in poor crisis management.

The audience

The general public, plus politicians, policy-makers, scientists and engineers, environmental and other pressure groups, and activists.

The business goals

Dow (www.dow.com) says that it has the long-term vision of being "A premier global company ... dedicated to growth ... driven by quality performance and innovation ... committed to maximizing our customers' successes ... always living our Dow values."[1] Its values are stated to include innovation, what it calls solutionism – solving many of the problems the world faces in relation to industrial processes and protecting scarce resources – and science and technology education. This last is an issue both for Dow, which as a high-tech researcher and manufacturer based in the US needs a skilled workforce to draw upon; and for the US, its economy and position as a world industrial power. The US has fallen behind compared to other developed nations in relation to what is known as STEM education – training in science, technology, engineering and mathematics. One of Dow's company story paths involves reporting on its engagement with this issue.

The brand journalism strategy and the platforms used

The purpose of any company news strategy is to present the organization effectively, both through the media and direct to members of the public through the use of social and owned media such as branded websites. Much more advanced, and interesting, is to identify an issue or problem and make a genuine contribution to its solution. Dow has done that with the issue of education in STEM subjects. It also has a strategy of enabling scientists to speak for themselves, enabling them to use social media to communicate with the next generation of scientists and engineers, as we'll see in a moment.

So, Dow's brand journalism strategy is geared towards reporting on itself and its activities as a solver of problems and as an educator. Dow handles the very basics of its company news storytelling on its main corporate website (www.dow.com/). Here it provides resources for the media to facilitate their storytelling about Dow, and also allows the general public, and specialist audiences such as investors, to hear what the company has to say for itself. But the focus of the Dow corporate website is actually on it doing its own storytelling. So while there is a media toolkit featuring company information, stills photography galleries, broadcast quality b-roll footage, a sign-up for news alerts, and an extensive Dow News area handling straightforward press releases; the homepage (at the time of writing) featured a number of Solutionism Stories.

For example, click on "Healthier Oil for Healthier Living" and you come to a page which introduces a YouTube video with the text: "Learn how Dow's Omega-9 Oils have helped eliminate over 1 billion pounds of bad fats from the North American diet."[2] The story is presented as the solution to a health problem, and beneath the video is more technical information. You are invited to "view our solutions" and to view or join the conversation around the story. The conversation takes place mainly on Facebook and Twitter, and the posts and tweets are pulled in there. Social share buttons enable you to post Dow's story or your views on the issue under discussion.

Another story is headlined "An Idea So Loud It Doesn't Make a Sound" and states: "As the global community continues to depend on railways for transportation, learn how Dow is implementing technologies to reduce vibration and noise for both passengers and passers-by."[3] With each story the format is to demonstrate what Dow is doing, via an accessible video, to give detail on the products and solutions the company has come up with, and to invite a conversation around the topic.

Here's how Dow tackles social media. At the time of writing, Dow had a neat "circles of influence" tracker that drew conversations on major issues Dow was interested in, such as sustainability and innovation, from across social platforms, and grouped them into hubs or circles so that they could be easily followed. The solutionism conversations and sharing take place on Twitter (twitter.com/DowChemical), Facebook (www.facebook.com/TheDowChemicalCompany), YouTube (www.youtube.com/user/-DowChemicalCompany?feature=watch) and Pinterest (pinterest.com/dow chemical/).

On Facebook, Dow also uses the timeline to feature landmarks in the company's history. It's done in an accessible way, with images and landmarks that a general audience can easily grasp, such as the invention of metal magnesium leading, in 1921, to "Tommy Milton wins the Indianapolis 500 auto race using pistons made with Dow metal magnesium".

There are many more inventions along the way: synthetic rubber, Saran wrap, polystyrene, plastics and the one-shot measles vaccine. In 1968, *Apollo* 8 re-entered the Earth's atmosphere protected by a heat shield made from Dow epoxy resins. Then there are compact discs, a non-sedating anti-histamine drug and disposable nappies. Mentioned along the way is: "Day One of the new Dow occurs on February 6, 2001, as Union Carbide becomes a subsidiary through a merger transaction." We'll look at what's not mentioned there in the next chapter.

Forbes reported that Dow was going beyond using social media simply for brand awareness and was using it "to make science a compelling career choice for millennials and the next generation".[4] It is doing this by partnering with schools, training teachers, sponsoring a large number of students at universities, and by letting scientists speak for themselves in channels such as a Pinterest board called "I'm a solutionist" (pinterest.com/dowchemical/i-m-a-solutionist/). There's an example on the *Brand Journalism* website.

Abby Klanecky, director of social and digital marketing for Dow, told *Forbes*: "What people may not realize is that millennials want to feel they are making a difference in the world. We are here to show them they absolutely can – directly – through choosing a career in science."[5] Dow's story[6] of how it has sponsored 300 sustainability fellows at the University of Michigan, had its scientists go into schools to evangelize about careers in science, designed courses for technicians at local colleges, and trained teachers in STEM subjects was picked up widely by the media.[7] This strategy is clearly a good example of how a brand can get its story across, but it is particularly significant as a demonstration of how brand journalism can become part of the DNA of a company. In achieving this, Dow is turning its scientists into effective storytellers.

Forbes reported: "[Dow's] Marketing [department] finds opportunities for engagement, PR and social media staff train and enable the scientists, and the scientists are actively leading the interactions."[8] Abby Klanecky told *Forbes*:

> Our partners, or universities, or customers want to hear directly from scientists who are engaged in cutting edge research. [Our] scientists care about their place in the world and how they can contribute. This passion comes through when they are allowed their own voice in these conversations. It builds immediate trust and a much more fruitful conversation – for everyone involved. As marketing, we train and then partner with our scientists to use these channels, to have active conversations and interactions with the world around them. It has been revolutionary in how they see the world – sharing and receiving unfiltered, real-time insights.

The social and digital marketing department works with Dow scientists, *Forbes* reports:

> … identifying communities, updating profiles, asking and answering questions, blogging, tweeting, etc. They get them to commit and block off hours each week for these sessions. The key here is to understand that you are helping these folks to fundamentally change how they interact with the world. You won't make that shift in thinking from an online seminar or a memo.

These trained scientists, says Abby, "have real power to tell their stories in a very human way that Dow would not get from a press release".

The result

The impact of the policy as not been quantified, but I believe the evidence of improved perception of the company is clear from the material cited here.

Assignment

Either analyse one brand's company news strategy or develop such a strategy for a brand that doesn't have one. Cover the full process, from establishing the target audiences for your company news and identifying business goals, to developing the brand journalism strategy to deliver those goals and the platforms used.

Notes

1 Dow on its long-term vision: www.dow.com/.
2 "Healthier Oil for Healthier Living", YouTube: youtu.be/Dx6aU4Gz9Ds.

3 "An Idea So Loud It Doesn't Make a Sound": youtu.be/45rS-KdS96w.

4 *Forbes* on Dow's use of social media: www.forbes.com/sites/sap/2012/05/08/dow-chemical-using-social-media-to-educate-and-train-the-next-generation/.

5 Abby Klanecky quoted by *Forbes*: www.forbes.com/sites/sap/2012/05/08/dow-chemical-using-social-media-to-educate-and-train-the-next-generation/.

6 Dow on how it has sponsored 300 sustainability fellows at the University of Michigan: mp125117.cdn.mediaplatform.com/125117/wc/mp/4000/7221/7254/13510/Lobby/default.htm?ref=WebCasterInvitationEmail%22.

7 Dow's sustainability fellows story picked up by the media: www.usnews.com/education/blogs/high-school-notes/2011/06/01/major-corporations-promote-stem-education.

8 *Forbes* on Dow's use of social media: www.forbes.com/sites/sap/2012/05/08/dow-chemical-using-social-media-to-educate-and-train-the-next-generation/.

23 Managing a Crisis

How Dow Chemical Failed to Tackle the PR Crisis over Its Association with the Bhopal Disaster

Goal of this module

Demonstrate how a failure to manage a crisis affects a brand – and how such a crisis could have been averted.

On the website

Find a contrasting crisis management case study, as well as further resources and links to all the sources quoted here.

Dow Chemical

Dow was a major sponsor of the 2012 London Olympics. The most visible manifestation of its contribution should have been Dow's logo on the £7 million fabric wrap it supplied around the Olympic stadium. But Dow decided to drop its branding. Why it had to do so is the story of a failure to manage a public relations crisis. We'll look at what Dow did and what it could have done. But first, here's the essential background.

In 1984, poisonous gas leaked from a pesticide plant in Bhopal, India, killing around 25,000 people and leaving around half a million with some form of health impairment. The plant was owned by the Indian subdivision of the American firm Union Carbide Corporation. Union Carbide was ordered to pay $470 million into a victims' fund set up by the Indian government. Bhopal victims called it a "pittance" – the average pay-out to almost 560,000 survivors who received settlements as of June 2001 was $580. The plant has still not been cleaned up, and hazardous waste left there means further health problems are being caused.

The plant was subsequently sold to another company, and in 2001 Dow Chemical merged with Union Carbide Corporation. Despite there being no direct connection between Dow and the Bhopal gas disaster, in 2012 Indian Olympics officials (instructed by the Indian government) protested that Dow was not a fit sponsor of the games. The International Olympic Committee (IOC) rejected their complaint, saying – as reported by the BBC:

The IOC and London Organising Committee for the Olympic and Paralympic Games were aware of the Bhopal tragedy when discussing the partnership with Dow. Dow had no connection with the Bhopal tragedy. Dow did not have any ownership stake in Union Carbide until 16 years after the accident and 12 years after the $470m compensation agreement was approved by the Indian Supreme Court.[1]

The audience

The general public internationally, politicians, opinion formers, the media.

The business goals (and how the controversy affected them)

The BBC reported:

> The world's second-largest chemical manufacturer became one of the 11 Worldwide Olympic Partners in 2010 in a multi-million pound deal which lasts until 2020. The resulting publicity has been almost entirely negative. Almost every story written about Dow's sponsorship namechecks its association with the 1984 Bhopal chemical leak.[2]

So what was Dow's business goal in sponsoring the Olympics? They were threefold, the BBC reported. One goal was to use the Olympics as a platform to talk about one of Dow's defining stories – what chemistry brings to the world in terms of supplying solutions in the field of water transportation, agriculture and energy – and to bolster its reputation in this field. The Olympic connection was also considered "good for employee morale for a firm focused on business-to-business relationships". Dow's 50,000 global staff were involved in contests to run in the torch relay.

There was also a great deal of business to be won. This was the most important:

> The bottom line from the company board's point of view is, as George Hamilton, vice-president for Dow Olympic operations put it: "Show me the money". During the 10 years of Dow's Olympic sponsorship, he estimates there will be £97bn ($150bn) spent on Olympic Games – building stadiums, venues, athletes' villages, roads and bridges, making a big marketing opportunity for a company ubiquitous in the field.

The *Wall Street Journal* listed Dow's goals as: "wooing top clients, sniffing out Olympics infrastructure deals in advance and attracting employees enticed by the Olympics affiliation".[3] It puts Dow's earnings goals over its ten-year Olympic sponsorship deal as:

Dow has set a target of generating $1 billion in sales through new business tied to the Olympic Games over the sponsorship period and intends to use projects at the 2014 and 2016 Olympics in Russia and Brazil as springboards to expand in those markets.

The brand journalism strategy

Dow wanted the conversation around the Olympics to be about how its science and technology could help solve many of the world's problems. It wasn't. Coverage of Dow's connection with the 2012 Olympics was almost completely negative. A BBC website timeline listed the key points of controversy, with Indian objections to Dow's involvement with the games surfacing in December 2010 and heralding 18 months of pre-games negative publicity.[4] A Special Olympics held with the children of gas victims of Bhopal on the day before the official opening of the London Olympics got wide coverage.[5]

So let's look at what Dow did, and what it should have done, in order to manage the crisis. Look at Dow's Olympics storytelling in its website's Solutionism area and you get a lot about Dow technology and how it is helping the games in so many ways.[6] But there is nothing about the controversy. A search on the Dow corporate website for Bhopal at the time of the controversy turned up few results, the top one dating from 2009 (three years before), entitled "The Dow Chemical Company and the Bhopal Tragedy".[7] It simply outlines Dow's argument that it bears no responsibility.

Dow denied it had any responsibility for compensating the victims of Bhopal, saying the liability rested with the Indian government.[8] The *Holmes Report* on PR crises said that Dow was wrong to do so.[9] Dow, it said, made the common mistake of confusing a court of law with the court of public opinion:

> It should have acknowledged publicly that it understood why people were uncomfortable about its sponsorship because of Bhopal and recognized why they were raising those concerns. Having done that gives you more legitimacy to then put your side of the argument.

Dow's critics said that its attitude over Bhopal made it morally unfit to sponsor the Olympic Games. The *Holmes Report* emphasized that Dow did not answer this point:

> The company made the critical, and typical, mistake of relying on a legal formulation, pointing out that only the courts could determine if it was required to take any more action. This sounds like a lawyer speaking and a legal answer to an emotional question rarely works from a PR perspective. If Dow really felt it had behaved properly in relation to

Bhopal; done all the right things; discharged all its obligations and behaved morally and ethically by the book, then why didn't it say so?

Dow said that its decision to remove its logo from the stadium wrap had been taken months before the protests – a claim which was received with some scepticism. Amnesty International, for example, said that Dow's toxic legacy could poison the Olympics.[10] Dow's Olympic video on a green, sustainable Solutionism theme[11] was parodied to include references to Bhopal.[12] The Motley Fool, an online resource for investors, saw Bhopal as an illustration of how multinational companies "can use legal loopholes to shirk their responsibilities in developing countries". It said: "We believe the story of Bhopal and Dow should be shared with investors to encourage corporate transparency around the world."[13] It argued that while Dow might not have a legal responsibility to act, it had a moral one:

> Dow's management team, employees, and shareholders should capitalize on the unique opportunity the company has as a sponsor of the 2012 Olympic Games. While Dow has no *legal* obligation, Dow has an ethical obligation to right this wrong, a move that will end up benefiting Dow in the long run ... Dow can reverse this public relations nightmare by taking responsibility for Bhopal on the global stage of the Olympics.

Motley Fool urged Dow to clean up the plant and provide healthcare to the victims in a £1 billion programme financed, in part, "through a public stock offering, a move that would boost Dow Chemical's reputation and, most importantly, provide the people of Bhopal with the services and healthcare they desperately need". It could also, said Motley Fool, use the Olympics as a platform from which to launch a Bhopal fundraising campaign:

> Dow should announce the launch of a $10 million campaign to raise awareness for the people of Bhopal, calling attention to its intent to remediate Bhopal during one of the most widely watched events in the world ... Dow's refusal to take responsibility for Bhopal has hit the company's bottom line well beyond the associated legal costs. The unaddressed liability has hurt its reputation, resulted in protests and media backlash, and even limited its ability to invest overseas.

You'll find more on this point on the *Brand Journalism* website.

Other commentators have drawn attention to Dow's commitment, among its Solutionism goals, to providing clean water to the world. Water around Bhopal is seriously polluted. In a post on the "Top 10 Social Media Nightmares", the Inventorspot blog noted:

> While Dow has refused to take direct responsibility, Andrew Liveris, Dow's Chairman and CEO, noted that "lack of clean water is the single

largest cause of disease in the world and more than 4,500 children die each day because of it." He went on to assert that "Dow is committed to creating safer, more sustainable water supplies for communities around the world."[14]

The question is: why haven't they started this work in Bhopal?

The result

It is difficult to quantify the impact that all this negative publicity has had on Dow. Despite the controversy, Dow claimed its Olympic sponsorship worked for the brand. The *Wall Street Journal* reported a Dow executive saying:

> "It was 100 per cent worth it," despite bad publicity around the sponsorship, Amy Millslagle, vice president of Olympic marketing for Dow, said in an interview at the Grosvenor House hotel in London. There, the company has a suite for the games to entertain 1,000 top clients who together comprise about $30 billion in business. Most of those clients – consumer-goods executives, architects, contractors and others – also get tickets to the Olympic Games. "While we had issues, all sponsors have issues," Ms. Millslagle said. "The benefits far outweigh all the issues that come with it."[15]

Assignments

1 Do you believe that Dow did not suffer over the negative publicity? Gather evidence and views on the Dow situation and write your own report.
2 Research a brand that has dealt with a PR crisis and analyse how they overcame it.
3 Identify a troubled brand and develop a crisis management strategy for it. Detail the brand journalism you would create to help it overhaul its image.

Notes

1 BBC report on the International Olympic Committee's views on Dow and Bhopal: www.bbc.co.uk/news/world-asia-india-17054672.
2 BBC report on Dow's sponsorship of the Olympics: www.bbc.co.uk/news/uk-16661107.
3 *Wall Street Journal* on Dow's Olympic sponsorship goals: online.wsj.com/article/SB10000872396390443991704577577370414589082.html.
4 BBC website timeline on the Dow Olympics controversy: www.bbc.co.uk/news/uk-16089139.
5 Report on a Special Olympics held with the children of gas victims of Bhopal: dawn.com/2012/07/26/bhopal-victims-hold-own-olympics-to-protest-dow/.

6 Dow's website Solutionism area: www.dow.com/solutionism/olympic.htm.
7 "The Dow Chemical Company and the Bhopal Tragedy": www.dow.com/sustain ability/debates/bhopal/index.htm.
8 *Daily Telegraph* report on Dow's denial of responsibility for compensating Bhopal victims: www.telegraph.co.uk/sport/olympics/9130231/London-2012-Olympics-Dow-Chemical-puts-blame-for-ongoing-crisis-in-Bhopal-at-Indian-governments-door. html#.
9 *Holmes Report* on PR crises: www.holmesreport.com/featurestories-info/11377/ The-Top-10-Crises-Of-2011.aspx.
10 Amnesty International on Dow and the 2012 Olympics: www.amnesty.org/en/ news/dow-s-toxic-legacy-still-tainting-london2012-2012-07-18.
11 Dow's Olympic video on a green, sustainable Solutionism theme: youtu.be/ szLgQi0GzvI.
12 Parody of Dow's Olympic video on a green, sustainable Solutionism theme: youtu.be/YlYuFH-9RvQ.
13 The Motley Fool on Dow and Bhopal: www.fool.com/investing/general/2012/07/ 27/how-dow-chemical-can-end-the-bhopal-tragedy.aspx.
14 Inventorspot, "Top 10 Social Media Nightmares": inventorspot.com/articles/ top_ten_branded_social_media_nightmares_30874.
15 *Wall Street Journal* quoting Dow: online.wsj.com/article/SB10000872396390 44399170457757737041458908 2.html.

24 Establishing a Personal Brand

How Richard Branson Has Built His Personal Brand

Goal of this module

Demonstrate how a personal brand can be built for a key individual within a brand using owned, social and traditional third-party media outlets.

On the website

Find further resources and information, as well as links to all the sources quoted here.

Richard Branson

Companies are about people. The standing of the boss, and other key individuals, can have either a positive or negative impact upon the standing of the brand. So building a key individual's public profile can benefit the organization too.

In this chapter we'll look at how you as a brand journalist can help to build a personal brand. We'll take as a case study Sir Richard Branson, chairman of the Virgin Group of 400 companies. Not every organization has a Branson, but by looking at how Branson has built his personal brand we can see how to apply those steps to any key member of an organization.

The audience

The audience for any personal brand of a chief executive officer (CEO) or other executive is fourfold: the customers and potential customers of the business; the industry in which the brand operates; the media; and the employees of the brand itself. We can add investors to that list in the case of public companies.

Virgin is a group of disparate businesses, with many markets and niches served. Hence, the customer audience for Richard Branson's personal brand is a very wide one.

The business goals

The aim of personal branding is to enhance the reputation of a key member of your brand's team, and through their improved profile to enhance the image of the brand. Why do you need a personal brand? Richard Branson said that "outstanding brands are built around great people who deliver consistently great customer service every day".[1] You need the communities around your brand to know about the great people who work for it.

Burson-Marsteller conducted a survey about the role of the CEO in the company's perceived image among investors, potential business partners and employees and found that, based on the CEO's reputation:[2]

- 95 per cent decide whether or not to invest in a company
- 93 per cent would recommend a company as a good alliance/merger partner
- 88 per cent recommend the company as a good place in which to work.

In a post entitled "Tomorrow's CEO Must Build an Authentic Personal Brand to Maintain a Competitive Edge", *Spice4Life* magazine said:

> There is no better poster-child for the benefits of CEO branding than Richard Branson; who has single-handedly proven that branded CEOs are a very precious commodity ... While Branson obviously has savvy operational skills, the key to him making the transition from successful businessman to building a multi-billion dollar enterprise has been the development of his CEO brand. Branson is known for his colourful personality and competitive spirit, he is a media darling and is loved by the public.[3]

In his time, Branson has created news by breaking world records, such as completing the first hot-air balloon flight across the Atlantic. He is involved in philanthropic initiatives and appears in commercials for his companies. It's not easy to create such a powerful personal brand, even if you are Richard Branson. Branson explained: "Branding demands commitment; commitment to continual re-invention; striking chords with people to stir their emotions; and commitment to imagination. It is easy to be cynical about such things, much harder to be successful."[4]

Your brand is what people think of you, what they say about you when you are not there. It's not your job title; that's just a role. So a successful personal brand has to be built on the reality of the person, not just their status in the company, industry or whatever. The individual has to take the lead in their brand-building; but you can guide them in what to do and support them. If you have to tweet on behalf of the CEO or blog for them, you really need to understand what they are about – and what the brand is about – and how to present them to their best advantage.

To help build a personal brand for a CEO or other executive, you have to decide what they want to be known for, and the key to presenting that is in the description they use of themselves. The person being branded must decide: what do I want to be known for? Here's how Richard Branson describes himself on Twitter (twitter.com/richardbranson): "Tie-loathing adventurer and thrill seeker, who believes in turning ideas into reality. Otherwise known as Dr Yes at @virgin!"

The brand journalism strategy and the platforms used

The channels through which a personal brand can be developed include social media, traditional media, public relations activities, philanthropy, books, speaking engagements and the way in which they treat their employees. Building a personal brand is not just about publicity – it involves activity in all the channels listed.

So, looking at Richard Branson: he is highly active on social media, and is said to write all his tweets and status updates himself, mixing posts about his businesses with the causes he supports, the issues that concern him, his family life, and simply sharing bits of fun. He is also highly active in traditional media, appearing as the spokesman for whichever of the 400-odd Virgin companies is in the news – this despite the fact that he is not involved in the day-to-day running of any of them. As for books, he has written an autobiography called *Like a Virgin: Secrets They Won't Teach You at Business School*, which is promoted on his Facebook page and elsewhere. He has a philanthropic organization called Virgin Unite, and a mentoring programme to help young entrepreneurs called Virgin Young Pioneers (www. virginmediapioneers.com/).

But many CEOs and other executives haven't even taken the first step into social media. Six Pixels of Separation reported: "Less than 30 per cent of the Fortune 500's top executives have (at least) one profile within a social media channel and the vast majority have none."[5] Should CEOs be busy on social media or are they legitimately too busy running their companies? The Branson case study would suggest that they can and should, but not everyone agrees (there's discussion on this point on the *Brand Journalism* website).

Let's look at the platforms Branson uses. As we do, I'll refer to a story that broke while I was researching this chapter: Virgin Trains' loss of a major rail contract in the UK to a rival, FirstGroup. Richard's blog (www. virgin.com/richard-branson) is at the heart of Branson's social sharing. Material here is pushed out to the social platforms he has a presence on. The blog addresses several audiences: the industries he works in, the media, his staff and customers. The Virgin Trains story was addressed through two posts. One, a thank you to staff,[6] the other an official statement for media and others.[7] On Facebook (www.facebook.com/RichardBranson), where Branson has 250,000 likes, that official statement is prefaced with this comment: "Fantastic job by all staff at +Virgin Trains. Proud of what's been achieved in past 15 years. Read my full statement here: virg.in/vt." There was also a picture of Branson with train staff.

Other Facebook posts – drawn from his blog in the main – are a mix of information about his companies and causes, such as this status update on climate change: "Do you believe in climate change? A leading sceptic has changed his mind – here's why: virg.in/ccr-."[8] There is also less serious stuff: "Watch Kira the dog swimming with wild dolphins. Perhaps we should invite Kira along next time we swim with whale sharks!"[9] And family life is present. When he once forgot his passport, Branson ran a competition to give a free holiday to one of those who tweeted an image of themselves holding their passport and using the #dontforgetyour hashtag.[10]

On Twitter (twitter.com/richardbranson), where Branson has 2.4 million followers, he has a promoted tweet anchored to the top of his page which invites interaction: "If you've got a question then ask away using the #askrichard hashtag, keep them coming!" On the trains story, Branson kept up a dialogue as reactions built to the story during the day. So tweets included:

- "We were planning no redundancies whatsoever. Hope FirstGroup keep all our staff & keep improving service for customers: virg.in/vt."
- "If you outbid somebody at auction you are smart if you do it by £1, less smart if by £1m & pretty worrying if by £750m! virg.in/vt."
- "The last 2 times UK government turned a Virgin bid down the companies they accepted both went bust: virg.in/vt."

Just as an aside, FirstGroup didn't have a Twitter account for the company, just for areas such as careers. The #firstgroup hashtag had been used for overwhelmingly negative comments. Nor was the story on their corporate website or in the media area (www.firstgroup.com/corporate/media/). Under "Latest news", the most recent story was unrelated and a week old.

On Google+ (plus.google.com/113544226688149802325/posts), where 2.8 million have Branson in their circles, the same feed is used as for Facebook. The Virgin Trains announcement received 92 comments in the first four hours, mostly positive and favouring Virgin over FirstGroup. On YouTube (www.youtube.com/user/richardbranson), where Virgin videos had 860,000 views, the trains story didn't feature. On the day, the top featured video was one posted four weeks before of Richard wishing Nelson Mandela a happy 94th birthday. Other videos included one of a record-breaking kite-surf across the English Channel and an interview on the 35th anniversary of the release of the Sex Pistols' "God Save the Queen" on Virgin records.[11] The Ask Richard featured playlist has short videos of him answering questions such as: how do you manage your time and do you get stressed?[12] The absence of a video on the trains story was a rare miss – Branson could easily have posted a video version of his statement.

Branson also uses LinkedIn, where his posts are about business and entrepreneurship, and build his status as a thought leader.[13] One post, written as I researched this chapter, was on the subject of personal branding and asked: "Why aren't more business leaders online?"[14]

The result

Let's look particularly at the trains story because it demonstrates how a chief executive with a powerful personal brand can aid the overall brand. Virgin, through Branson, led the news agenda. Most headlines began "Virgin loses ... ". Only the *Financial Times*'s headline began "FirstGroup wins ... ".

The top line on bulletin stories during the day on the BBC was Branson's annoyance that he had lost the contract, and his case that it was a worse deal for the government and passengers. FirstGroup, which had a case to make that they were promising faster and more frequent trains and lower fares, were not interviewed, while Branson was.

While Branson's personal brand and use of social media gave media the material they needed, and a recognizable figure to put on bulletins, First-Group did not have the story on their corporate site (not even in the media section), did not have a Twitter account, and failed to contribute to the story as it unfolded. Indeed, searches for FirstGroup on both Twitter and Face-book on the day of the story brought up a Dubai-based property company of the same name.

Away from the trains story, Richard Branson's personal brand clearly has great power, and is a huge asset for his companies.

Assignments

1 Think further about the subject of personal branding. Could Branson's personal brand be too strong for Virgin? With him gone, would the companies be weakened? How have companies that have lost a high-profile leader fared once that person left? What happened to Apple's brand after Steve Jobs's passing?
2 Draw up a personal branding strategy for an individual with whom you work.

Notes

1 Richard Branson quoted in *Wealthy Matters*: wealthymatters.com/2012/08/09/learning-from-sir-richard-branson/.
2 Burston-Marsteller survey on CEOs' impact upon company image: issuu.com/burson-marsteller-emea/docs/b-m_info_ceo_study_engl_final.
3 *Spice4Life* magazine on brand image: www.spice4life.co.za/content/tomorrows-ceo-must-build-authentic-personal-brand-maintain-competitive-edge.
4 Richard Branson quoted in *Wealthy Matters*: wealthymatters.com/2012/08/09/learning-from-sir-richard-branson/.

5 Six Pixels of Separation on CEOs and social media: www.twistimage.com/blog/archives/grow-your-company-or-be-active-on-social-media/.

6 Virgin Trains story, "Thank-you to staff": www.virgin.com/richard-branson/blog/dear-colleagues.

7 Virgin Trains story, official statement for media and others: www.virgin.com/richard-branson/blog/on-virgin-trains.

8 Branson post on climate change: virg.in/ccr.

9 Branson post, "Watch Kira the dog swimming with wild dolphins": virg.in/dsd.

10 Branson post on losing passport: www.virgin.com/travel/news/dont-forget-your-passport.

11 Virgin YouTube video on 35th anniversary of the release of the Sex Pistols' "God Save the Queen" on Virgin records: youtu.be/LvuCGqkbZ1M.

12 Branson's "Ask Richard" feature: www.youtube.com/watch?v=390mu3k7N00&feature=channel.

13 Branson on LinkedIn: www.linkedin.com/profile/view?id=204068115&authType=name&authToken=mlJ9&goback=%2Empd2_*1_*1_%2F20121019130632*5204068115*5why*5aren*5t*5more*5business*5leaders*5online.

14 Branson on LinkedIn on "Why aren't more business leaders online?": www.linkedin.com/today/post/article/20121019130632–204068115-why-aren-t-more-business-leaders-online?trk=mp-details-rr-rmpost.

Part IV

Measuring the Results of Your Brand Journalism Strategy

This final section of *Brand Journalism* looks at monitoring your performance and measuring what you have achieved through your brand journalism strategy. In the following chapters we cover:

- monitoring your performance on social media and analysing your success in terms of business goals and brand journalism strategy
- using Google Analytics to examine the performance of your branded websites and to improve your content
- understanding search engine optimization and the growing importance of good content, and authoritative writers, in earning a brand good search engine rankings.

25 Social Media Monitoring and Analytics Tools

Goals of this module

In this chapter we will answer these three questions:

- What should you be monitoring and analysing on each of the main social platforms that you use for your brand journalism?
- What tools should you use to do that?
- How can you measure your success?

A number of the tools we look at are also effective in monitoring mentions of your brand more generally – on blogs and websites.

On the website

Find links to tutorials on the monitoring and analytics tools discussed, as well as videos and links to all the resources mentioned here.

There is no shortage of data available to you. Social platforms such as Facebook and YouTube, and both free and paid-for social media dashboards, will tell you a great deal about who interacts with you and how. In fact, it's easy to get so overwhelmed with data that you are unable to make sense of it. You must decide what measurements are significant for each of the platforms you are using.

It's important, when looking at the data monitoring and analytics tools given to you, to relate what you are being told to your brand journalism strategy and, hence, to whether you are meeting your business goals. One of those goals may well be to build brand awareness so that the number of likes, fans and comments on Facebook, and of followers and re-tweets on Twitter, can in itself fulfil one of your key goals. But if your goal is thought leadership, you need to consider data in this context. The same applies to lead generation, becoming a trusted news source, improving customer service or any other goal.

We'll run through the main social media platforms we discussed using in Chapters 8 and 9, and we'll identify which measurements are valuable to you, depending on your business goals. We covered establishing business goals in Chapter 3. As ever with this learning programme, you'll find it most valuable if you are able to apply what we cover to a real-life brand journalism operation or to a brand-specific project that you are working on.

We need to remember that social media engagement is often not an end in itself – although it is an important way of engaging with our community. For many brands, social media engagement is just the first contact point in what we hope will be a progressively deeper relationship with our brand. It's about generating leads and converting those leads into customers. So while total number of Twitter followers, Facebook fans, YouTube subscribers and so on is one measure of success, what is often as important for our business goals is how many of those contacts are converted into visitors to our website, subscribers to our email bulletin, sharers of our content and, ultimately, customers or supporters.

In deciding which social media platforms work for you, the first task is to make sure that you fish where the fish are: go where your community hangs out. If you don't know where that is, it makes sense to experiment on a wide range of platforms, analyse the responses you get and then direct your resources where you have identified communities that want to engage with you. The tools provided by social media platforms can only tell you how you are doing on those platforms. They don't tell you how much traffic they are pushing to your branded websites and blogs. For that we need tools such as Google Analytics, which we look at in the next chapter.

Twitter

What you should be monitoring on Twitter

Monitor:

- tweets and conversations about your company
- tweets about your rivals
- tweets about your industry
- requests for help or information
- feedback
- positive and negative comments
- the sentiment around your brand.

One important purpose in monitoring is to identify your most important followers and the influencers in your industry. These are the people who tweet the most about your brand/your industry, and have the largest number of followers. They are key influencers, and have the power to help or hinder your brand journalism strategy and, hence, your business goals. If one of your goals is thought leadership, then such information helps you to identify the elite you need to be interacting with and impressing with your knowledge.

To keep in the loop, you should set up keyword searches for each of the keywords that will bring up the important conversations that you need to follow. Use a tool that lets you save keyword searches as a live stream.

The tools to use (including those that help you to manage all of your social media accounts)

Unlike Facebook, YouTube and others, Twitter doesn't have inbuilt monitoring and analytics tools. Social media dashboards such as Hootsuite (hootsuite.com/) or Tweetdeck (www.tweetdeck.com/) can assist you in listening, engaging, contributing and learning. They enable us to pull all our social presences, and different elements within each of those presences, together on one dashboard and to display them alongside each other, typically as a series of columns, in one browser.

There are also sophisticated paid-for social media management tools such as Sprout Social (sproutsocial.com/) that are designed to let a social media manager oversee all accounts in one place and assign work on them to individuals and groups, hence coordinating the implementation of a social media strategy. Social Sprout offers a 30-day free trial of its services. It says this about what it offers: "You can organize individuals into teams large or small, giving some teams or individuals access to some social media accounts, but not to others. You can also monitor all your incoming contact from customers and followers, then assign individual tweets or other tasks to people in your organization, such as replies to certain customers."

Sprout Social offers this advice on management and coordination:

> The most common problem with managing a team responsible for social media promotions is coordinating who's publishing what – and when. Sometimes team members will publish on top of each other, and sometimes important updates will go unpublished because someone thought someone else was responsible for making it happen.

You'll find a user's assessment of the service on the *Brand Journalism* website.

Hootsuite or Tweetdeck are probably all that individuals and small teams will need. With them you can, for example, have your Twitter stream present, as well as – in a series of separate columns – more focused information streams such as your own tweets, tweets that mention you, re-tweets of your tweets, tweets from specified groups of your Twitter contacts and so on. If you are a brand journalist responsible for several Twitter accounts relating to different aspects of your employer's business or for a range of different clients, you can group all of these accounts together on a social media dashboard. You can also have your Facebook, LinkedIn, Foursquare, some other accounts and really simple syndication (RSS) feeds visible, depending on the tool you are using and whether you are using the free or premium versions. These social media dashboards make posting easier too – they allow us to direct a particular post to one, some or all of our platforms at once.

Social media dashboards also allow you to schedule your tweets so that when you have planned events in your schedule, you can write and schedule tweets about them in advance. They also enable you to monitor mentions of your brand and your rivals from across the web. Dedicated automated posting devices such as Buffer (bufferapp.com) let you publish your non-time-sensitive tweets at appropriate times and intervals.

You can use the social media dashboards discussed above or social media monitoring tools such as Crowdbooster (crowdbooster.com/) to alert you to important follows and connections. Crowdbooster measures the performance of your tweets, advises you when to tweet for best results, and gives you a weekly analysis graph of your most successful tweets. It also shows you the growth in followers, who your most influential followers are, as well as your top re-tweeters. Such services can tell you when to tweet for maximum impact and identify influential individuals you should follow back.

On Twitter itself, you can use Twitter searches to regularly check up on discussions in your areas of interest. Search on Twitter is in real time. You can save important search terms so that you can easily re-run the searches whenever necessary. Conversocial (www.conversocial.com/) allows you to manage your Twitter account by alerting you to communications from your followers, using terms and parameters you have set and directing them to the person who can deal with them. So you can use such a tool to sift the tweets you get, many of which will be routine, and to identify the important ones that need to be dealt with swiftly and, perhaps, by a senior person.

Tools such as Social Mention (www.socialmention.com/) facilitate real-time search and identify real-time buzz around a topic. Social Mention enables search across one, several or all main social platforms, and identifies how many people are talking about a subject, the sentiment associated with those mentions, the keywords employed, the main people mentioning the topic, the hashtags and the platforms used. You can set up RSS feeds and email alerts for the terms you need to monitor regularly.

Tools such as Topsy's (topsy.com/) pro version let users see the historical context of a topic or brand (both yours and a competitor's), identify the most influential tweeters and tweets, and index tweets by various time-frames – from within the last year down to the last hour, or within a specific date range. Users can analyse topics by location and see what sentiment was attached to the topic by measuring positive or negative comments.

Mashable also recommends Spredfast (spredfast.com/) "for agencies managing social media for several companies", and Engage121 (www.engage121.com/) "for franchise companies looking to maintain consistent messaging while giving local branches a hand in social media strategy".[1]

How to measure your success

These are the essential measurements to use:

- How many followers do you have compared to your competitors?
- How fast is your following growing?
- How many times are you re-tweeted (a measure of your influence)?
- How many hashtags are used to re-tweet or comment on your tweets (an indication of the buzz around your brand)?
- What are the positive and negative comments (a measure of the sentiment towards your brand)?

You should monitor these analytics in relation to particular brand journalism projects that you run, see how successful these projects are comparatively, identify those that really resonate with your community, and then refine your brand journalism to deliver more of what people want. You can also identify points at which your brand is both succeeding and failing to get its message across, and react accordingly.

Facebook

Things to monitor on Facebook

Monitor:

- growth of your fan base
- the level of "talking about this"
- comments – look for spikes in comments around particular content
- the level of "likes" – look for spikes
- reach
- viral reach
- your level of subscribers (if you allow subscribing www.facebook.com/about/subscribe and unsubscribes – look for spikes and see whether particular posts caused them).

Your monitoring should be a mix of assessing the overall level of "likes", "talking about this" and so on, and a detailed examination of individual status updates and how successful they were.

Using Facebook Insights

Facebook Insights gives you very detailed information on how your Facebook presence is performing. Insights provides:

- your page views and number of unique visitors
- your "likes" by gender, age and location

- your demographic reach, again by gender, age and location, and how users found you: through organic search (they put a term into a search engine), by paid means such as an advert or sponsored story, or by viral means, which involves a friend of theirs interacting with your page in some way
- your "talking about this" total.

"Talking about this" is a key metric because it shows exactly how many among your Facebook community have actually engaged with you recently. The full list of ways in which people can be reached virally, and the actions of individuals that go to make up your "talking about this", is down to EdgeRank, the algorithm Facebook uses to assess your performance. Steve Goldner outlines the actions that make up a "talking about this score", which he defines as "the unique users that have interacted with the brand on Facebook".[2] This includes:

- liking a page
- posting on the page wall
- liking a post
- commenting on a post
- sharing a post
- answering a question
- RSVPing to a page's event
- mentioning the page in a post
- tagging the page in a photo
- checking in at a place
- sharing a check-in deal
- liking a check-in deal
- writing a recommendation.

He says: "All of these activities are very important. When a Facebook user 'talks about this' (the brand), the action shows up as a post on their friends' news feed. Thus the action and exposure of the brand is shared ... the brand is shared with a larger audience." With all the analytics that Facebook gives, you can drill down to a number of categories that further refine the data – so you can see how many "likes" come from your posted videos, for example, or how much of your reach is down to stories posted by others on your page. Here, from Social Media Today, is how EdgeRank works:

> Facebook wants users to be engaged, so EdgeRank is a critical aspect of their business. The EdgeRank factors are:

- Affinity – how often you interact with others (be it visiting a friend's profile or commenting on a page's picture).
- Edge Weight – the type of content it is. A few types are: Photos, Videos, Status, Place Check-ins, becoming friends with someone, liking a page,

changing your profile picture, etc. Keep in mind, there are general rules, but everyone's Edge Weight is different and Facebook has carte blanche to tweak things at will

- Recency – the older something is, the less likely you are to see it.[3]

You can check your EdgeRank rating here: edgerankchecker.com/.

Because Facebook wants users – including brands – to engage on the platform, rather than posting material to it from an external application programming interface (API) such as a social media management tool, it downgrades content that is generated in this way. Social Media Today estimates that using an external application to post on Facebook decreases engagement by an average of 80 per cent because Facebook penalizes content delivered to it in this way.[4]

The evidence is clear – if you want to use Facebook effectively as a brand journalist, you have to be actively engaging on it.

How to measure your success on Facebook

These are some of the essential measurements to use:

- How many fans do you have compared to your rivals?
- How many likes do you have compared to your competitors?
- How fast are your likes growing?
- What is your "talking about this" score compared to your competitors?
- How you are engaging with your brand's chosen demographic?

YouTube

Things to monitor on YouTube

Monitor:

- number of times your videos have been watched
- number of subscribers
- engagement – likes, dislikes, comments, shares, favourites added, favourites removed
- your top-performing videos and the number of views they received
- demographics – locations, age and gender of viewers
- discovery, including top playback locations (whether on a YouTube page, a mobile device or embedded in another site)
- top traffic sources (whether the video was found via YouTube search, Google search, as a YouTube suggested video, on an embedded player, mobile apps or an external website)
- keyword searches – the search terms used to find your videos.

Using YouTube's analytics tool

YouTube's analytics tool gives you the above information for the time period you specify.[5] It can also analyse audience retention for a given video and show when people stop watching. That's a useful guide, when compared to the average, of when a video has been more or less interesting than usual.

You can also learn more about your YouTube channel with Google Analytics, which we cover in the next chapter.[6]

How to measure your success

You can't make comparisons with rival brands using YouTube Analytics other than by observing publicly available information such as subscriber numbers, but you can measure the improvement in your own performance. These are some of the essential measurements to use:

- What is the growth in viewing figures for your videos?
- How many subscribers do you have compared to your rivals?
- How are you succeeding in reaching your target audience in terms of age, gender and location?
- What is happening to your level of engagement according to the various measures of engagement you have available?

Using Google Analytics, you can track how much traffic your YouTube videos are driving to your website or affecting the time visitors spend on your site. If your goal is to generate sales, then you can measure sales generated by YouTube traffic.

Deluxe for Business has this suggestion if your goal is more nebulous, such as building your brand image: "You may want to conduct some sort of market research before and after a YouTube campaign to gauge what customers think of your brand and how they heard about it."[7]

Google+

As we mentioned when we discussed Google+ in Chapter 8, this platform's performance as a social network is nowhere near that of the big operators. There is, however, one very important reason for seeing Google+ as central to your brand's web presence. It has to do with the Google profile you set up when you create a Google+ page, with a Google algorithm called AuthorRank, and with its impact upon your brand's ranking in search results. Google has integrated Google+ and other social platforms in Google Analytics in an area it calls Social Reports. We look at that in the next chapter.

Meanwhile, here is what you can learn on Google+ itself.

Things to monitor on Google+

Monitor:

- what people are saying about your brand
- who is sharing and re-sharing your content and who is influential
- +1s of your pages and re-shares of your pages via Google+ (do that on Google Analytics)
- user demographics.

Using Google+'s own analytics

Here are key points from Google's own explanation of how to use its Google+ analytics.

Google+ search

Google says: "Search on Google+ can help you as much as it helps your customers. You can search keywords, names or anything else, and use your search results to understand better what people are saying about your brand, reward superfans with rebate coupons or even jump in to help resolve customer service issues."[8]

Ripples

Google says: "Ripples let you see your posts spread across Google+, who's sharing and resharing your content and whose opinions matter. Use it to identify influencers and add them to a circle, or see how communities are formed around your content."

At the time of writing, Google was planning to provide information on "who's interacting with your page and how; your users' demographics; and info about their social activities like +1's, shares and comments."

Measuring your success on Google+

Here are some of the key measures of your brand's performance:

- What is the level of positive comments about your brand?
- What is the growth in interaction with your content?
- How successful are you in reaching your brand's chosen demographic?

LinkedIn

LinkedIn has analytics on its company pages[9] and on its groups, available to those who run them.[10]

Things to monitor on company pages[11]

Monitor:

- who is visiting your company profile
- who is following your page, as well as their industry, company and function (position)
- visitors to your careers tab
- visitors to products and services tab
- promotional banners; and
- which visitors make contact with your employees.

Things to monitor on Groups

Monitor:

- demographics
- growth in group over time
- activity levels.

Using LinkedIn's analytics

Hubspot says:

> The Demographics tab is the most thorough tab. It uses your members' LinkedIn profile information to give you a deep dive into their overall career level, job function, location, and industry. Use this information to figure out what type of members your group attracts. Are you bringing in the right people for your business? Can you use this data to supplement your buyer personas?[12]

We covered buyer personas in Chapter 2.

Group growth shows whether the content you are creating is working. Hubspot asks:

> Is the content you're providing attracting more members to your group, growing your LinkedIn reach? The Growth tab lets you know how many members you've added per day as well as your total member growth over time. You can also dig into your week-over-week growth. The Activity tab offers this: "Are people discussing content and commenting more over time? Find out through the Activity tab."

How to measure your success

Among the measures you can use on company pages are:

- the increase in follows for your company page
- the demographics on those follows and how relevant they are to your brand and its business goals

- the increase in visits to features such as your products and services tabs and how many visitors do business with you.

Among the measures you can use on groups are the:

- growth in reach of your group
- growth in engagement among group members
- growth in activity surrounding your content.

Pinterest

Traditional monitoring tools work with text rather than images, so Pinterest and other visual platforms present a challenge.

Things to monitor on Pinterest

Monitor:

- Who are your influential pinners?
- Which pins are trending?
- Which users are most engaged?
- Which boards are most viral?
- Which pins drive e-commerce?
- How do you compare with your competition?

Tools to use to monitor Pinterest

Pinterest is a relatively new platform and at the time of writing there are no analytics available on the platform itself, but there are a number of external analytics providers.[13] None offers comprehensive analytics, but the following all offer key parts of the analytics jigsaw.

Curalate (www.curalate.com/) can find and match images to your brand and then track where they are seen, shared and talked about. It lets you discover and join in those conversations. Curalate says:

> Use Curalate's service for enterprise-level Pinterest analytics. Your brand will learn about its most engaged followers and be able to join the conversation by accessing Curalate's consolidated communication tab. You'll be able to strategize existing Pinterest campaigns and future content by identifying trends of a viral nature.

Reachli (www.reachli.com/landing) offers brands the ability to launch "campaigns" by linking your pins to analytics tools, which measure clicks and reach. Reachli says you can compare selected campaigns against one another, and measure engagement over time: "It's a helpful way to judge the impact of certain types of content."[14]

Repinly (www.repinly.com) lets you "research the habits and trending content around top pinners and discover the type of content that's trending right now." Compare with Pinfluencer (www.pinfluencer.com), which enables brands to track its most influential pinners and most engaged users, and compare what it calls Pinfluence against competitor brands. It tracks the level of repins of your content against the competitors you specify, the level of engagement with your brand, influential pinners, and the impact of boards and pins. For ecommerce brands, it can track the process from pin to purchase.

How to measure your success on Pinterest

Among key measures of success, depending on your brand's business goals are:

- the increase in reach of your pins and boards
- the increase in level of engagement with your brand via pins and boards
- levels of purchase resulting from individual pins and boards.

Instagram

Things to monitor on Instagram

Monitor:

- follower growth
- engagement: likes, comments and most engaged followers
- most popular photos – so that you can give people what they want
- posts featuring your products and those of rivals
- the use of hashtags featuring your brand or products.

Tools to use to monitor Instagram

Instagram's purchase by Facebook is likely to lead to the inclusion of analytics for it in Facebook Insights. Currently, in the absence of analytics on Instagram itself, Statigram and Nitrogram are the best tools.

Statigram (statigr.am/tag/analytics) covers all of the above, while keeping a record of how often you post, at what times, and the filters and tags you use. Its optimization analytics tell you the best times to post, average photo lifespan (when engagement ends) and the filters that are the most popular. It also tells you how popular the tags you use are and lists the most popular tags on Instagram. Using popular tags (and posting photographs in the most popular categories) improves engagement. Statigram analyses your community in terms of "follows" – which are reciprocal, who you don't follow back and who doesn't follow you back.

Nitrogram (nitrogr.am/) offers brands a way to keep track of what people are capturing and sharing about them. The Next Web reports that Nitrogram allows you to monitor official brand accounts, as well as specific employees or celebrities who are endorsing your (or a rival's) products by using its "track a new term" facility:

> Each account then brings up data analysis ... such as the number of photos that have been taken and the number of people who have liked or commented on it, as well as the number of people who have been 'reached' through the uploads collectively ... Nitrogram pulls in the last 3,000 photographs uploaded to Instagram on any given account or trend ... On top of this is the ability to analyse hashtags ... This is particularly useful for seeing what your customers are uploading about your product. In our testing we searched for #converse and found that, well, a lot of people really love multi-coloured Converse All Stars.[15]

How to measure your success on Instagram

Among key measures of success are the:

- increase in follows for your brand's account
- level of likes for the pictures you post
- level of increase in posts featuring your products.

Flickr

Things to monitor on Flickr

Monitor:

- how many views each of your photographs attracts
- your most popular images
- reuse of your images
- search terms used to find your images
- groups sharing photos relevant to your brand.

Tools for monitoring Flickr

You have to activate analytics on Flickr by clicking on stats and confirming that you want them. Their frequently asked questions (FAQs) on the service explain that their stats:

... are designed to give you insight into the ways that people are finding your photos. There are stats available for people surfing on Flickr itself – where the referrer is flickr.com – and stats about people coming from other websites. We can show you the sorts of things people search for on search engines where your photos turn up, and tell you how many views your photos have.[16]

The Blog Studio gives this rundown on what Flickr analytics can tell you:

The most useful section of the Flickr analytic report is the Referrers section. Here you can see how people found your images, right down to the individual web pages and search terms they've used. Examining the search terms will give you more ideas on how to better tag your photos so more people will find them, by adding these search terms to the tags when you add new images. Since you can see the places where your work is appearing on the web, you can drop by those pages and leave a comment. Let the people who've used your work know that you're flattered they picked your photo, and leave your URL to help get the word out. It's a method of expanding your circle of online contacts without being a spammer.[17]

Flickr only offers analytics for the past 28 days and suggests that you search for external apps in the Flickr App Garden if you want more historic information.[18] One such app is Statsr. The premium version of Statsr (statsr.net) offers more extensive Flickr analytics, including URLs and geo-locations of those who look at your images, information on groups whom you are a member of, and stats on any sets and collections of pictures that you create.

How to measure your success on Flickr

Among the key measures of success are:

- growth in views of your images
- positive feedback within groups set up by you or others that are relevant to your brand
- the level of searches using the keywords relevant to your brand that people are employing to find your photographs.

Foursquare

Things to monitor on Foursquare

Foursquare offers analytics[19] to brands which have claimed locations via a merchant dashboard.[20] The stats they give you include:

- total daily check-ins over time
- your most recent visitors
- your most frequent visitors
- gender breakdown of your customers
- Foursquare activity, such as number of friends, mayorships and followers
- where customers come from
- what time of day people check in
- the kind of tips people leave at your venues
- the portion of your venue's Foursquare check-ins that are broadcast to Twitter and Facebook.

As Social Report notes, you can receive daily email alerts containing a summary of all check-ins, tips and new users across your venues, and export your Foursquare analytics and general data to Excel.[21] They add: "For managers of chains and multiple venues, you will be able to choose how to view your data – individually by venue, by certain venue groups, or for all venues."

How to measure your success on Foursquare

Among the key measures of success are:

- the ratio between Foursquare activity such as check-in rates and increased business
- how effective you are in attracting your target demographic, as reflected by check-ins and other stats
- the level of positive feedback in recommendations left at your venues
- growth in the number of your venue's Foursquare check-ins that are broadcast to Twitter and Facebook.

Assignment

1 Set up a comprehensive monitoring and analytics strategy for your brand. Road test the services discussed here and decide on the combination that best serves the needs of your brand
2 Conduct monitoring over an extended period and record how it enables you to improve your content, develop your brand journalism strategy and move closer to your business goals.

Notes

1 *Mashable*'s social media management recommendations: mashable.com/2010/10/21/social-media-management-tools/.
2 Steve Goldner on "talking about this" scores: www.econtentmag.com/authors/AboutAuthor.aspx?AuthorID=.

3 Social Media Today on how EdgeRank works: socialmediatoday.com/bigsea/
370308/writing-effective-facebook-posts.

4 Social Media Today on how Facebook penalizes posts from external applications:
socialmediatoday.com/bigsea/370308/writing-effective-facebook-posts.

5 What YouTube's analytics tool does: www.blueglass.com/blog/video-
optimization-and-analytics-a-closer-look-at-youtube-insight/.

6 YouTube and Google Analytics: ytbizblog.blogspot.co.uk/2009/05/google-
analytics-now-providing-data-on.html.

7 Using Google Analytics with YouTube: www.deluxeforbusiness.com/learning-
center/article/372/top_5_metrics_for_measuring_youtube_success?.

8 Google on Google+ search: www.google.com/+/business/measure.html.

9 LinkedIn analytics on company pages: learn.linkedin.com/company-pages.

10 LinkedIn analytics on groups: blog.hubspot.com/blog/tabid/6307/bid/28736/
LinkedIn-Launches-Analytics-Tool-for-Groups.aspx.

11 Things to monitor on company pages: kherize5.com/linkedin-launches-new-
analytics-for-company-pages/.

12 LinkedIn analytics on groups: blog.hubspot.com/blog/tabid/6307/bid/28736/
LinkedIn-Launches-Analytics-Tool-for-Groups.aspx.

13 *Mashable* on Pinterest analytics tools: mashable.com/2012/09/21/pinterest-
analytics-tools/.

14 Reachli on its services: www.reachli.com/landing.

15 The Next Web on Nitrogram: thenextweb.com/socialmedia/2012/10/04/nitrogram-
allows-brands-to-take-instagram-analytics-and-marketing-campaigns-to-the-next-level/.

16 Flickr FAQs: www.flickr.com/help/stats/.

17 The Blog Studio on Flickr analytics: www.theblogstudio.com/2011/08/making-the-
most-of-flickr-promoting-your-brand-your-business-and-yourself/.

18 Flickr App Garden: www.flickr.com/services/apps/search/?q=stats.

19 What Foursquare analytics offer: support.foursquare.com/entries/196050-what-
are-analytics.

20 Foursquare merchant dashboard: support.foursquare.com/entries/21725352-the-
merchant-dashboard-viewing-your-free-data-and-analytics.

21 Social Report on Foursquare analytics: support.socialreport.com/entries/
21030668-foursquare-venue-analytics-are-here.

26 Monitoring and Analysing Your Branded Websites, Blogs and Email Bulletins

Goals of this module

In this module we concentrate on Google Analytics as a tool for examining and improving the performance of our branded websites and blogs.

Our specific goals are:

- Analyse where the traffic to our branded websites originates: organic search, referrals and direct.
- Identify what we need to monitor on our branded websites and blogs.
- Track how visitors use our websites.
- Identify successful and unsuccessful content.
- See how our websites help us to meet our business goals.

We also look at analysing the performance of blogs and email newsletters.

On the website

Find links to primers on using Google Analytics and other tools, essential updates, videos and other supporting material on what we cover here, as well as links to all the resources discussed.

In the last chapter we looked at how to monitor and analyse our performance on social platforms, mostly using tools that those platforms provide. As we saw, such analysis can tell us a lot, but it doesn't give us anything like the full picture. In the main, our goal in using social platforms is to reach and begin to build a relationship with potential customers/clients/supporters of our cause, or whatever. We hope to draw those with whom we connect back to our branded online presences in order to build our relationship with them. So we need analytics to tell us how successful we are, on the social platforms we use, in driving traffic back to our websites and blogs.

Once we have them on our brand sites, we need to track how visitors behave on them, to analyse the performance of the content we publish there, to learn how to improve our content, and to use what we discover to set goals for our brand journalism. We looked at a range of business goals in

Chapter 3. Sometimes our goal is to increase brand awareness, so getting additional traffic to our websites can in itself fulfil one of our key goals. But most brands want more. A business will want to identify leads and potential paying customers; a charity will want to increase support and donations.

Monitoring and analysing our performance is vital. If you are joining an established brand journalism department you will probably find that the company has a system of monitoring in place. It may use Google Analytics in either the free (www.google.co.uk/analytics) or premium (www.google.co.uk/analytics/premium) versions. It may well be that there are dedicated people, or departments, that work on your search engine optimization (SEO) and analyse your site performance, in which case what we cover here is already taken care of. But what follows is still valuable because it shows you what they are doing – how they are measuring and why they will reach conclusions such as that your brand journalism is failing in some important way.

If you are establishing a brand journalism department, or have been hired as a sole content creator, you'll need to get analytics in place. Without analytics you can't demonstrate your success to the various stakeholders. If you need a primer in installing and using Google Analytics, you'll find some useful links on the *Brand Journalism* website.

Monitoring your websites

There are various free and paid-for monitoring and analytics tools available. Google Analytics is the most popular, and what we cover here follows more or less chronologically the layout of the Google Analytics browser. This chapter will work best for you if you have installed Google Analytics on a site and can refer to the results that it is showing as you read.

These are some key measurements and what you should see from them.

Unique visitors over time

You are looking for an upward trend. Compare uniques in different time periods, particularly periods in which you launch new campaigns online or publish significant new content. Which campaigns were the most successful? Which didn't work as well? You need to learn over time what content best fulfils the information needs of your community.

By default, Google Analytics shows you results over the past month. You can change that period and also compare two periods – this month with last month, yesterday with the same day last week, and so on.

New compared to repeat visitors

A new business, or one seeking to increase its reach, will want to see a high proportion of new visitors. An established business may want a higher number of repeats because that shows they are building their base of loyal customers. Repeat visitors have demonstrably found your content valuable – it's fulfilled whatever need they had, whether information, problem-solving, advice or entertainment – and are coming back for more.

So what levels of new and repeat visitors should you be looking for? Hubspot (www.hubspot.com), a premium analytics tool we'll look at later, recommends a repeat visitor rate of around 15 per cent, saying that if it is above 30 per cent you may not be attracting enough new people to grow your business. If your repeat visitors rate is below 10 per cent, you are probably not offering enough valuable information on your website to fulfil the promise that your social media campaign has made to the new visitor – the click they made on the link to your website didn't get them the information they wanted.

As well as the overall percentages for each group, you should also look at the actual numbers. You'll always have more new visitors than repeat ones. It's important that, in real numerical terms, both groups are growing. Always relate the figures to your business goals. If you are building a brand, a high level of new visitors is a sign that you are getting the word out about yourself.

Of course, you may work for a brand where repeat custom is low because the purchase or other type of engagement you offer is a very occasional one, perhaps a one-off. So you always need to relate what analytics seem to tell you to the nature of your brand.

How often people visit you

Really engaged members of your community will come back regularly. The majority of your visitors will only come to you once. A smaller number will appear twice, and from there the number coming three, four or more times follows a downward curve. What is most significant is the number visiting you five, six, seven times or more. It's hard to give absolute numbers to aim for here, but they should be growing. If you run a site with a large amount of fast-moving news about an industry and, hence, one of your business goals is to become a trusted news source, then you want to see a good proportion of visitors coming multiple times, perhaps daily.

The "days since last visit" metric is also significant. How many repeat visitors come back daily? How many weekly? What are your business goals for frequency of visits? If, for example, you are posting content daily, but a significant proportion of visitors are coming back weekly, perhaps you need to adjust your brand journalism strategy to cater for them by producing a weekly digest of news, with links to material published over the last seven days.

Other demographic information about visitors

Depending on your business goals, you may wish to monitor where in the world your visitors come from, so you can measure how effectively you are reaching a particular geographic market.

Metrics on the sex ratio and age range of your visitors would also be valuable. But an analytics platform can only give you the information it has from users. That's why bringing Google+ into Google Analytics (as mentioned in Chapter 25) is significant. People on Google+ have created profiles in which they give a good deal of other valuable information. If, for example, you are seeking to build brand awareness among women aged 25 to 34, living in New York, and your analytics service has access to such personal information, you can see how you are doing in meeting that goal. If you can compare the content you publish over time with levels of engagement with your target market, you can see what content has worked and what hasn't.

Pages that draw the most/least traffic

This enables you to see which are your most popular pages. Some, the homepage and other main content pages, will naturally feature prominently. The popularity or otherwise of other pages is down to how useful or interesting people found them.

Page popularity is a useful indication of what content is working and what isn't, and can help you to refine the topics you cover. Popular pages are ones where you are achieving the most engagement, and are good places to put opportunities for people to engage with you further – so they are a good location for links to more content, opt-in forms for email bulletins, contact-us forms and so on.

Landing pages – popular entry points

A landing page, in Google Analytics terms, is the first page a visitor sees at your site. Often that's the homepage, but it can be any other page which brings them to you. The list of these gives another indicator of the means by which you've hooked the visitor, and is another measure of successful content. They are also key pages on which to give visitors other useful information and to encourage them to explore your site further.

Landing page conversion rates

You can track the percentage of visitors who take a desired action. Depending on your business goals, that might be visitors who become leads (e.g. they fill in a form asking for more information) or who purchase from you or make a donation if your brand is a charity. If your site doesn't feature ecommerce, you might see one good conversion goal as signing up for an email bulletin or clicking a button to follow you on Twitter.

An analytics tool such as Google Analytics will let you set a series of goals, such as visit duration or number of pages visited, and collect data on how successful you are in achieving them. This is all about seeing how well you have been able to engage those who were persuaded to visit your site.

Visitor engagement and flow

Engagement is measured by how long visitors spend on your site and how many pages – Google Analytics calls this page depth – they visit when they are with you. What you are looking for is significant engagement which shows that visitors are consuming your material. Measuring it over time, and comparing engagement levels with significant content postings, can show you how effective your engagement is.

The visitor flow on Google Analytics demonstrates in graphical format the path visitors took through your site, from the particular landing page that got them to you and the subsequent pages they went to. It also shows you the drop-off at each point – those that exit your site. Monitoring flow over time, and analysing the ways in which new content affects the flows, helps you to see popular paths through the site and understand what visitors want from you, and where there are opportunities to improve retention. It also indicates which pages are performing poorly in terms of keeping readers interested in the site.

If a page that brings in a lot of visitors also has a high drop-off rate, this can indicate a problem with the content. And if there is a large drop-off from a page which is designed to move readers on to a further page – perhaps a bookings page – that also needs examining.

Comparing the different places new and return visitors go can show you what works for each category. Typically, you may get a large number of new visitors who are using your site as one among many that they conduct research on. The proportion that later returns may have decided to make a purchase, a donation or fulfil some other call to action, such as subscribing to your mailing list. There will often be distinctly different paths for new visitors compared to repeats. It's important that those paths are smooth and clearly laid out, or you'll get unacceptably high drop-off rates.

Bounce rate

The bounce rate is the percentage of visitors who leave almost immediately. They either came to you by mistake or can instantly see that your site is not for them. Bounce rates vary widely between industries and it's hard to set a rate that is acceptable. The *Make Use Of* guide to Google Analytics suggests that a bounce rate below 80 per cent is good, and one of 50–70 per cent shows you are "doing an excellent job keeping the interest of your readers".[1] Monitoring the bounce rate, and working to bring it down with compelling content on your landing pages, is an important part of your brand journalism strategy.

The technology and devices visitors used when finding you

Your analytics tool will tell you what technology your visitors used when coming to you. You'll get the percentage using the web and that using mobile devices. There will be a breakdown of the Internet service provider, browser and search engines employed. You should see a fairly level split between the big browsers: Internet Explorer, Chrome, Firefox and Safari. Among search engines, since Google is the most popular, it will bring you the most visitors.

For mobile visitors, you'll see the devices – for example, what proportion used iPads. This information enables you to make sure that your site is optimized for use on the most popular devices your visitors use. It can also indicate, if you have low traffic from a popular device, that your site may render badly on it.

Traffic sources – where visitors come from

There are three types of traffic:

- direct
- organic
- referral.

Direct traffic comprises people who have typed your URL into a browser, have you bookmarked or have clicked on a link you supplied to them, perhaps through an email bulletin. Organic traffic involves people who found you on a search engine. Referral traffic comes via a link on another website. Hubspot recommends a rate for organic traffic of 40 to 50 per cent.

Referral traffic shows how successful your link building is on other websites, and will include any adverts with links to your site that you place there. Hubspot says 20 to 30 per cent of overall traffic should come from referrals. Referrals are important because they are highly valued by search engines as indications that yours is a useful, reliable site; hence, they help your SEO. However, as we will see in the next chapter, the relative importance of such links is declining.

You should track your referrals month by month to see how links are working. By specifying particular periods, and comparing them, you'll be able to track the performance of particular links. You'll get a breakdown of all the sources visitors came from, alongside indications of whether these sources are organic, direct or referral, and what they did when they got to your site – how many pages they visited, how long they stayed, how many were new visitors, and how many left immediately (the bounce rate).

Search engine optimization (SEO)

The SEO area in Google Analytics shows you what is happening to your listing at the search engines. For each specific query which brought you into search results, it tells you how many impressions you got, how many clicks on your listing, your average position in the results, and your click-through rate. You really need a position in the first ten on the results, as few searchers go beyond the first page. Such a position should give you a high number of impressions, which ought to give a good click-through rate if you have the wording within your listing right.

Keywords

Keywords are the words visitors typed into a search engine and with which they found you. These are the top search phrases that draw people to your website. Your analytics tool will list them for your site.

Keyword ranking and performance

How well your site is optimized for search engines determines where you appear in the list of results and, hence, how much traffic you will get. Choosing the right keywords is one of the roots of good SEO. You should be monitoring the performance of your keywords in search, and seeing how well your site ranks for searches conducted using them, as well as how effectively those keywords are delivering traffic to your site. Google Analytics and other tools monitor keyword performance.

In a large organization, you will be able to call upon a dedicated department that works on this; in a small one it may be down to your department or to you. But there is a balance to be struck between writing content that works for search engines and content that works for human readers: search engines are striving to improve their performance in delivering the latter (see Chapter 27). Get your content right – give people what they need, and you'll do well in SEO.

As mentioned above, around 40 to 50 per cent of your traffic should come from organic search. If it's lower, you should review your keywords, see if there are others you should be using, and build content to support their use.

Branded and non-branded search traffic

Of this organic traffic, some will come from keywords related directly to your brand – company name and other words and phrases closely associated with your brand. That's known as branded search traffic. The rest will come from non-branded search, using keywords that are generic to your industry or the broad products or services that you provide.

Branded search comes from people who have already heard of you and, hence, could put your brand in their search terms. These are rather like repeat traffic. Those who find you by using non-branded search terms have either not heard of you or for some reason didn't consider that your brand name would help their search. If most of your traffic comes from branded search, you need to work harder on attracting non-branded search with the adoption, and content support, of keywords applicable to your industry generically. You'll then be able to broaden the community around your content and your business.

The full list of search terms driving traffic to you

The list that analytics tools provide of all the search terms which resulted in a visit to your site shows how many – or how few – ways your content is pulling in visitors. A long list of search phrases is good; it means you are attracting readers with a wide range of information needs. You also need to monitor what percentage of visits comes from the use of a particular search term.

Your targeted keywords should be prominent in the list. If they are, your content is doing its job. If they aren't, you need to improve your content. Consider whether your content supports the search terms with which people are finding you. If it doesn't, they may be disappointed when they arrive at your site. Also consider whether there are search terms that are important to your business but which are not resulting in visitors. You need to build content that will attract people interested in these areas and satisfy their information needs once they are with you.

Inbound links

These are links from other websites. Search engines value links to you, particularly from high-traffic, authoritative sites, and use them when deciding how to rank you. You can see which of the inbound links are most important to you from the amount of traffic they deliver. Knowing where people come from can also help you to determine their information needs, and work to ensure that your content satisfies them.

Conversion rates from organic search

We looked above at how many visitors you should expect from organic search. But getting them to you is just the first step. What's significant once they are with you is whether they complete one of the tasks that are important to your business goals and which your brand journalism strategy is designed to deliver. Those goals can be anything from completing a purchase to signing up for your email bulletin, depending on what your business goals are. Monitoring conversion rates and working to improve them is crucial.

Measuring paid search

If your brand uses pay-per-click sponsored search results or adverts on search engines, you'll need to know how much it costs you to get a visit from each person who responds to those ads and how much business they deliver. The platform you use, whether Google or any other, will have that information, but there are five key metrics in evaluating it:

- click-through rate (what percentage of those who saw the ad clicked on its link)
- average cost per click

- conversion rate (what percentage of those who click complete the task the ad was there to encourage)
- cost per acquisition (what it cost to get each piece of business)
- return on advertising spend.

Click-through rates vary widely, but if you run regular paid-for campaigns you can use the variance in those rates to determine how particular subjects worked. It's usually possible to run more than one version of the ad simultaneously, so you can adjust headlines and other wording to see whether one gives a better click-through rate than another.

It's important that the content on the relevant landing page works well with the ad and delivers on what the ad promised. If it does, you should get a good conversion rate. If you get a low conversion rate, then those who clicked decided for some reason that what initially interested them wasn't worth pursuing once they got to the landing page. You need to analyse where things went wrong. For example, if the goal was to get people to register with you, did you ask for too much information?

Cost per acquisition is your total spend divided by your conversion rate. Return on advertising spend is your total spend divided by the revenue generated by your acquisitions. This is the bottom line: was the campaign worth it?

Social traffic

This area charts your social relations – how effectively you are engaging with members of your community on social sites. Google Analytics gathers this information for you and explains the process like this: "The social web connects people where they share, critique and interact with content and each other. Social analytics provides you with the tools to measure the impact of social. You can identify high-value networks and content, track on-site and off-site user interaction with your content and tie it all back to your bottom-line revenue through goals and conversions."[2]

Google Analytics offers an overview, which shows how many visitors come from each of the social platforms you are on. If you are active on a particular social platform, you should see a significant number of visits from it. You'll be able to see how many visitors were delivered to your site by a URL that you shared in a tweet or status update. It also shows you the reactions you get from social plug-ins that you have on your site – such as an "embed" of your Twitter stream or Facebook status updates. These visitors are tracked across the pages they visit once they have got to you. On Google Analytics, a social visitors flow tool, the equivalent of the social flow tool discussed above, shows where those visitors go on your site.

You can use this analysis to identify particular social posts that have worked well, and whether there are areas of content that those on one social platform prefer when compared to those on another.

Analysing the effectiveness of your content

The content section of Google Analytics drills right down into your content. We got an overview before; but this section shows you how each individual page on your site is performing. This is extremely valuable information that lets you identify well- and poorly performing pages. We see how many page views each gets and how many unique visitors are drawn to them.

Site speed

You want your site to load quickly – any delay and some visitors will just go elsewhere. An average response time of one to two seconds is desirable, with a page load time ideally of ten seconds or below. This tool shows you whether you are achieving it. Google Analytics will break the response down by the browsers that visitors were using.

You may notice some spikes in page load times: odd days over a month when it took a good deal more than ten seconds for pages to load. You can trouble-shoot by clicking on page timings to try to identify pages that are loading slowly for some reason. Perhaps a large picture has not been compressed.

Content experiments

Google Analytics lets you experiment to see if you can improve the performance of pages within your site. You can create up to six variants on a particular page and paste the URLs into the experiments interface. There's a video explaining this on the *Brand Journalism* website.

Setting goals

Google Analytics also allows you to set goals for improving your engagement with your visitors. Goal reports are found under the conversions tab. Here's some advice from *Mashable* on how to use goals:

> The Goals area is where your data tracking can really help you make a difference. These outcome-oriented metrics help you dive deeper into your site performance and learn whether you're achieving what you want with your website.
>
> The first step is defining your business objectives: Are you driving visitors to make online purchases? Getting them to view a specific piece of content? Aiming for more newsletter signups? Once you've pinned down your site goals, make sure your site administrator enables Goals in Google Analytics in the Account Settings page. Then you can choose one of four Goal types to track:
>
> - URL destination: this metric is best if your goal is to get visits to a key page of your site, such as your homepage or a post-purchase message page.

- Time on Site: if you're looking to measure engagement, this will track visitors spending a defined amount of time on your site.
- Pages per Visit: also important for engagement, Pages per Visit will keep tabs on a defined number of pages visitors view in a session on your site.
- Events: Event Goals allow you to track specific actions visitors are taking on a page. This includes anything from downloading a PDF to watching a video.[3]

In-page analytics

Another useful Google Analytics tool is the in-page one, which brings up the page on your site that you want to examine and overlays it with percentages of visitors who clicked on a particular link. That's a great way of seeing at a glance which calls to action are working and which are not.

Custom reporting

Everything we have discussed above is conducted under standard reporting. But Google Analytics also offers custom reporting. It includes the following.

Real-time data

What is happening on your site right now? This can be highly useful if you aim to be a trusted news source and have a fast-developing news story. A flurry of activity on a particular story can be an indication that users are hungry for more information on that topic. Respond to that demand immediately and you should find a further boost to engagement.

Intelligence events

This picks up on any unusual data in your site's performance – anything out of the ordinary that might be significant, such as an increase or decrease in traffic, or a rise or drop in average time spent on the site. As well as standard alerts, you can set your own. This is a much easier way of spotting potential problems, or opportunities, and reacting to them than having to trawl through data yourself.

Other analytics tools

Hubspot (www.hubspot.com/products/) is one of the paid-for Internet marketing software products available. It is a full content management system on which you build your website, blog, email marketing and run your social presences. It sells itself as a one-stop-shop that both monitors performance, flags up opportunities, and analyses performance across search engine optimization, marketing analytics, blogging analytics, and social media integration. As you create content on the site, it is assessed for SEO and tips given on improving it. Essentially, it takes data in the form that

Google Analytics presents it, and develops from it a list of notifications and recommendations for action.

Any trained journalist is likely to find its recommendations over-prescriptive. It sees one optimal length for a blog post or example, and flags up if you fail to use an image or include a call to action. There is a video overview of Hubspot on the *Brand Journalism* website.

Hubspot offers a 30-day free trial, which is well worth taking so that you can experience what a premium web and social media management service can do. We'll have a rundown on the current other best services to take a look at on the *Brand Journalism* website.

Blog monitoring and analytics

Your blog may have a number of goals attached to it. One may be to get your content findable. If so, you probably promote it on Twitter and other social media and use it as a staging point designed to generate visitors to your main corporate website. Many blogs are used for comment and analysis on news developments in a brand or industry; others are designed to generate leads. So, as with website analytics, you need to keep in mind what business goals your blogging strategy is designed to support.

If your blog is hosted on your website, you will be able to analyse it through Google Analytics. If it is hosted on a popular blogging platform such as Blogger or Wordpress, you'll find analytics built in there. Much of what you should be monitoring with your blog is the same as with your website, but here are the main points.

Your traffic

This involves:

- total traffic
- where it comes from: social media, referrals, organic search.

Traffic from organic search is down to the effective use of keywords. That from social media is due to the effective promotion of your posts via tweets, Facebook status updates and so on. Traffic from referrals can be down to people linking to your blog, perhaps on their blogroll, and is a measure of how authoritative the blog is.

You also need to look at the demographics of your blog. The geographic distribution of your readers may well have a bearing on what content is relevant.

Your content

There are a number of measures of the effectiveness of each of your posts, depending on what your business goals are. In general, seeing what sort of content is popular is obviously a useful guide to what to write about. You may find some topics have an enduring popularity, with a long tail of hits. Such topics may suggest areas you should develop on your main branded website.

The effectiveness of each post

You'll want to monitor how many views each post gets so that you can identify popular topics and less popular ones. As with everything else you write, it's important to identify the most effective use of headlines. Know what works for you: is it How … or Why … headlines? Headlines with numbers in them?

Conversions per post

If your blog is there to generate leads, you need to monitor how effective each post is in generating those leads. This can mean that your total readership on a post is less important than the number of conversions it generated.

Response to calls to action

Blogs with a commercial focus often have a call to action of some kind in each post.

Email newsletter monitoring and analytics

Your email newsletter host will give you the tools you need to monitor your email campaigns. Popular hosts include MailChimp (login.mailchimp.com) and Constant Contact (www.constantcontact.com).

What to monitor

The main thing to monitor is subscriber list growth rate. According to Marketing Sherpa, the churn rate (loss of readers) can be 25 per cent a year or higher, which means you must constantly replace lost subscribers just to stand still.[4] Churn will be reflected in the bounce rate, which indicates how many emails could not be delivered.

Open rate

This involves the percentage of recipients who open a particular email bulletin. Open rate can be unreliable because it doesn't mean they read any of it. Maybe they opened it to delete it. Click-through rate is a much better guide to the success of a bulletin.

Click-through rate

Click-through rate is the percentage of subscribers who click on one of the links in your bulletin. Reading it is one thing, but if you have structured your bulletin well, readers will need to click to get to the meat of any of the topics covered on a link and that will take them to your main website.

Forwarding rate

If your email has an invitation to pass it on to someone whom the recipient thinks might appreciate it, this can be a useful guide to its perceived helpfulness.

Conversion rate

If your email contained a call for recipients to carry out some action, such as purchasing a product, you can track that.

Revenue generated per bulletin

If your bulletins contain opportunities to purchase, you can monitor what revenue was generated from each.

Assignments

1   If you have access to analytics on a site that you work for, examine its performance using the measures discussed in this chapter. Compile a report on that performance, identify strengths and weaknesses, successes and failures, and come up with a brand journalism strategy with content designed to better meet the brand's business goals.
2   If you don't have access to existing analytics, set Google Analytics up on a site that you do have access to (it can be one which you are developing as part of a university or other training project) and apply the procedure described in the last paragraph to it.

Notes

1   *Make Use Of* guide to Google Analytics: soc.li/SjPm43C.
2   Google Analytics: www.google.co.uk/analytics/.
3   *Mashable* on goal-setting in Google Analytics: mashable.com/2012/01/04/google-analytics-guide/.
4   Marketing Sherpa on churn rate: www.marketingsherpa.com/.

27 The Last Word

Good Content = Good SEO

Goals of this module

- Demonstrate the central importance of good content to any brand's search engine optimization (SEO) strategy.
- Outline how to optimize your site's status as a source of good content.

On the website

Find links to primers in SEO, essential updates, further resources and all sources quoted here.

We haven't spoken much in this book about search engine optimization, and there's a reason for that. The trend among search engines has been to improve their results-finding service and to make good quality content the key determinant of what is offered up high in results. Since this book has been all about creating great content – content that serves your brand and its business goals – good SEO has been at least a by-product, and in some ways central, to what we have been doing all along. You'll find links to primers on search engine optimization on the *Brand Journalism* website; but just to put the discussion that follows in context, here are the essentials of SEO.

Put at its simplest, SEO is the process of formatting the HTML mark-up and raw content of a website or web page such that search engines correctly understand its content.[1] Fundamental to this, as far as the content we write is concerned, is optimizing the meta tags such as "title", "description" and "keywords", which are the places a search engine looks to identify what your page is about. Search engines use complex algorithms to rank the pages they find in order of importance, determining the order in which they appear in search results. Algorithms differ between search engines and are constantly tweaked and updated. SEO experts are employed to know exactly how those algorithms rank content and to ensure that content is presented in such a way that the algorithm ranks it highly. Increasingly, good content = good SEO.

Matt Cutts,[2] head of web spam at Google, talks in his blog of how the company has been invigorating its anti-spam efforts to ensure that only good content ranks well in its search results.[3] And by spam he means poor-quality content dressed up to look authoritative and informative though SEO trickery. The other search engines are doing the same. Matt makes clear that Google is out to stop sites using SEO techniques to push content up the rankings which, in terms of the information it provides, doesn't deserve to be there. The key to good rankings for any brand is to offer content that is frequently updated, well researched and newsworthy. That's the only way to rank well consistently on Google and other search engines.

The techniques we have discussed in this book support that strategy. A good SEO-friendly policy includes having informative business landing pages, frequently updated blogs, and effective engagement on Twitter to promote those first two. Tweets help Google index content faster and therefore get your news noticed. Writing on Search Engine Watch about the impact of search engines' focus on content in determining rankings, Kevin Gibbons says:

> Google is now valuing authorship, natural links, and social signals far more highly. So the next natural step is content marketing [with brand journalism as a vital part of that]. Content marketing is a great SEO strategy – even better than link building. Shifting your strategy from search marketing to content marketing is increasingly leading to higher search rankings and more organic traffic.[4]

Link-building is the process of establishing mutual links with other authoritative sites to increase search engine rankings.

Kevin gives a number of reasons why concentrating on content pays off. One is that focusing on creating good content rather than thinking of all the links you can cram in is a more natural way of writing: "You are writing content and naturally generating links as a result of writing great content. People are choosing to blog about it, share it socially, and generally create a buzz because it's interesting to them."

Another is that "authoritative writers are the future". Kevin says: "Google wants to know about the people who write on websites and blogs – and if they know this they will have more trust in you. If you write frequently for authoritative sources and you've built a strong social footprint, they'll like you even more." Google shows its interest in authorship partly through something it calls Google Authorship or AuthorRank, which involves tying a Google+ profile to pieces of content by the person who has that profile. In doing so it is seeking to identify authoritative authors and the places where good content can be found.

In early 2013, Google was still developing AuthorRank, so look for updates on this topic on the *Brand Journalism* website. Mike Arnessen on the SEOmoz blog outlines how AuthorRank is likely to work:

> Google considers over 200 ranking factors when determining where our sites rank in organic search, so it's safe to say that they'll be using plenty

of signals to calculate AuthorRank. Here's my shortlist of factors that Google is likely to use in their calculation:

- The average PageRank of an author's content [PageRank is Google's existing way of ranking web pages].
- The average number of +1s and Google+ shares the author's content receives.
- The number of Google+ circles an author is in.
- Reciprocal connections to other high AuthorRank authors.
- The number and authority of sites an author's content has been published to.
- The engagement level of an author's native Google+ content (i.e. posts to Google+).
- The level of on-site engagement for an author's content (i.e. comments and author's responses to comments).
- Outside authority indicators (i.e. the presence of a Wikipedia page).
- YouTube subscribers and/or engagement on authored videos ... .
- Any number of importance/authority metrics on social networks that Google deems trustworthy enough (Twitter, Quora, LinkedIn, Slide-Share, etc.).
- Real world authority indicators like published works on Google Books or Google Scholar.[5]

Kevin Gibbons writes of the results of analysis he did on the impact of Google+ upon organic search results:

I analysed two sets of clients I was working with and categorized them as:

1 websites with strong social profiles;
2 websites with weak social profiles.

What this analysis showed was:

- Websites with weak social profiles saw a 19.5 percent reduction in organic traffic
- Websites with strong social profiles saw a 42.6 percent increase in organic traffic.[6]

So, as he says, "set up Google Authorship and encourage social promotion around your content from your authors and bloggers". You'll find a primer on setting up Google Authorship on the *Brand Journalism* website.

Another reason Kevin Gibbons gives for focusing on content in your SEO strategy is that good content will stand up well, whatever changes Google makes to the algorithm it uses to rank sites:

The days of chasing Google's algorithm, and finding the next quick fix or SEO tactic, are disappearing quickly. So instead of focusing on whatever type of link hasn't been hit by a penalty yet – make content marketing the center of your SEO strategy instead. You're likely to see much greater rewards this way and it's long-term. So you'll be the one looking forward to Google's next algorithm update, instead of being the one scared if you've been caught out and worrying that your whole business model has to be re-visited.

He also says (and this might be another way of persuading a CEO that they should build a brand journalism team):

> Hiring good SEOs is hard. Link builders in particular. However, hiring a good copywriter really isn't that difficult. There are lots of people out there with strong copywriting skills – you just need to identify the creative ones who are good at blogging and generating social attention.

I disagree with him on one thing. He talks about copywriters. I believe brands need fully trained and qualified brand journalists to make a content strategy work for them. That belief formed the impetus for writing this book, and I hope the book makes the case for brand journalism and brand journalists. If you'd like to talk to me about any aspect of brand journalism, or need advice about anything we have covered (or haven't covered) in these pages, you'll find me on the *Brand Journalism* website.

Assignments

Assignment relating to this chapter

Set up AuthorRank for yourself and/or each of the journalists who work for your brand.

Assignment relating to the whole of Part IV

If you have access to all the monitoring and analytics data for a brand, use that material to evaluate the success of its web and social media presences. Identify strengths and weaknesses, and develop a strategy for improving performance.

Notes

1 SEO definition: www.brafton.com/glossary/search-engine-optimization.
2 Matt Cutts's blog: www.mattcutts.com/blog/.
3 Matt Cutts on search engine spam: googleblog.blogspot.co.uk/2011/01/google-search-and-search-engine-spam.html.
4 Kevin Gibbons, writing at Search Engine Watch, on content's role in determining rankings: searchenginewatch.com/article/2186953/Why-Content-Marketing-is-a-Great-SEO-Strategy-Not-a-Short-Term-Tactic.

5 Mike Arnessen writing about AuthorRank on the SEOmoz blog: www.seomoz. org/blog/how-to-prepare-for-authorrank-and-get-the-jump-on-google.
6 Kevin Gibbons, writing at Search Engine Watch, on content's role in determining rankings: searchenginewatch.com/article/2186953/Why-Content-Marketing-is-a-Great-SEO-Strategy-Not-a-Short-Term-Tactic.

Index